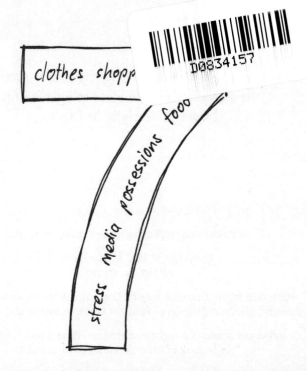

clothes shopp...

stress media possessions food

an experimental mutiny against excess

UPDATED AND REVISED

Jen Hatmaker

Convergent
New York

Dedication

For Jesus, who lived so lightly on this earth,
He didn't even have a place to lay His head.
I want so deeply to be like You.

2020 Convergent Books Trade Paperback Edition

Copyright © 2017 by Jen Hatmaker
All rights reserved.

Published in the United States by Convergent Books, an imprint of
Random House, a division of Penguin Random House LLC, New York.

CONVERGENT BOOKS is a registered trademark and its C colophon is a
trademark of Penguin Random House LLC.

Previously published in the United States by Jen Hatmaker in 2017,
and in a slightly different form in 2012.

Unless otherwise noted, all Scripture quotations are taken from the
Holman Christian Standard Bible®, Copyright © 1999, 2000, 2002, 2003,
2009 by Holman Bible Publishers. Used by permission. Holman Christian
Standard Bible®, Holman CSB®, and HCSB® are federally registered
trademarks of Holman Bible Publishers. Scripture quotations marked NIV
are from the Holy Bible, New International Version, copyright © 1973,
1978, 1984 by International Bible Society. Scripture quotations marked
NASB are from the New American Standard Bible®, Copyright © 1960,
1962, 1963, 1968, 1971, 1972, 1973, 1975, 1977, 1995 by The Lockman
Foundation. Used by permission (www.lockman.org). Scriptures marked
NKJV are from the New King James Version. Copyright © 1979, 1980, 1982,
Thomas Nelson, Inc., Publishers.

ISBN 978-0-593-23744-1
Ebook ISBN 978-0-593-23745-8

Printed in the United States of America on acid-free paper

convergentbooks.com

2 4 6 8 9 7 5 3 1

Contents

The 7 Hatmakers: Brandon & Jen with Gavin, Sydney, Caleb, Ben, & Remy

7..Seven Years Later

Welcome! Welcome to this story, Risk Takers, Trouble Makers, Rule Breakers, Status Quo Upenders, World Changers, Question Askers, Rabble Rousers. I'm guessing you fit in at least one of those categories or you wouldn't be interested in a story like this one. Something is under your skin. Something feels...off - about how much you have, how much you spend, how much you waste. Maybe it is all completely undefined, as it was for me when I first began this adventure seven years ago. Or maybe you are just munching popcorn and here for the free show.

Either way, I couldn't be happier to welcome you in to a little social experiment that changed our lives for good. I can say that now, because although this specific season is in my rear view mirror, as I've read back through every word recorded during 7, I was surprised how many ideas were new to me then, because they are the air we breathe today. Let that be good news to you: no matter if anything you read here seems too hard or too crazy or too overwhelming, maybe it will just be Step One into a new idea and in seven years, you'll discover an assimilation so deeply embedded in your life, you won't even remember not thinking that way.

Also, you may say in seven years: I'M GLAD THAT PART IS OVER. Let's just be honest. Eating the same seven foods for four weeks is bananas (a food item I sadly did not partake in during that month). What we learned during and since 7 was that the mechanics of it all were temporary but the lessons were permanent. And that is exactly why I am glad you are here.

Let me tell you what is different now than when I first wrote 7. This will be obvious if you've followed along with me since, but we only had three kids at the onset of this experiment. During the last month of 7, Stress, we were matched with Ben and Remy, our two youngest adopted children from Ethiopia, which I wrote about here in such raw form, I sobbed through it upon re-reading. We brought them home the year after 7 was over. So now we have five kids, and they are such a normal, treasured part of our family now, I can't even remember who is adopted. In fact, I felt something close to sadness going back through 7 because Ben and Remy weren't here for it. Shared memories before they joined our family are bittersweet; still precious because those years count too, but with the reverse knowledge that our little tribe was incomplete and our two youngest were suffering while the rest of us were thriving. (But I'll tell you right now that Ben Hatmaker would have had exactly none of Food Month. He'd have moved in with my parents. That boy loves food.)

Another difference is that *The 7 Experiment* was created. If you visit the7experiment.com, you will see that this book is just part of a bigger picture. *The 7 Experiment* offers a 9-week workbook study, a 9-part video series, and a private Facebook group. It was created for added support as you journey through your mutiny of excess.

Life has also gotten a bit bigger and more public which has made it a touch lonelier than I like, and there are certainly way more of you now, but that has been a joy, not a burden. I've seen more of the world since too; I got my very first passport during the writing of 7. We've been to Africa a dozen times now, and even though I mentioned I'd never been to Italy in the intro, I literally returned from there two days ago where I took the trip of lifetime with Brandon and Council Members Jenny and Shonna and their husbands. I've fallen hard for the world, you guys. It is beautiful and marvelous, and it has much to teach us on living simply, living well, living smaller, slowing down. There is nothing like trying to visit a store in Spain around 1:00pm and finding it closed for a siesta until 3:00, the owner having coffee with friends or a nap, lost profits be damned. The world has been my best teacher since the completion of 7, a continuing education program that awes me.

Other than that, we are still pastoring our beloved Austin New Church. We still have the same friends you'll read about. We still retreat at my mom and dad's ranch every Thanksgiving. (Oh! One other new development: Dad put a double-wide trailer on the ranch so we are no longer sleeping on 40-year-old sofas in the barn. See Day 26 in the last section. We're fancy now.) We still eat pretty clean except when we don't. We still protect the Sabbath pretty fiercely, although we observe it on Sundays, the only true day of rest in our weird life with our weird schedule. We still live in Buda, Texas just south of Austin, although we moved into a 1908 farmhouse four minutes away that we remodeled on HGTV, which I don't have time to explain here because what in the world?

We still love Jesus so much and believe in this life He asked us to live. We think He knew what He was talking about when He told us to not store up too many treasures on this earth but to live well and love well, because as it turns out, that is what matters more than anything. And listen, Jesus has seen us through some suffering in the last seven years - real, desperate, unexpected pain - so we believe Him more than ever. He is exactly who He said He is, and when literally everything you hold dear falls away, Jesus remains. So yeah, we're still all in here.

On Day 17 of Month Four, I wrote:

"I giggle to imagine what 2017 Jen would come back to teach me; I don't even know what I don't know."

I love that I wrote that. I love that I decided to be a lifelong learner who is less attached to certainty and being right and more interested in paying attention and developing. One thing the 2017 Jen would say to the 2010 Jen that originally experienced 7 is this: Number one, use sunscreen. I'm serious. You are in your final days of irresponsible sunning with no consequences. But number two, this weirdo little life you are constructing where you follow Jesus to strange places doing bizarre things and taking risks is all worth it. Every day of it. It only gets more exciting and meaningful. When God asks you to do something, do it. He is such a trustworthy leader. Don't be afraid. You've put your chips all in on the right number. I am delighted you are here, reader. As I've said a thousand times since, 7 is not a template. It is not a list of rules. It is not a program. It is simply an imperfect social experiment to help us find God in an overcrowded, overindulged, overscheduled life. And it did. If any word, any sentence, any section you read helps you cut through the chaos and simplify down to something meaningful, I will count it nothing but privilege that I was able to walk alongside you in some small way. This has absolutely nothing to do with rules or guilt and everything to do with freedom. Much, much love to you, dear reader. Welcome to 7.

Jen

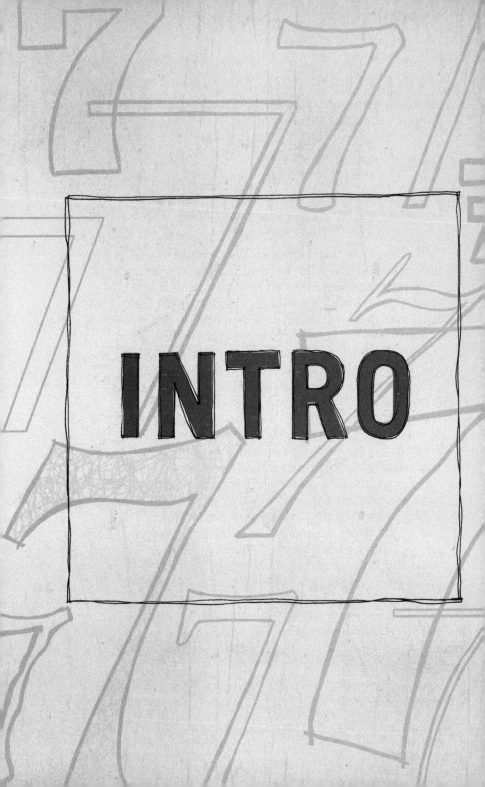

INTRO

This is all Susana's fault. She had to trot out her little social experiment, "Pick Five" right when God was confronting me with my greed, excess, materialism, consumerism, envy, pride, comfort, insatiability, irresponsibility, and well, there was other stuff but I want you to like me, so I'll shelve the rest for later. (Did I mention "need for approval"?) Let me back up. My husband, Brandon, and I have undergone profound transformation in the last three years. Let me sum it up: God really messed us up. We were happy-go-lucky; Brandon was a pastor at a big ol' church making excellent scratch, and we spent our money however we wanted (on ourselves). We were climbing the ladder, baby. Fortunately, we didn't have to worry with the poor because we were paid pros serving the saved. We spent so much time blessing blessed people, there was nothing left over. Besides, that wasn't really "our thing."

Then, let's see, a bunch of stuff happened, the Holy Spirit leveled us and laid our motives bare, we turned into crazy people, yada yada yada . . . we started a new church centered on justice. Sorry for the gaps, but it's too much (but my book *Interrupted* will walk you through the thrilling account of God turning our world upside down).

Our adventure in relearning the essentials of faith, Austin New Church, has been on the ground for two years. It's a little faith community that has, quite simply, changed my life. Our mantra is "Love your neighbor, serve your city." Taking a cue from Francis Chan, we take the Scripture "love your neighbor as yourself" seriously, and we give away half of all we receive. We won't spend more on ourselves than our poor neighbor.

A poor church plant operating on half of its intake means

we rent a worship space with dancing frogs painted on the back wall and carpet that saw the Nixon administration. Our front door won't open properly, which resulted in one guy leaving during church to get something, not being able to get back in, and sitting on the curb until service was over. Our parking lot looks like it was hit by an earthquake—and then patched up by drunken monkeys. We have no support staff, no secretaries, no copy machine. Our band is almost entirely homegrown. When we needed a drummer, one of our guys reported playing "a few times in college." He was on stage the next week where he kicked over a cymbal and accidentally launched a drumstick into the crowd. These are deficiencies most pastors would never stand for (or most churchgoers), but we won't buy carpet at the expense of orphans. $10,000 for a new parking lot could fund a hundred thousand tree seedlings to reforest Africa's decimated land and stimulate their local economy. It's kind of a no-brainer.

But before you launch a parade, let's revisit my description in the first paragraph. Granted, we descended many rungs in the last three years, and transformation did not come cheaply or without pain. We suffered loss—relationships, reputation, position, security, approval, acknowledgment—all the stuff I used to crave. But here is what I gave up the least:

Comfort.

I might have disagreed two years ago when having a conversation with a homeless man was the most uncomfortable situation I could envision. When God first sent us to serve the poor, every moment was awkward. Each confrontation was wrought with anxiety. In

Interrupted, I made this statement:

"I thought I'd never be happy again."

However, God changed me and grafted genuine love for the least into my heart. I looked forward to every encounter, rejected service that was labor-intensive rather than relationally focused. I became a girl who loved the marginalized. I couldn't get enough of them in my personal space.

So what used to be comfortable (being a big fat consumer Christian) became uncomfortable; then what was uncomfortable (engaging the poor) became comfortable. Follow? Perhaps I gave up emotional comfort for awhile, but then God affirmed Himself as our provider, established the vision He gave us, and taught me how to love. The uncomfortable turned into our life's mission, and we would never go back.

That said, a new tension began lurking. The catalyst was the week we housed twelve evacuees from Hurricane Ike. Our little church, four months old at the time, took in eighty strangers from the coast that had nowhere to go. We moved our three kids into our bedroom, washed sheets, blew up mattresses, rolled out sleeping bags, and readied the house for an onslaught. As carloads arrived and we welcomed them in, one ten-year-old boy walked into our home, looked around with huge eyes, and hollered:

"Dad! This white dude is RICH!"

We are.

For years I didn't realize this because so many others had
more. We were surrounded by extreme affluence, which
tricks you into thinking you're in the middle of the pack. I
mean, sure, we have twenty-four hundred square feet for
only five humans to live in, but our kids have never been on
an airplane, so how rich could we be? We haven't traveled
to Italy, my kids are in public schools, and we don't even
own a time-share. (Roll eyes here.)

But it gets fuzzy once you spend time with people below
your rung. I started seeing my stuff with fresh eyes,
realizing we had everything. I mean *everything*. We've
never missed a meal or even skimped on one. We have a
beautiful home in a great neighborhood. Our kids are in a
Texas exemplary school. We drive two cars under warranty.
We've never gone a day without health insurance. Our
closets are overflowing. We throw away food we didn't eat,
clothes we barely wore, trash that will never disintegrate,
stuff that fell out of fashion.

And I was so blinded I didn't even know we were rich.

How can I be socially responsible if unaware that I reside
in the top percentage of wealth in the world? (You probably
do too: Make $35,000 a year? Top 4 percent. $50,000? Top
1 percent.) Excess has impaired perspective in America;
we are the richest people on earth, praying to get richer.
We're tangled in unmanageable debt while feeding the
machine, because we feel entitled to more. What does it
communicate when *half the global population* lives on less
than $2 a day, and we can't manage a fulfilling life on
twenty-five thousand times that amount? Fifty thousand
times that amount?

It says we have too much, and it is ruining us.

It was certainly ruining me. The day I am unaware of my privileges and unmoved by my greed is the day something has to change. I couldn't escape the excess or see beyond my comforts though. I wrung my hands and commiserated with Brandon but couldn't fathom an avenue out. We'd done some first-tier reductions, freeing up excess to share, but still . . . the white dude *was* really rich.

Which brings me back to Susana. About this time she announced her Pick Five project: only five foods for forty days subtitled "Simplified Life, Amplified God." My first reaction was, "She's so crazy." (I really love food, and that will be become apparent in the next section.) But as the experiment unfolded and I heard what she was learning, I became a teeny bit enamored.

See, I am an extremist. I don't learn lessons easily, subtly, or delicately. I can't be trusted with loose boundaries. If God gives me an inch, I will take a marathon. Dipping one toe in doesn't work for me; it simply hastens my return to the couch where I can return to my regularly scheduled program. I am a difficult student who is extremely bullheaded. Total immersion is the only medium that can tame me.

I was where all my best ideas happen (the shower), and in forty minutes—I apologized to God for the egregious waste of water—"Pick Five" turned into 7. It had sloppy edges and "undeveloped" is too kind, but I realized this extreme social experiment was my ticket out of nauseating consumerism. Or at least it would start the engine.

I ruminated for six months, letting it marinate, forcing my friends to discuss it with me. I started praying about what God wanted; what would move me closer to His agenda and further from mine? How could this be meaningful, not just narcissistic and futile? What areas needed the most renovation? How am I blind and why? Where have I substituted The American Dream for God's kingdom? What in my life, in the lives of most westerners, is just *too stinking much?*

Food   Clothes   Possessions   Media   Waste   Spending   Stress

Seven months, seven areas, reduced to seven simple choices. I'm embarking on a journey of less. It's time to purge the junk and pare down to what is necessary, what is noble. 7 will be an exercise in simplicity with one goal: to create space for God's kingdom to break through.

I approach this project in the spirit of a fast: an intentional reduction, a deliberate abstinence to summon God's movement in my life. A fast creates margin for God to move. Temporarily changing our routine of comfort jars us off high center. A fast is not necessarily something we offer God, but it assists us in offering ourselves. As Bill Bright, founder of Campus Crusade for Christ, said, "It is exchanging the needs of the physical body for those of the spirit."[1]

"'Even now,' declares the Lord, 'return to me with all your

heart, with fasting and weeping and mourning. Rend your hearts and not your garments. Return to the Lord your God, for he is gracious and compassionate, slow to anger and abounding in love" (Joel 2:12–13). According to Scripture, fasting was commanded or initiated during one of six extreme circumstances:

Mourning Inquiry Repentance

Preparation Crisis Worship

As I write this, I enter the next seven months for (at least) two of these extreme reasons. First and foremost, repentance. 7 will be a tangible way to bow low and repent of greed, ungratefulness, ruined opportunities, and irresponsibility. It's time to admit I'm trapped in the machine, held by my own selfishness. It's time to face our spending and call it what it is: a travesty. I'm weary of justifying it. So many areas out of control, so much need for transformation. What have we been eating? What are we doing? What have we been buying? What are we wasting? *What are we missing?* These questions grieve me, as well they should. I'm ready for the deconstruction.

My second reason is for preparation. Most of my life is in front of me yet. I'm thirty-five and only six years into my assignment as a writer and Bible teacher. The bulk of my work lies ahead. My children are young—still entirely impressionable. It is not too late to untether them from the lie of "more." Our church vision is new, and our mission is really just beginning. I'm hungry for the reconstruction.

I'm ready to adopt Jesus' version of *rich, blessed,* and *generous.*

He had plenty to say on the subject. I look forward to what God will accomplish in the next seven months. He will meet me, I'm certain. I'm anxious about turning the soil, but I'm so eager for liberation that I'm still willing to become weird and eccentric for the next seven months. It's the means to the harvest.

Jesus, may there be less of me and my junk and more of You and Your kingdom.

Here we go.

The Council

I have a personality that would land me in prison without a steady influx of wise intervention. I'm something of a loose cannon. Left to my own devices, I'd be a recurring character on *Dog the Bounty Hunter*. Luckily, I married Mr. Responsible who has rescued me from disaster more times than I'd like to admit. Brandon senses when I am about to self-destruct:

"Take your fingers off the keyboard and back away from that e-mail."

"You have that look in your eyes. Go for a nice drive in the country."

"Now is a good time to stop allowing words to flow out of your mouth."

"Once that picture goes on the Internet, it's there forever."

So a project like 7 sounds straightforward to you, but to me it sounds like a wealth of opportunities to hedge. I've already polished up the phrase "extenuating circumstance" to use regularly for the next seven months. What about a wedding? What about the airport? What about a season finale? What about a *series finale*? For the love of the land.

I will clearly need help to keep me on the straight and narrow.

Enter The Council. Six friends, six personalities, six chances to keep this thing from derailing. The seven of us will confer on all things 7 for the duration of the project. They are advisors, cheerleaders, decision-makers, counselors, collaborators, and brainstormers. They are my personal think tank.

When I encounter a weird situation or roadblock, these girls are the Supreme Court. They helped develop the framework for 7 already and hinted at probable participation. Their creative ideas go straight into the 7 bucket, although Trina insists that her angle on Month One could become a best-seller and net her millions which she won't share. (Jenny argued that she was codeveloper of the angle and is entitled to half. I'm going to let them fight this out in the courts, knowing they will not land on the Oprah Network and instead will just advise some random author for seven months for no pay.)

Meet the Council

Becky earned a clear spot on my Friend List with her dry-as-dry-can-be humor and self-deprecating wit, two qualities I rank above honor and integrity. Out of sheer will she just dropped 85 pounds and is so smokin', we worry she might go for friend upgrades. She's a massage therapist, which seems so exotic, like being a belly dancer or geisha girl. Becky brainstormed three brilliant topics for my last book when my brain turned to cornmeal and I couldn't remember how to spell J-E-S-U-S.

Jenny became my first friend in Texas twelve years ago when she asked me over fajitas if I'd had a nose job. Jenny and Tray packed up their life in Corpus Christi, home for eighteen years and forever respectively, and moved to Austin to start our church with us. We bought houses on the same street and started our campaign for neighborhood domination. The only Council member more likely to land in jail than me is Jenny. She uses hot glue for everything, including custom curtains and Girl Scout badges.

Molly laid down a string of sarcasm during our first conversation in our 'hood, and I vowed to make her mine. Appealing to the nerd in me, she brought notes on a legal pad to our first 7 brainstorming session; words failed me. She has three DVRs because there is not enough recording space on one (or two) for all her shows. Molly executed a perfect herkie jump during a recent football party, which we captured on film and still marvel at with regularity.

Shonna adopted me as a friend through Jenny, and now we spend a piece of nearly every day together. When talking about my girlfriends recently, a woman asked, "You and your friends have so much fun. Do you have any time left to parent?" Shonna and I are both adopting, and we are raging bleeding hearts; pass the Kleenex to the girls crying over sermons and orphans. At the above-mentioned football party, Shonna completed a toe touch that was so stunning it generated forty-three responses on Facebook. She's still got it, folks.

Susana has long red hair that defies comprehension; she's like Samson. She is an excellent banter partner and loyal disciple to the Texas Longhorns, so if you don't get why we became fast friends, you clearly don't know me. Susana's "Pick Five" project was the inspiration behind 7, so I will either copy everything she does in the future or absolutely nothing. Let's see how it plays out. She bakes gourmet cakes and sews and creates handmade cards, and *I still like her*. She's that cool.

Trina was my first friend in Austin ten years ago, even though she forced me into women's ministry, which terrified me (it all worked out). She pretends to be a hard-nosed, tough-as-nails broad, but she cries over refugees and volunteers as a horse therapist with special needs adults. Whatever, Treen. We're all onto you. If you're ever around her without a conversation topic, just ask her about dogs, beaches, or how to transition from boxed wine. She's an expert, I tell you.

This is The Council who will keep the wheels on 7. You'll notice their input throughout. A social experiment of this scope requires good friends, and I have the best. Should you have any questions about food limitations or green living, feel free to call them because I'm sure they'd be happy to boss you around too.

Some Stuff I Thought to Tell You After I Was Already Finished with 7

Guess what I'm doing? Trolling Twitter while watching a Texas basketball game with a bowl of salsa on my lap. I'm wearing whatever I want, and ten minutes ago I ordered Melissa Fay Greene's new book *No Biking in the House without a Helmet* on my Kindle. I am clearly liberated from the confines of 7, which I finished two months ago. (Wish you knew what happened?? Sorry. You'll have to read the actual book to find out the goods. No spoilers here.)

I started this project with some vague boundaries and a fuzzy notion of how this would all go down. Now, on the other side of it, I've collected the FAQs lobbed my way for the last year, and I'm going to preemptively answer your questions because there is a 100 percent chance they are the exact same ones every person in the universe has asked me over the course of this zany thing.

1. How are you organizing this book? I wrote 7 sort of like a blog, sort of like a diary. I decided to write it in real time rather than retro-report on each month. I didn't give myself time to sanitize an experience or gloss it over with pretty words or a hazy memory. It went like this: experience it > feel it > write it. So at the end of a day, I sat down with my laptop and typed, "Day 13: If I eat one more bite of spinach, I am going to start stabbing people." Or some such. I didn't follow exact calendar months, but each "month" of 7 was four weeks long. The book is organized by month, then by day, with a conclusion at the end of each month. I took about two weeks off between each new month of 7. This was to fine-tune the writing, elaborate on any sections I truncated for time, and take a blasted break before wrapping my head around the next collection of reductions. 7 started in mid-January and ended the week of Thanksgiving. Much like my husband crammed four years of college into five, I squeezed seven months of 7 into ten.

2. Are your kids doing this? Yes and no. If my children were reduced to eating avocados, spinach, and eggs, they would've starved to death before we ever reached the second month. Some months of this project were simply not kid friendly. I did not feel like answering to their therapists one day for why I made them wear the same seven clothes for a month of fourth grade. The kids bowed out of the first two months: seven foods and seven clothes. The rest of the months were whole-family endeavors. They gave up their Wii and Gameboys, they gave away a ton of clothes and toys, they took eighty trips out to the compost bin, and they observed the Sabbath, among a bunch of other 7 stuff. Sometimes they were delightful and sometimes they were hostile. So pretty much exactly like normal.

3. Are you going to be bossy and make us feel guilty? I don't think so, but I can't be sure. Sometimes conviction is mistaken for guilt, and I can't promise you won't traverse that gray area a bit. And I feel my feelings really strongly so my fanaticism could sound like bossiness. I don't know. But I'll tell you this: 7 was most assuredly written from a place of repentance, not arrogance. You'll find I included a smorgasbord of my own personal failures and bad attitudes so don't imagine I'm writing from the cardboard house I chose to live in next to the homeless refugees I feed with money diverted from our health insurance. I'm so not here to boss you or make you feel guilty. I don't have an agenda with you other than sharing our little journey of reduction, and if you find a point of connection meaningful to your story, marvelous. If not, well, this book only cost you $14 or so, and you spent twice that amount on dinner at P.F. Chang's last week. No big loss. Carry on.

4. Are you weird? Because 7 is weird, and I'm not sure if this is for normal people. Well, obviously. But here's the lowdown on my vanilla existence: I married my college sweetheart, and we had three kids who look just like us. We live in the suburbs and we're into church. My house is painted pretty colors, and I wear cute shoes sometimes. I spend twenty minutes straightening my hair with a Chi I bought off an infomercial for $115, which I hid for a month after FedEx delivered it. I like my toenails painted. My kids are in public school. I love trips. I have a book collection that is embarrassing. We go on date nights. I love to cook and eat and laugh and watch movies. I go on every class field trip and bring cupcakes to school on Teacher Appreciation Day. I really, really like to have fun with my friends. I'm kind of normal. So is my family. And that's the problem. More likely, 7 would sound weird to a *real* radical living in the Congo or sharing all his worldly possessions; that person would read all this and deadpan, "Wow, everyone. Stop the presses. Jen turned off the Internet for a month. Let's throw a party and give her a book contract." I wrote this from the middle of the American pack, nauseated from the normalcy. So did I answer your question? I kind of dodged it. But then again, weird people never really know they're weird.

5. I need to know something else, and you didn't answer it in this cute little section. Come ask me. You can find me on Twitter at @jenhatmaker, on Facebook (how many Jen Hatmakers can there be?), or through my Web site at www. jenhatmaker.com.

Month 1

FOOD

Picking seven foods is like trying to pick my favorite kid. Some people eat to live, but I live to eat. I come from a long line of eaters; my sister is in culinary school in New York City as I write this. We long-distance foodie talk once a week until Brandon gives me the *I just can't take it anymore* look. I would positively get rid of cable tomorrow if it weren't for the Food Network. I read cookbooks like they are Jodi Picoult novels.

Food is the centrifugal force that draws together my people. According to me, a party needs no other activity than eating. I shoo the kids out of my space around 5:00 every day, put on some music, pour a glass of Cabernet, and enter cooking heaven. I love to chop. I love to sauté. I love to deglaze. I can't live without shallots. Sauces, spices, herbs, marinades, slicing, julienning, rough chopping, butterflying, searing, slow roasting, whipping, braising—these put a tear in my happy little eye.

So I've thought hard about my seven foods, perhaps more than any other month in the project. I've consulted experts and Web sites and less-skilled advisors like my girlfriends. I've gone on some trustworthy nutrition Web sites[1] to determine healthy ratios of vitamins and minerals. I researched super foods and organic produce. I've prayed over my choices and here they are:

Cheeseburgers   Tortilla chips   Fresh salsa

Mozzarella sticks Veggie Lovers pizza

Dark chocolate   Coffee

I'm kidding, people. These are some of my favorite foods, and I will miss them sorely. Farewell, *mis amores*. I love you, but you have given me a situation with my pants. I'll be back to enjoy you all in moderation, but for now this good-bye hurts me worse than it hurts you. Find someone else to make fat and happy for a month. Here is my real cast of characters:

Chicken   Eggs   Whole-wheat bread

Sweet potatoes   Spinach   Avocados   Apples

This healthy roll call will be washed down with water, and that's that. Don't get me started on "no coffee"; I'll begin wailing and gnashing my teeth. The Council approved salt and pepper and olive oil in modest increments. That's it. No rosemary. No onions. No oregano. No Salt Lick barbeque sauce. These foods are a good balance of protein, calcium, fiber, vitamins and minerals, and good fat. There are some decent mixy-matchy options in there, and since The Council gifted me with salt, I might stay sane.

Because Michael Pollan and Barbara Kingsolver and Eric Schlosser and all their little "eat real food" friends are in my head (more on this later), I'm going with organic produce and free-range, cage-free chickens and eggs. I realize "free-range" can be as misleading as labeling Lucky Charms "heart healthy," but it's a baby step toward healthier food and more humane farming practices. I'm deviating from my giant grocery store for the first time, so let me imagine my birds roamed the countryside in chicken bliss eating grass and frolicking with their fowl pals while the farmer pet their wee chicken heads and gave them all names.

Four members of The Council are adopting a version of seven foods: They chose seven of the most impoverished countries, and for three days each, they are eating like that nation's poorest. During those three days, we will pray for that country and its people, learn about its struggles, and in some small way identify with those who suffer there. They will eat the humblest of food from Haiti, Ethiopia, Uganda, Afghanistan, Bolivia, Cambodia, and Sudan.

So with that I begin Month One with excitement, anxiety, and a little trepidation. As you read the first few pages, kindly take note of these findings by researchers from the University of Vermont College of Medicine and Johns Hopkins School of Medicine: "The team demonstrated that stopping daily caffeine consumption produces changes in cerebral blood flow velocity and quantitative EEG that are likely related to the classic caffeine withdrawal symptoms of headache, drowsiness and decreased alertness."[2] All right? So nothing is my fault for the next five days, including bad writing and/or aimless ranting. If you encounter either, just attribute it to my *condition*.

Day 1

Lemon cheesecake, spinach and artichoke dip, salsa, crab dip, White Russian cupcakes, pimento cheese sandwiches (from Central Market and can't be disrespected with inadequate words), a plethora of tortilla chips/crackers/ Wheat Thins/bread chunks to shovel all this goodness into my mouth: This was the buffet last night at my girlfriend's baby shower. I kept telling my girlfriends it was The Last

Supper. They pretended to still care after the ninth time I'd referenced it. I took my last bite at 11:28 p.m.

Let 7 commence.

However, the experiment started today in the most unnormal way. My kids are out of school, and I scattered them around so we could sleep in. Thus, Brandon woke me up at 10:15 (don't hate—I did my time in baby prison and can now enjoy the occasional leisurely morning) and said, "We have lunch with that couple at 11:00, remember?"

If by "remember" he meant write it down or put it in my calendar, then no. So I found myself in a bloody restaurant for my first meal of 7. The menu caused an instant panic attack. I'm still operating by the letter of the law here. I don't know if I'm going to be flexible in social settings or eat something with parsley. I'm just not sure. I'm a total legalist at this point. I haven't even had a chance to follow the rules, much less break them.

I see spinach salad with chicken, but its covered in honey roasted walnuts, goat cheese, baby tomatoes, and red onions and tossed in homemade vinaigrette. This description alone could send me to the fetal position. How will I endure this kind of temptation?

You don't understand how much I love food. *Good food.* I adore innovative ingredients with fresh produce and perfectly cooked meat, especially the kind that is doused in condiments. I believe food is simply a vehicle to devour sauces. I am a flavor junkie, and my happiest moments take place with a fork in my mouth.

Perhaps I am being dramatic because my head is pounding out of my skull. Council Member Susana advised me to step down my caffeine intake for a few days before I started. And then some other words came out of her mouth that sounded like blah, blah, blah. So I weaned myself off coffee, meaning I only had two cups yesterday instead of four. Why would I deprive myself of coffee before I had to? I said I'd rather suffer through withdrawal, which is precisely what I am enjoying right now.

Awesome.

But back to brunch. If I followed my food rules, I'd have to ask the chef to make something that didn't exist on his menu. Or the instructions would be so annoying that I would probably regret whatever the chef sent out to the impossible granola weirdo girl at Table 12:

"Can you hold everything on that spinach salad? Can you not flavor the chicken? And can you not use the onions and seasonings and eggs in my sweet potato cakes? Is the bread prebuttered? Are the apples cinnamoned?"

Then I saw it: á la carte. This was my answer, and by divine intervention, breakfast was served at Galaxy Café until 1:00 p.m. Plain scrambled eggs (yes, I asked), dry wheat toast, and a side of sliced avocado. And water. I was in business. The Council approved salt and pepper, so my first meal fell nicely within the boundaries of 7.

I tried not to look at my friend's heaping pile of French toast smothered in fresh strawberries, maple syrup, and powdered sugar. I certainly didn't concentrate on his side of bacon. (If you think there is a better combination than bacon and syrup, drive to Austin and I'll fight you.) I chose gratitude that neither of these two fresh faces ordered coffee, and thus I didn't have to resort to violence or hate.

I also had a love surge for Brandon who is doing this month with me, even though he asked if he could substitute cheeseburgers for spinach. I held my tongue when he ordered a tortilla wrap with eggs, spinach, and avocados, because everyone knows a tortilla doesn't count as bread. I tried not to be judgmental. He didn't eat the salsa, which took such unfathomable heroics, I can hardly fuss about the tortilla. It's bread-ish. And he's not getting paid for this.

Quick note: my stomach was growling at 3:00, so I grabbed an apple. I deviated from my normal cheap, from-wherever apples and splurged on organic Fuji apples. Let me tell you something: Yum. That thing was good. It was the antithesis to my bland eggs, dry toast, and avocado from breakfast. I'm feeling the love for apples. Let's see if it holds.

Reader, don't worry that I am going to bore you with the minutia of every meal and snack for the next forty pages. I have other stuff to talk about. But it's Day 1, and the reduced menu is distracting me from (what will certainly be) terribly impressive spiritual observations. But for today my head hurts, and ordering at a restaurant traumatized me. Give me grace to worry that starting tomorrow—Day Stinking 2—I'm speaking at an event for two days. My weird food limits are about to become someone else's minor problem. Can I pack a sweet potato in my carry-on? I don't even know.

Okay, back to today, dinner was somewhat of a nice surprise. Not nice like "a filet covered in peppercorn sauce" but nice like "this didn't stink as bad as I thought." I had a sweet potato and sautéed spinach. These food items are not unfamiliar, but the stripped down cooking process was. Normally, I'd bake sweet potatoes in olive oil and sweet onions or slather them in butter and cinnamon. I love them whipped up with half-and-half and cream cheese. And spinach? Give me mushrooms, shallots, red pepper flakes, olive oil. Give me creamed spinach with nutmeg and butter.

A microwaved sweet potato with just salt and pepper? Spinach sautéed in water? Surprisingly, not bad. There is nice natural flavor in both, which I couldn't have possibly known since I condiment-up food (this is a verb) before taking my silverware out of the napkin. Again, it could be that I bought organic, local produce, notoriously more flavorful than its mass-produced, imported counterpart. But regardless, both tasted yummy, even though they were the not-as-cute wingman version of my usual hot chick dishes.

Admittedly, I felt unanchored in my own kitchen today. I had a cupcake—a strawberry daiquiri cupcake with cream filling and fresh strawberries *I made from scratch* yesterday—on my counter looking at me. It was strange not to pinch a bite off. I stared it down, trying to own it with my mind. I opened my pantry and uttered, "You're dead to me." It was all bizarre.

Which reminds me: I'm doing this for a reason. This is a fast, a major reduction of the endless possibilities that accompany my every meal. It is supposed to be uncomfortable and inconvenient. Not because I'm a narcissist but because the discomfort creates space for the Holy Spirit to move. This shake-up of my routine commands my attention. I can no longer default to normal, usual, mindless, thoughtless. It's like having an eyelash under my contact all day.

What will the Spirit do with this new space? I don't know. We'll see. It's His to engineer. I won't box Him in or assume I know what He'll say. I'm not going to project my goals onto His movement. I have simply said, "Jesus, may there be less of me and my junk and more of You and Your kingdom." I will reduce, so He can increase.

Admittedly, the spiritual waters were stagnant today. I was distracted by the mechanics, the launching. I struggled to find a spiritual rhythm. Ingredients and headaches sidetracked me. Perhaps this is the philosophy behind the biblical fasts of three days, seven days, and forty days in the Word. Maybe we need more than one day to push through the inauguration onto the business of communion. After the shine wears off, the real spiritual work begins.

And maybe these blasted headaches will wane.

Dear coffee: I miss you already. We're just on a break. Don't worry. They say if you love something, set it free; and if it comes back to you, then it was truly addicted to you in the first place. Hold onto that. Mark it down: Jen/Java reunion in thirty days. Be strong.

Late Night E-mail from Brandon Hatmaker

Dear Jen Hatmaker:

tor•til•la

–noun, plural -til•las   [-tee-uhz; Sp. -tee-yahs] Mexican Cookery.

A thin, round, unleavened **BREAD** prepared from cornmeal or sometimes wheat flour, baked on a flat plate of iron, earthenware, or the like.

Day 2

I'm sitting in the Dallas airport, happy to discover I've completed half a day on the road with no major incidents. I made my own breakfast, which was, well, exactly what I ate in the restaurant yesterday, but cheaper. I ate lunch during my layover, and this dawned on me:

I eat a lot of food in airports. Like, a lot. Layovers are the bane of my existence so I eat in airports or I don't eat sometimes. I walked past ten places before I found one that would work: That's right . . . Subway, Jared's yellow brick road to skinniness.

Wheat bread, chicken breast, raw spinach, and avocado. Dry. Not only were these fast-food caliber ingredients; they were airport fast-food ingredients. Blech. The girl in front of me, possibly a lost sister, had not one, not two, but three sauces ladled on her sandwich: sweet chicken teriyaki sauce, honey mustard, and oil and vinegar. She even had him spread the sauces with a spatula for even coverage, which is exactly what I do (hello, OCD). I need my condiments and layers represented in exact ratios.

This is a good time to tell you that I take sandwiches very seriously. Ask my friends. I'm not going down with peanut butter and jelly or plain ham and cheese. Those are for amateurs. I pile up the ingredients: tomatoes, shredded cheddar or gruyere, thinly sliced honey ham, romaine, banana peppers, avocado slices, bread and butter pickles, honey mustard. The honey mustard is so essential that I would not make a sandwich should I find myself without it, which I would never allow to happen. Ever.

I like my bread lightly toasted, then I pile the meat and cheese on one slice and slide it under the broiler for a meltdown. The cold ingredients go on the other piece, and then they get married and live happily ever after in my belly. I am a sandwich diva. I eat one almost every day.

But I digress.

Once I arrived to the church where I was speaking, my adorable hostess had a plain grilled chicken sandwich for me from—wait for it—Chick-fil-A (be still my heart). I'd sent an e-mail vaguely explaining my food limits and asking ever so nicely if I could stay within the boundaries of 7.

Insert the scenario I was dreading:

As we arrived at the church, my event planner said, "I want you to meet our pastor!" We trotted into his beautiful office, and he welcomed me by saying:

"We've been hearing all about your weird food requests!"

I knew it.

I won't be remembered as the funny author or the fascinating Bible teacher but as the high-maintenance girl who sent a list of culinary demands like I was Beyonce. So I babbled uncontrollably trying to explain 7 (which I haven't done yet in under eight minutes), hoping to resurrect my reputation as low maintenance. I came across as a bizarre hippie who was a below average communicator.

Anyhow, I had a Spirit encounter later that redeemed the day. I spoke to a group of young women, and at the end I invited them to leave something at the altar: tangible sacrifices for a homeless mission—shoes, coats, gloves, scarves; or intangible offerings like a relationship, a habit, a heartache, a dream.

As I watched these dear girls leave their treasures for God's safekeeping, we sang:

> *I believe You're my healer.*
>
> *I believe You are all I need.*
>
> *I believe You're my portion.*
>
> *I believe You're more than enough for me.*
>
> *Jesus You're all I need.*

So I stood there with tears, hands raised, trusting Jesus to be enough. As I reduce, He is enough. As I simplify, He is enough. He is my portion where food and clothes and comfort fall woefully short. He can heal me from greed and excess, materialism and pride, selfishness and envy. While my earthly treasures and creature comforts will fail me, Jesus is more than enough. In my privileged world where "need" and "want" have become indistinguishable, my only true requirement is the sweet presence of Jesus. So I wrote my offering on an index card and left it:"All of me."

Day 5

I ate a whole plate of nonsanctioned food today. I was still full five hours later. The only item remotely permissible was chicken, but it was covered with such rich sauce and exotic spices it isn't even related to my bland chicken-with-salt-only.

(Warning: impending justification.) The Council just transitioned to Ethiopian food, and they decided to experience genuine food prepared by a true national: enter Aster's Ethiopian Restaurant. Here's how the justification unfolded:

Molly: You definitely want to come. Just eat first.

Me: Of course I'm coming. Where is it?

Molly: Well, I-35 and something. I mean, come on! It's the little restaurant that faces the highway with the GIANT PICTURE OF AFRICA AND THE ETHIOPIAN FLAG.

Me: Oh yeah.

I have an inexplicable, boundless love for Ethiopia, a country I have never set foot in. I've memorized pictures,

I've poured over Web sites, read heaps of African books. I
have thirty Ethiopian blogs bookmarked, which I devour
with envy and pleasure. The beautiful people of Ethiopia
frequent my dreams and nightmares. I know its history,
nobility, its strength, its tragedies. I've mourned its losses
and celebrated its triumphs. All this for a country I've
never even been to.

But we are adopting two of its children.

Ironically, I mailed our adoption application today.

So I had a clear dog in this hunt. I couldn't miss an
Ethiopian restaurant to breathe its smells, its character.
I joined my girlfriends and enjoyed a fascinating tutorial
by Judy Kassaye, Aster's daughter. She taught us about
Ethiopian cuisine, how to eat it with injera bread. She
explained each dish on the buffet, a veritable feast from
the cradle of civilization.

When she left us to our dining, my girlfriends closed ranks.

"You have to eat this.""It's a crime if you don't."

"You're going to have to cook this stuff soon!"

"We can't eat Ethiopian food before you do."

"We have Council Majority here. We say yes."

So we agreed on a 7 moratorium, and I grabbed a plate,
thrilled to share in the Ethiopian spirit and palate. On
Judy's advice we took a spoonful of every dish, around
twenty varieties of a few meat dishes and mostly
vegetarian fare. Onions, garlic, ginger, turmeric, Berbere,

cinnamon, fresh lemon, tomatoes, green peppers; I died and went to flavor heaven. I'm an adventurous eater anyway, but this was a whole new frontier.

Admittedly, some got spit into my napkin. (I'm sorry, Ethiopia. You would spit out our processed American cheese food and McDonald's "chicken" nuggets, trust me.) We all had, um, intestinal issues by the day's end because I'd been eating bland whole foods, and The Council ate like homeless Haitians all week.

However, we marveled together and discussed favorites and surprises. In fact, everyone but me went back for seconds, because I was already in seriously gray territory and one round of prohibited food was all my Type-A conscience could handle. The Council came back with desserts that looked like chocolate cake and lemon cake. When they pushed it over to me, I said: "That just looks like cake. Do you think it's uniquely Ethiopian?"

Silence.

Crickets.

"Whatever, Jen. It was made in an Ethiopian restaurant. Stop ruining our fun." All right. But I passed on what was clearly *chocolate cake and lemon cake* you could get at Applebee's.

Aster immigrated to the U.S. from Addis Ababa when Judy was two, but Judy didn't join her until she was nine. In so many ways she was like the children we're adopting: changing countries in elementary school, joining parents who were basically strangers, starting over with Ethiopia cemented in her blood, her language, her heart.

"Judy? I'm adopting children from Ethiopia who will be around the age you were when you moved to Austin. If you could give me one piece of advice, what would it be?"

"The kindest thing you can do is keep them connected to their country. Teach them the proud history of Ethiopia and instill love for their mother country. Cook our food. Pray our prayers. Take them back to walk on the soil where they were born. They might push back because sometimes adopted children just want to be American, no different from the other kids around them. But when they are grown, they will be so grateful you kept their heritage alive."

At this point Shonna and I were bawling (we're both adopting and that's what we do), and all of us were enraptured. I wanted to kidnap Judy and make her be my best friend. We came for Ethiopian food but left with Ethiopia in our hearts. Plus, I bought a pound of Ethiopian coffee beans and a hand-painted mug Aster made. It will be the first thing I enjoy twenty-three days from now, but who is counting not me of course.

I came home floating.

Cut to dinner.

I made the kids breaded fish fillets, baked and crispy, which they have eaten a thousand times. I put a few goodies on the side (my seven-year-old Caleb loves "cold broccoli," which I consider a parenting victory and might mention on my adoption paperwork). Since Brandon and I had finished our chicken and spinach, I ran upstairs to do something terrifically exciting like sorting laundry or washing it or drying it or folding it or putting it away.

(Jealous?) I came down five minutes later to find all three kids in the living room.

"Did you finish eating already?"

"Yes."

"Did you eat everything?"

Long pause.

"Pretty much."

I went to the trash and saw five of the six fish fillets uneaten, even *unbitten*.

When the kids saw my face, they mumbled: "We didn't have any ketchup."

Maybe it was the headache I couldn't shake this week. Maybe it was the pizza commercial I saw that caused me actual pain. But probably it was my afternoon in an Ethiopian restaurant where I prayed for my African children and worried they were hungry and wished desperately they knew I was coming. It was probably the haunting knowledge that East Africa is suffering drought for the sixth year in a row. I wish I didn't know that Ethiopian Disaster Prevention Minister Mikitu Kassahas denied reports that millions need urgent food aid and claimed the government was helping those hit by the drought. He argued, "In the Ethiopian context, there is no hunger, no famine."[3]

My children live in the ninth poorest country in the world where 46 percent are undernourished with a global hunger index listed as "extremely alarming." Tragically, the World Food Programme, that assists eleven million people in Ethiopia, reduced the emergency food ration by one third, just when food assistance is critically required.[4] Meanwhile, embarrassed government officials are insisting the sky is not falling and international intervention is not needed. The chances my African children are going to bed hungry are so high I almost don't need to waste a line space speculating.

And tonight my kids here with me in the land of plenty threw away a pound of food because they didn't have ketchup.

How can we extract our children from this filthy engine where indulgence and ignorance and ungratefulness and waste are standard protocol? Where they know they can throw perfectly good food away because there is always more in the pantry?

I wept for all my children tonight, my Ethiopian children orphaned by disease or hunger or poverty who will go to bed with no mother tonight and my biological children who will battle American complacency and over indulgence for the rest of their lives.

I don't know who I feel worse for.

"Tell me about the world before. What was it like?"

"We didn't even know what was precious.

We threw away things that people would kill for today."

—The Book of Eli

Day 7

I could arguably be the Christian poster child. My dad is a pastor, and I went to church three times a week as a fetus. I am fluent in Christianspeak and can navigate the (wacky) world of Christian subculture blindfolded. I can still sing a few Petra songs by heart, and I used to pretend to be Sandy Patti belting out "Via Dolorosa." I burned my secular tapes and re-bought them all twice. There isn't an Acquire the Fire, One Day, Passion, or Women of Faith conference I haven't sat through. I once wore a T-shirt to high school that said, "This is your brain. This is your brain in hell. Any questions?" I wish I were kidding. (If these references make no sense to you, then you obviously didn't grow up in the Bible Belt, or you've repressed the memories. Carry on.)

Consequently, I have heard more sermons, talks, messages, and lectures on Christianity than can possibly be impactful. I have spent half my life listening to someone else talk about God.

Because of this history, I've developed something of an immunity to sermons. Typing that is embarrassing; it makes me sound so unteachable. Teaching by example, radical obedience, justice, mercy, activism, and sacrifice wholly inspires me. I'm at that place where "well done" trumps "well said." When I see kingdom work in the middle of brokenness, when mission transitions from the academic soil of the mind into the sacrificial work of someone's hands, I am utterly affected. Obedience inspires me. Servant leaders inspire me. Humility inspires me. Talking heads dissecting apologetics stopped inspiring me a few years ago.

Like this rhetoric I stumbled on:

I have been thinking lately about how to classify different types of theology. What I am interested in here is only secondarily connected to the sorts of theological positions taken by those doing theology in any of the modes that I will explicate. The modes themselves are what interest me. It seems to me that one can fall anywhere on the continuum between orthodoxy and heterodoxy while working within any of these modes. Of course, some modes may make it easier than others to lean toward one or the other pole on this continuum, but that is beside the point.[5]

What the what? I would suggest this entire line of thinking is beside the point. I'm over this. Before I lose my doctoral students, trust me, I know theology has its place. And I appreciate the irony of a Bible student, paid speaker, and pastor's wife penning these thoughts. But when the exhaustive exegesis of God's Word doesn't create people transformed into the image of Jesus, we have missed the forest for the trees. Or perhaps Jesus explained it better: "You diligently study the Scriptures because you think that by them you possess eternal life. These are the Scriptures that testify about me, yet you refuse to come to me to have life" (John 5:39–40).

The careful study of the Word has a goal, which is not the careful study of the Word. The objective is to discover Jesus and allow Him to *change our trajectory*. Meaning, a genuine study of the Word results in believers who feed poor people and open up their guest rooms; they're adopting and sharing, mentoring and intervening. Show me a Bible teacher off mission, and I'll show you someone with no concept of the gospel he is studying.

The ivory-tower approach to sermonizing just wore me out after twenty-five years. I developed resistance to sermons because so many have been heard but rarely seen. This detachment is clearly not good. If I cannot be moved by God's delivered Word, I've set myself up as untrainable. That is some seriously dangerous territory.

So today in church, Matthew, our missions pastor, was at the helm. (A quick insert: my husband and our other two pastors are so on mission, they run out of time for church stuff. Two of them, including Brandon, are bi-vocational with their second jobs in nonprofit work. Brandon has never made it through one sermon without choking up. These dudes are not just talking about it, yet my sermon resistance has flared up even at my own beloved church.) Matthew is our resident theologian/activist. He's the guy who reads Tozer, then drives off to work with refugees.

Note that 7 is a one-week-old baby today. Spiritually, I've noticed a thaw. I can't pin it down yet except to describe a general softening. God has His eye on a couple of these hardened areas. He is showing me that my emotional barrier is throwing the baby out with the bathwater; I've missed some really good babies because they were once immersed in the bathwater of stale organized religion. The Spirit is whispering, "You are fighting a straw man here."

Matthew's sermon today confirms this. Or rather, my response to his sermon confirms this. After some smack-you-around Bible teaching on Acts, he asked three questions:

1. What in my life, if taken away, would alter my value or identity?

2. What causes an unhealthy change of attitude, personality, or focus when "it" becomes threatened?

3. What is the thing outside of God that you put everything else on hold for?

I sat there in a tsunami of convictions.

Rather than the arrogant, hard-edged, I've-heard-this-stuff-before reaction, I asked God the three questions. And lo and behold, He had some answers. Not surprisingly, I am unhealthily attached to the very things I'll be giving up during 7: approval, stuff, appearances, money, recognition, control.

That critical perspective has to go, too. Cynicism wreaked some havoc on my gentleness, my humility. When God interrupted our lives a couple of years ago, He deconstructed some toxic paradigms and rebuilt them on a sturdier foundation. However, unwilling to address them, I left a few in rubble, never reconstructed or reimagined. The debris proved fertile soil for cynicism, as it always does for the obstinate.

So I repent today, acknowledging my reflection in the Scripture we studied: "You stiff-necked people . . . you always resist the Holy Spirit!" (Acts 7:51). That is not the legacy I want to leave. I want to live gratefully, humbly, hopefully. Clinging to criticism has not made me happier; it just made me cynical. It played a bit part when Jesus used discontentment to move me, but now it is simply baggage I must shed if I hope to carry on with integrity.

Day 8

Hey, guess who I hate? That's right, you, Chicken Breast. I can't believe I ever had feelings for you. You're so dry, and you only taste good when someone covers up your blahness. Salt and pepper is just lipstick on a pig or, in this case, a fowl. I spent forever making a sweet potato and apple hash and stuffing it into your innards, only to be sorely disappointed by the Sahara Desert dryness of your boob meat. You need to be breaded, coated, injected, and smothered to be decent. We're going to have to part ways. I'm shacking up with your little friends Thighs, Legs, and Weird Parts Underneath That Taste Good. You've ruined my last dish.

However, I had a glorious culinary moment today, quite by accident. Like an addict returns to her crack house, I watched the Food Network today during lunch. Listen, I can't quit the FN. Those people are my friends, my muses. I sent an e-mail to the Neeleys once asking if they would adopt me. I mute Rachael Ray to avoid her wordy words but copy her oh-so-marvelous dishes. Giada gets lots of play as long as the hubs is gone, since I'm not all about her low-cut shirts near my man. There aren't words to express my devotion to Paula Deen. I enjoy watching thirty minutes of food preparation as much as watching Brandon do the dishes.

So while I dined on spinach (again) and half a sweet potato (again), what to my hungry eyes should appear, but Ina Garten, Mrs. Barefoot Contessa, pulling out ingredients for a dish that looked 7-approved. It was like watching lottery balls pop up while I held my precious ticket with its seven small numbers:

"Butternut squash . . ." I can sub sweet potatoes!

"Nice tart apples . . ."

(gasp) Check.

"Sweet onions . . ."

(sigh) I can omit.

"Olive oil . . ."

Oh my stars.

"Salt and pepper . . ."

Come on, come on . . ."

And a little chicken stock."

OH MY GOSH! OH MY WORD! I can't believe it! I won! These are all my ingredients! I called my friends and sent out a mass e-mail. It was thrilling. I emerged from food poverty with one magnificent windfall.

Following directions to a T, I roasted the cubed sweet potatoes and apples in olive oil and salt and pepper, making good use of their natural sugars as they caramelized in the oven. A quick buzz in the food processer to smooth it out. Back into a saucepan to thin out with chicken stock (which I made the day before) and cracked pepper.

Gavin: What's chicken stock?

Me: It's basically chicken-flavored water.

Gavin: Awesome! Will you put some in my lunch tomorrow instead of juice?

Me: You're telling me you want to drink chicken water?

Gavin: Who wouldn't?

So anyway, the soup started bubbling, the caramelized bits rose to the top, and I did a happy hand clap. I sliced up half an avocado for the perfect topping, took a picture of my precious new dish, and let me tell you something: I blacked out a couple of times. It was soup divinity, and I became its disciple. I can't fathom how good it will taste when I add roasted onions and a dash of cream and fresh thyme. Oh, mama. Thank you, Ina Garten. Goes to show you: Never trust a skinny cook, but always trust one with a nice big squishy middle because *that* girl understands her some good food.

Day 10

Brandon is insisting I tell you that I ate a tortilla in the airport with my eggs. They didn't have toast, okay? Plus, everyone knows a tortilla is a thin, round, unleavened bread prepared from cornmeal or sometimes wheat flour, baked on a flat plate of iron, earthenware, or the like.

Day 11

I just got off the phone with Trina, and it's official: 7 draws a strong response. Intentional reduction is so uncommon people just don't know what to do with it. Folks are adding, not subtracting.

We're encountering two responses. For those hungry for simplicity too, they beg, "Take me with you!" 7 resonates with people already carrying tension about what *enough* really means. They immediately pledge devotion to 7, complete with a dissertation on how tired, broke, unhealthy, and disappointed they are with the American rat race.

"I'm doing this with you. Send me everything you have so far."

"My whole family is in."

"This is the best idea I've ever heard next to the Bible."

"I feel violated, like you've been reading my thoughts!"

"My wife came home ranting about gardening and adoption after eating lunch with you." (Sorry, Luke.)

Ironically, studies show that increased consumerism comes at a steep price. A rise in prosperity is not making people happier or healthier. Findings from a survey of life satisfaction in more than sixty-five countries indicate that income and happiness track well until about $13,000 of annual income per person. After that, additional income produces only modest increments in self-reported happiness. It's no wonder. We are incurring debt and working longer hours to pay for the high-consumption lifestyle, consequently spending less time with family, friends, and community.

"Excess consumption can be counterproductive," said Gary Gardner, director of research for Worldwatch. "The irony is that lower levels of consumption can actually cure some of these problems."[6] That makes sense: If we buy only what we need and can afford, debt becomes a moot point. When accumulation is not our bottom line, we are liberated to disperse our time and resources differently. I know working to pay off The Man and keep the house of cards intact has not made me a happy camper. A bunch of us are wondering if there is a better way.

But not everyone. I'm developing a thick skin for the other reaction 7 draws. The Council concurs. It goes more like this:

"Why would you do that?!"

"Weird."

"Don't you think this is a little extreme?" (Um, yes.)

"You're turning eccentric."

"What is the point?"

"Hmmm."

"You always have to have something, don't you?" (I don't even know what this means.)

I can tell who is going to dig it and who so isn't. I'm getting used to the "I-thought-you-were-normal-but-now-I-see-I-was-plainly-wrong" face. Maybe I *am* turning into a girl who always has to have something, I don't know. What I do know is that my "something" is a desire to look more like Jesus. I am pierced by Gandhi's astute observation: "I like your Christ. I do not like your Christians. Your Christians are so unlike your Christ."

Would Jesus overindulge on garbage food while climbing out of a debt hole from buying things He couldn't afford to keep up with neighbors He couldn't impress? In so many ways I am the opposite of Jesus' lifestyle. This keeps me up at night. I can't have authentic communion with Him while mired in the trappings He begged me to avoid.

I wouldn't dare call this reaction to 7 persecution since that would be laughable. I'm not sure "I think you're stupid" is in the same category as "I'm going to kill you" as far as spiritual backlash goes. But it does forge a small sense of solidarity with Jesus, as He was always misunderstood for His countercultural ideas.

The least shall be the greatest.

Blessed are the meek.

Humble yourself like a child.

Sell all your things and give to the poor.

Don't gain the world only to forfeit your soul.

I can't imagine these were popular ideas either. I'm sure Jesus got the "I-thought-you-were-normal-but-now-I-see-I-was-plainly-wrong" face plenty of times. He seriously knew how to thin out a crowd. He always gunned for less, reduced, simplified. He was the most fully and completely unselfish, ungreedy, unpretentious man to ever live, and I just want to be more like Him. It's as simple and hard as that.

So if eggs and apples, bread and spinach, sweet potatoes and chicken, avocados and water can help Jesus overcome me, then so be it. I'm okay with my oddball label.

Day 12

I had a glorious, marvelous 7 evening.

It started with a dinner invite, although this would typically be disastrous. (When consulting The Council on what to do when people cook for me or take me to dinner, they advised: "Don't be an imbecile.") I tell people the basics of 7 and hope for the best when I'm not in control of the kitchen.

Sidebar: This position resulted in two extraordinary food oases this month. First, an event planner in Texarkana catered a dinner, anchored by chicken salad sandwiches. Striving not to be an imbecile, I ate it. Oh, did I eat it. Chicken and mayonnaise should spawn sandwiches like this one forever and ever, amen. Second, my event team in Columbia hosted a dinner involving creamed spinach. I couldn't speak because *there were no words*. I ate every bite before my fork acknowledged the chicken. I don't care what it is—drown it in cream and Parmesan, and, as we say in Texas: It'll eat.

Anyhow, this dinner invite was safe because it was Council Member Susana's parents, Dale and Laurel, who'd already navigated Pick Five with her. Laurel asked about my seven foods in advance, so I didn't waste any emotional space worrying about an impending evasion.

Dale and Laurel are Messianic Jews who go to our church along with most of their giant family/commune. We arrived at 6:00, just as the sun was setting. The table boasted a beautiful presentation of all seven foods. It was so dear and thoughtful, I almost burst into tears.

Traditionally, on Friday afternoon, observant Jews begin Shabbat, or Sabbath, preparations. The mood is like preparing for the arrival of a special, beloved guest: the house is cleaned, the family dresses up, the best dishes are set, and a festive meal is prepared—in our case, a 7-inspired meal. Shabbat candles are lit and a blessing recited just before sunset. This ritual, performed by the woman of the house, officially marks the beginning of Shabbat.

The two candles represent two commandments: *zakhor* ("remember" creation and God's deliverance from captivity) and *shamor* ("observe" the day of rest God initiated at creation). Dale led us through a traditional Kiddush, a prayer over wine sanctifying Shabbat while passing a loaf of challah, a sweet bread shaped into a braid.

We shared some beautiful readings of Scripture together (until the Hebrew parts when Brandon and I stayed silent to not butcher this lovely moment with atrocious pronunciation). Dale and Laurel sang a few sections, and the whole thing was beautiful. Between the communion, the food prepared with loving hands, the Scripture, and the ancient rhythm of it all, I was overjoyed.

There are many Shabbat readings available, but this one I love:

> There are days when we seek things for ourselves
> and measure failure by what we do not gain.
> On the Sabbath we seek not to acquire but to share.
>
> There are days when we exploit nature
> as if it were a horn of plenty that can never be exhausted.

On the Sabbath we stand in wonder before the mystery
of creation.

There are days when we act as if we cared nothing
for the rights of others.
On the Sabbath we are reminded that justice is our duty and a
better world our goal.

Therefore we welcome Shabbat.
Day of rest, day of wonder, day of peace.

Day 16

Facebook status/thread by Brandon:

**I'm tired of avocado and eggs. And I hate spinach
without a bunch of ranch. There. I said it.**

Jen Hatmaker: Don't forget dry chicken breast. I hate you,
chicken breast.

Brian J: Try stewed spinach. Had some in grade school.

Scarred me for life!

Becky F: I love avocados and eggs, but I include sausage,
sour cream, and cheese. Is that helpful?

Matt F: Are you on a reality show?

Brandon H: Feels like it, Matt. Feels like it.

Becky M: Dear Sweet Jesus, Please make the chicken juicy.
Amen.

Day 17

So I had my first 7-induced cry. I felt it coming on. I alerted
Brandon that at some point today I would probably cry,
and it wouldn't be his fault, but I might blame it on him.
He was warned.

It was the perfect storm of factors. I was ousted from
my house for the last three days, making 7 adherence
profoundly difficult. I've had five coffees/breakfasts/
lunches in three days, meaning other people drank coffee,
and I pretended to listen while fixating on their java.

Or they ate tomato-basil soup at La Madeline's while I
picked at plain chicken and dry spinach. Cashier: "So you
don't want the bacon on your salad?" No. "What about the
candied walnuts?" No. "Red onions or feta cheese?" No. Just
spinach on a plate, dude! Gah! It still came out tossed in
vinaigrette and I had to send it back.

Plus, I burned my third batch of baked sweet potato chips.
I JUST WANT A SNACK FOOD, FOR THE LOVE OF PETE. I
need a handful of little somethings I can pop in my mouth.
Listen, this is how sweet potato chips bake: too soft, too
soft, too soft, burnt. I can't get it right. They need to be
fried in oil, or just forget about it.

Then, last night, some pastor friends from Chicago were in
town for a conference and wanted to have dinner. "We've
heard all about Hula Hut!" they chirped. "Can we meet
there?"

%@*#!!

Hula Hut is the greatest Mexican/Hawaiian fusion restaurant ever, a total Austin icon. They make homemade tortillas and salsa I would commit actual murder just to have. My craving for tomato products is so severe, I think I've developed a disorder. I dream about salsa, marinara, spaghetti sauce, and pico de gallo. And ketchup. I feel lightheaded just typing it. Sitting at Hula Hut with its glorious salsa six inches away was torture. So was my condiment-free entrée while our friends were all experiencing food spasms.

Plus, it's been raining for five days.

Plus, Texas lost to Baylor in overtime. *Baylor*.

Plus, the Super Bowl is Sunday, and 7 is going to ruin it.

So that's why I looked at an avocado next to yesterday's chicken and burst into tears. I just want to eat. Other stuff. All my foods except apples are soft and bland. (If it weren't for apples, I'd be bereft.) I had a nice, dramatic lament while Brandon commented helpfully, "This whole thing was your idea, you know."

I tried to redirect my emotions toward Jesus, but I struggled to maintain composure. Everything felt dark; I couldn't find center. I retreated to my bedroom and sat on the edge of the bed and prayed:

"Jesus, please help me find gratitude. This whole thing feels stupid."

It took a minute, but here is what came to mind:

I remembered how my friend Krista made a test version of her sweet potato soufflé with only 7-sanctioned ingredients, declared it still delicious, offered to bring it over, and sent me the recipe with happy thoughts and encouragement.

I recalled the twenty phone calls and e-mails this week from friends who love me, checking on 7 and cheering me on.

I thought about these seven healthy foods jam-packed with nutrition, fueling my body. My energy has doubled and I feel really good. I have the luxury of eating healthy, organic food, an extravagance in most of the world.

I remembered The Council, sticking by this project with absurd enthusiasm. I recalled *their* diet as they ate like the poor: rice, cornmeal, some beans, simple breads. These girls are deeply living 7 alongside me, and I'm so grateful.

I realized my slightly reduced life is still extraordinary in every way. There is no end to my advantages. For whatever reason I was born into privilege; I've never known hunger, poverty, or despair. I have been blessed, blessed, blessed— relationally, emotionally, spiritually, and physically. My life is so happy it's almost embarrassing.

So I thawed into a gratitude puddle, exchanging my physical aching for spiritual communion. It was a good trade. I exhaled and breathed, "Thank You."

Oh! I also remembered the dried apple slices I found at Sprouts, my favorite new natural grocery store, which I do believe counts as a snack. Lots of little somethings I can pop into my mouth that don't taste like tree bark and make a decent substitute for the chips and salsa I would sacrifice a child to have.

Thank You, Lord.

Day 19

At the DFW airport today, I almost bought a coffee. I stood four feet from Starbucks and nearly ordered. These were the sinister thoughts I entertained, nay, *coddled* for two minutes:

No one would ever know.

It would just be one cup.

I need the caffeine. For energy.

The letter of the law is not the point.

It would make me happy and, thus a better speaker tonight.

I want a soy vanilla latte so bad I could spit.

In one teeny moment of resolve, I sent an SOS text to The Council: "I'm about to buy a coffee. I-am-this-close. Somebody help me." The texts started buzzing in.

Susana: It probably tastes like dirty underwear anyway.

Shonna: Ask for hot water in a coffee cup.

Becky: I should say something spiritual about Jesus being your caffeine, but really that just sux.

Jenny: I say coffee is acceptable. Love, Your Favorite Council Woman. (This permissiveness is why Jenny was selected for The Council.)

I escaped narrowly by chewing gum like a quitting smoker. I should tell you that every time I've been in Sprouts, I've put my nose directly on the glass cases of bulk coffee beans and inhaled like a deranged weirdo. I mean, deeply inhaled. For at least ten seconds. Nose to the glass. The only possible way I could act more disturbing is if I ground up some beans, made a line with a razor blade, and snorted it in the middle of aisle 9.

My gosh. I think I have a problem. A friend asked if I was quitting coffee after this month was up. I told her I'd considered renouncing coffee exactly zero times, and if she ever brought up such foolishness again, I was going to quit *her*. Yeah. I definitely have a problem.

Day 21

So, between my pantry, refrigerator, and freezer, I have around 240 food items. This is the kitchen my kids holler in about having nothing to eat. Nearly everything in my pantry is processed. We may not eat enough raw broccoli, but we are getting plenty of soy lecithin and sodium acid pyrophosphate. Most have at least fourteen ingredients, and there is an excellent chance our blood has turned to straight high fructose corn syrup.

This bothers me.

Occasionally I come across a book that is so insightful it is a real struggle not to plagiarize the entire thing. If I could insert the entire content of In Defense of Food right here, I would do it. It has revolutionized my ideas about food and nutrition. This is the main premise: Eat food. Not too much. Mostly plants.

What author Michael Pollan means by "food" is "real food" that came from the ground, a tree, a plant, or an animal without messing with it, food that hasn't been loaded with corn syrup or injected with hormones. He writes not as a nutritionist overcomplicating something simple, but on the authority of tradition and common sense.

By the 1960s or so it had become all but impossible to sustain traditional ways of eating in the face of the industrialization of our food. If you wanted to eat produce grown without synthetic chemicals or meat raised on pasture without pharmaceuticals, you were out of luck. The supermarket had become the only place to buy food, and real food was rapidly disappearing from its shelves, to be replaced by the modern cornucopia of highly processed foodlike products.[7]

Our grandmas ate local meat and vegetables from their gardens; we eat Pop Tarts and Velveeta. Today in America the culture of food is changing more than once a generation, which is historically unprecedented. This machine is driven by a thirty-two billion-dollar food-marketing engine that thrives on change for its own sake, not to mention constantly shifting nutritional science that keeps folding in on itself every few years.

Pollan explains:

Like a large gray cloud, a great Conspiracy of Scientific Complexity has gathered around the simplest questions of nutrition—much to the advantage of everyone involved. Except perhaps the supposed beneficiary of all this nutritional advice: us, and our health and happiness as eaters. For the most important thing to know about the campaign to professionalize dietary advice is that it has not made us any healthier. To the contrary: it has actually made us less healthy and considerably fatter.[8]

Clearly. Four of the top ten causes of death in America today are chronic diseases with well-established links to our industrialized diet: coronary heart disease, diabetes, stroke, and cancer. These health plagues remain rare in countries where people don't eat like us, even if its local diet is high in fat or carbs, the two straw men America decided to fight. The basics of the Western diet include:

- The rise of highly processed foods and refined grains

- The use of chemicals to raise plants and animals in huge monocultures

- The abundance of cheap calories of sugar and fat

- The massive consumption of fast food

- The shrinking diversity of the human diet to a tiny handful of staple crops, notably wheat, corn, and soy (thanks to vigorous lobbying and strategic subsidization by our government)

- The conspicuous absence of fruit, vegetables, and whole grains[9]

This bodes terribly for us, and it is downright disastrous for our children. In fact, U.S. life expectancy was projected to rise indefinitely, but a new data analysis from the *New England Journal of Medicine* suggests this trend is about to reverse itself due to the rapid rise in obesity, especially among children. Our kids are the first generation in the history of America that has a shorter life span than their parents.[10]

There is a way out of this madness.

We get to vote three times a day against this toxic food supply with our forks.

Do you know what happened this month? After eating only whole foods and virtually no fast food, my pants are falling off. I feel energetic during my typical afternoon slump. My cheeks are rosy. My allergies disappeared. I haven't had a single digestive issue. My canker sores went dormant. I swear, my eyes are whiter.

There's more. What used to take two hours shopping at the big store now takes thirty-five minutes at the farmer's market. I've spent only half my grocery budget by not buying extra garbage. Plus, you can't imagine how much we've saved by eating mostly at home. We're wasting less; you better believe leftovers get eaten—this was rare before 7 because we had so many other choices. (Why eat yesterday's food when you could have new food?) More than ever, the family has gathered around the kitchen, chopping and stirring and rehashing our day.

Maybe food simplification is a good idea for all of us, and for more than one reason. Spiritual clarity and health come to mind. Waste reduction and time management and financial responsibility and gratefulness deserve some line space, too. There are other things, but that's a decent start list.

Barbara Kingsolver is a better foodie (and writer) than me, so let's wrap up with her oh-so-good thoughts:

When my generation of women walked away from the kitchen we were escorted down that path by a profiteering industry that knew a tired, vulnerable marketing target when they saw it. "Hey, ladies," it said to us, "go ahead, get liberated. We'll take care of dinner." They threw open the door and we walked into a nutritional crisis and genuinely toxic food supply. . . . But a devil of a bargain it has turned out to be in terms of daily life. We gave up the aroma of warm bread rising, the measured pace of nurturing routines, the creative task of molding our families' tastes and zest for life; we received in exchange the minivan and the Lunchable.[11]

I'm hoping for a way back home.

Day 26

I've read *In Defense of Food, Animal Vegetable Miracle, The Maker's Diet, Fast Food Nation,* and watched "Food, Inc." with my horrified children, who I am not ashamed to brainwash. Here's my conclusion:

I feel had.

I've been drinking the Kool-Aid the marketing industry, food lobbyists, nutritional "experts," and the FDA have been selling. You say oat bran is the new messiah? Check. Include in every recipe from 1988 to 1991. Fat is our enemy? Got it. Enter margarine, only one molecule away from plastic. Now carbohydrates are evil? Delete from menu. Insert angry feelings toward orange juice and other sneaky foods conspiring to make me fat. High fructose corn syrup is healthy because it's made from corn? Bring on the, well, ten million products it is pumped into.

After all, according to its Web site[12] high fructose corn syrup "*can* be part of a balanced diet", and these people would never lie to us. Evidently, our obesity epidemic has nothing to do with a highly processed sugar diet, but "a decrease in PE classes and other plausible explanations." (I know I haven't had a decent PE class since 1991.) Also? Good news! Its expert panel concluded that frequently consuming soft drinks will not increase our obesity risk at all.[13] Sweet surprise indeed! Dr. Pepper for everyone and pass the Oreos.

But beware of the carrots. They have an *agenda*. Honestly, I have swallowed this whole. I haven't had a glass of orange juice in four years, but I've had no problem drinking Diet Coke, with substantiated links to cancer and kidney failure. But it's fat free. My nutritional perspective is so tainted by marketing I've lost touch with common sense.

I thought I was safely bubble wrapped within 7 since my menu contains all whole foods except bread, but that's as wholesome as a toddler with dimples, right? Then I read this little gem under Pollan's food rule of thumb:

Avoid food products containing ingredients that are

a. unfamiliar,

b. unpronounceable,

c. more than five in number, or that include

d. high-fructose corn syrup:

Consider a loaf of bread, one of the "traditional foods that everyone knows" . . . As your grandmother could tell you, bread is traditionally made using a remarkably small number of familiar ingredients: flour, yeast, water, and a pinch of salt will do it. But industrial bread—even industrial whole-grain bread—has become a far more complicated product of modern food science (not to mention commerce and hope). Here's the complete ingredients list for Sara Lee's Soft & Smooth Whole Grain White Bread:

Enriched bleached flour [wheat flour, malted barley flour, niacin, iron, thiamin mononitrate (vitamin B1), riboflavin (vitamin B2), folic acid], water, whole grains [whole wheat flour, brown rice flour (rice flour, rice bran)], high fructose corn syrup, whey, wheat gluten, yeast, cellulose. Contains 2 percent or less of each of the following: honey, calcium sulfate, vegetable oil (soybean and/or cottonseed oils), salt, butter (cream, salt), dough conditioners (may contain one or more of the following: mono- and diglycerides, ethoxylated mono- and diglycerides, ascorbic acid, enzymes, azodicarbonamide), guar gum, calcium propionate (preservative), distilled vinegar, yeast nutrients (monocalcium phosphate, calcium sulfate, ammonium sulfate), corn starch, natural flavor, beta-carotene (color), vitamin D3, soy lecithin, soy flour.

There are many things you could say about this intricate loaf of "bread," but note first that even if it managed to slip by your great grandmother (because it is a loaf of bread, or at least is called one and strongly resembles one), the product fails every test proposed under rule number two. . . . Sorry, Sara Lee, but your Soft & Smooth Whole Grain White Bread is not food and if not for the indulgence of the FDA could not even be labeled "bread."[14]

For the love of Michael Pollan.

Sure enough, my 100 percent whole wheat bread had twenty-eight ingredients. I counted. I felt smug about this choice just weeks ago, but it has more ingredients than the most heinous box of sugared cereal I've ever bought.

So I decided to make my own bread. This sounds like nothing to you who roll out piecrusts and can your own tomatoes or whatever, but this was seriously new territory for me, so give me this Laura Ingalls Wilder moment. When I mentioned this brainchild to my girlfriends, I had a tsunami of offers for bread machines:

- "I have one in storage."

- "I have one in the attic."

- "I have one I couldn't sell in my garage sale."

- "I have one to set out when my mother-in-law visits."

So I borrowed a bread machine, and with four days left I've made six loaves. I want to report that homemade bread has changed our lives, making us more grateful and connected to the earth. I'd planned to wax nostalgic about the smell of baking bread and the delectable, warm goodness of eating the first piece. I mean, if homemade bread isn't the bull's-eye of domestic excellence, I don't know what is. Reading Barbara Kingsolver's accounts of rising dough and general delight in hearth and home made me want to build a brick oven and milk some cows. Here is my actual report:

My loaves have been gross.

I've used different mixes and different settings; I've sliced it super thin and as thick as bricks. I've eaten it warmed, toasted, baked, and room temp. I've tried wheat, half wheat, 9-grain, and rye. My bread was slathered with baked apples, used for a sandwich, toasted as croutons, and employed as a sponge for over-easy eggs. I've tried, people. *I've really tried.*

But it's just icky. My first loaf was as hard as cement and about as flavorful. The next five didn't fare much better. Maybe the wheat mixes are the problem. There is a reason people love white, fluffy bleached flour—nutritionally void but oozing with white-bread deliciousness. Perhaps I'm so used to bread sweetened with HFCS and lightened up with chemicals that I can't appreciate four-ingredient bread anymore. Maybe the omission of butter on fresh bread is just too criminal. Maybe this just needs to be done the old-fashioned way, um, whatever that is.

I don't know.

My sixth loaf came out an hour ago, I spent twenty minutes chopping apples and cooking them down into a spread, only to take one bite and nearly gag.

I guess I need to call my mom for cooking instruction like I did during the first few years of marriage when I was a domestic tragedy. I still believe in you, homemade bread! I know you can be delicious and soft. I won't be thwarted by my false starts, because clearly I have no idea what I'm doing in the baking department. It's like trusting a monkey with a baby; I need to be trained before handling another innocent mound of dough. Bread will not defeat me, I say! I have a college degree, I'm raising three decent humans (and none have perished), and I haven't run out of gas in six years.

I can make bread.

Day 29

I recant. The homemade bread is cement. I'm buying my bread. So what.

Day 30

God bless The Council. What began as an innocuous e-mail ("Hey girls! Anyone want to come over for appetizers and brainstorm an idea with me?") turned into a group project that involved me getting avocados and sweet potatoes while they ate cornmeal. After letting this first month settle a bit, Shonna wrote her thoughts on the food fast, and I dropped it back in here for your reading pleasure:

> *Fasting has always seemed like a radical thing to me. People like Gandhi fast. Not people like me. I have never really even considered a fast as a way to gain clarity or to better hear God's voice. My biggest problem with fasting is: I like to eat! I have seriously considered keeping breakfast bars in my*

nightstand. When my belly is empty, I feel less clear-headed, not more focused. I get grouchy and quick-tempered when I have not eaten in a few hours (or so I'm told).

When I volunteered to be a part of 7, I thought, sure, this is really not about me, it will be easy! I figured my participation would be in the support role. During the month Jen ate only seven foods, a small group of us chose an alternative. We selected seven countries and ate what the poorest residents of each country would eat for three days.

There was rice and plantain. There was rice. There was rice and plantain. People in underdeveloped countries don't eat much, and when they do, it's most commonly rice. I ate rice at home, I ate rice with my friends, I even ate rice at a restaurant. That last one got a funny look from the waiter; he must have thought that I was trying a new diet fad to lose weight. To be honest, I got a lot of comments. One friend even told me that I had become a bit "eccentric." I mean, look at me: eating rice and talking about Haiti and Ethiopia!

I found out so much about these seven countries. I was spouting facts left and right at people. When someone asked why, I talked about the countries and how little the people eat every day. I have never visited a single one of them, yet I love them all. And I yearn for the day when I can travel to each one and experience them firsthand.

So how did a girl like me, one that eats and eats, manage during these four weeks? Prayer. When I felt hunger, I prayed. I prayed for the country, for the people, for their leaders, for the children. I prayed more during those days than I ever have. I had a physical reminder to pray. I felt no hunger after praying for a child in Haiti that would be going the entire day on a cup of rice or less. I was amazed by what

*God showed me during those weeks. 7 was my introduction
to fasting. After those weeks of rice and prayer, I knew I
could do it again. And I have. (I recently finished a twenty-
day fast from one of my favorite things.) Yes, I am embracing
my eccentricity. When I take away what I enjoy, what I feel
like I need, and replace it with prayer, I have felt that clarity.*

Fasting: it's not just for Gandhi!

Day 31

It's the last day of Month One, and I have some
conclusions. The ordering of the seven months was fairly
random; food received Slot 1 because I copied this concept
from Susana, and that's what she did. Rest got the seventh
slot because God rested on the seventh day, and that
seemed poetic. Other than that, the months were listed in
brainstorm order.

That said, I'm grateful food launched me out of the
starting blocks. There was no shirking possible, no viable
semi-attention. Seven foods required my concentration
from morning until night every day. Each meal was
intentional, each bite calculated. There was no escape
from 7; I never had longer than five hours between meals
to mentally slip away. The concept of reduction was never
further than my next meal.

This held me fast to the heart of Jesus.

Just as a forty-day fast inaugurated His public ministry,
this month has paved the way. It's gently erased parts of
the palette. I don't know nearly as much as I think I do.
My riches aren't genuine. My story includes some fraud.

Certain elements don't belong on the canvas. I don't know what this means yet, but the counterfeit parts must be whitewashed before they can be redrawn.

In *Simplicity*, Richard Rohr wrote,

> On the way to contemplation we do the same thing that Jesus Christ did in the wilderness. Jesus teaches us not to say, "Lord, Lord," but to do the will of his Father. What must primarily concern us is that we do what Jesus has bidden us do. Jesus went into the wilderness, ate nothing for forty days, and made himself empty. . . . Of course, emptiness in and of itself isn't enough. The point of emptiness is to get ourselves out of the way so that Christ can fill us up. As soon as we're empty, there's a place for Christ, because only then are we in any sense ready to recognize and accept Christ as the totally other, who is not me.[15]

Honestly, I've said a lot of "Lord, Lord" without simply doing the will of my Father. My mission is clouded by a thousand elements with no eternal value. The canvas is muddy. I know the correct Christian rhetoric—emptiness, surrender, humility—but those words are meaningless until they are more than words. While my life is marked by ambition, accumulation, and perceived success, then no matter how much I squawk about Jesus, I'm a resounding gong, a clanging symbol; I am nothing.

After Jesus' fast, He began healing, rescuing, redeeming. The Spirit filled up the emptiness Jesus created, launching Him into ministry. In some supernatural way the abstinence from food was the catalyst for Jesus' unveiling; the real fireworks were next. Never again would Jesus fly under the radar. His powerful ministry was activated, inviting worship and opposition, salvation and death. After thirty years on earth, His story truly began.

"He ate nothing during those days, and at the end of them he was hungry." (Luke 4:2)

I am hungry.

Month 2

CLOTHING

This morning my seven-year-old Caleb went to school in "matching clothes": a green camouflage T-shirt, brown camouflage cargo shorts, and a gray camouflage hoodie. Back in the day I would've marched him upstairs to change into some Gymboree collection. But now? Three real kids later? I'm over it. This is not the hill I'm going to die on when I have bigger fish to fry, like raising them to leave my house one day and not move back.

Frankly, I've always taken my son to Target in his Batman costume and let my daughter wear a leotard and boots to church. It was never worth the drama; plus, there would always be another mom pushing a little Teenage Mutant Ninja Turtle around.

On any given day I wear jeans and a T-shirt. My style is utterly unsophisticated; I look like a college girl who rolled out of bed five minutes before class—but who has prematurely aged. Anyhow, I'm a simple or possibly lazy dresser who doesn't spend much time thinking about my wardrobe.

Clothes are just not a huge deal to me.

So, why clothes then? Why reduce radically in a neutral category I say I don't care about? Because although that sounds true in my head, my closet tells me a different story. I walked through all five of our closets, and I realized we spent real cash on every single item. I did some fuzzy averaging, and if we spent around $10 on each item, our closets represent an expenditure of, well, a lot of money. (I'm a writer not an accountant.) It is such a high total I had to sit down. Especially considering we don't wear half of the items.

I counted, and I have 327 items from which to choose. You read that right. No other category even comes close to this one in quantity. And let's be honest, most of these didn't average $10. If I spent $20 on each item, that's $6,540 spent on just my clothes in about the last five years. If the average is closer to $30, that means I've spent $9,810. This doesn't include anyone else in the family.

Sadly, I only wear a tiny percentage of these clothes. So while my mouth is yammering about my laissez faire attitude toward my wardrobe, my hand keeps reaching into my wallet to buy more. If I am serious about addressing overindulgence and irresponsible spending, I need not look any further than our closets. I spend more just on clothes in one year than the average Ethiopian family earns in almost five.

So we are starting Month Two: seven articles of clothes. Besides the obvious crazy factor, the main wrench in the machine is speaking engagements. I have three this month. I live two separate fashion lives: my daily, one-notch-above-a-vagrant wardrobe, and my weekend, speaker-on-a-stage collection. These two styles are so opposite I've lost sleep trying to choose seven items that will work for both.

Advising me this month, The Council is divided between the permissive girls and the Catholic-nun-slap-your-hand-with-a-ruler girls. Half think this month should be duplicable should any brave reader want to try it. The other half just wants me to suffer (this is my assessment). So we've compromised on a couple of items:

Shoes will count as one item. However, I will only rotate through two pairs of shoes: my cowboy boots and my tennis shoes. Every working woman has two fashion lives, so two pairs of shoes is not an indulgence on par with 327 items of clothes. This still leaves twenty-one pairs untouched, lined up on shelves in my closet like I am Imelda Marcos.

Underwear doesn't count. It just doesn't, okay? Between bra, panties, and socks, I'd use up half my allotment before I got my pants on. I considered omitting understuff from my wardrobe, but unleashing my free-swinging lady self onto this innocent world is probably a felony. No one deserves that kind of visual assault. So undergarments get a free pass, and if that makes me a 7 slacker, well, at least I'm a slacker wearing a bra.

Here are my clothes for the month:

- One pair of jeans, dark wash, kind of plain

- One long-sleeved solid black T-shirt, fitted

- One short-sleeved black "Haiti relief" T-shirt with white print

- One short-sleeved gray "Mellow Johnny's Bike Shop" T-shirt with yellow print

- One pair of gray drawstring knit Capri pants

- One long silk dark brown dress shirt

- Shoes: cowboy boots and tennis shoes

At one point I was going to designate a scarf as one item, but Council Member Molly told me she was losing

sleep over the scarf; that it wasn't *substantial enough*. So
I replaced it with a second T-shirt, which was probably a
good move so I don't wear my Haiti shirt for thirty straight
days. In case you don't fully understand some of the core
items I'm leaving out of life for the next month, here are a
few pieces that are being left in the closet:

- No coat (it's February)

- No jewelry, except my $45 wedding band from Walmart

- No accessories

- No belts

The Council is doing a few variations of this month along
with me. Jenny and Shonna are also sticking to seven
clothing items, but they are adding seven accessories, each
from a different country. Every day, they'll pray for the
country that produced the hat, scarf, earrings, necklace,
or bracelet they are wearing. Molly and Trina are putting
each item they don in a separate part of their closets to
determine what percentage they actually wear, suspecting
their closets are full of clothes that cost real cash but
never even get worn. Susana is wearing only handmade
clothes for seven straight days. Incidentally, the fact that I
have a friend with enough handmade clothes to last her a
week is hysterical since my children have to bring pants to
my mother-in-law to sew on missing buttons.

Month Two begins with this wee pile of clothes. I'll turn a
blind eye to the four bars, six shelves, and one dresser full
of other garments and make my peace with these seven
items which I just realized are all black, gray, and brown.
I'll look like a member of the Addams family or a mime.

Maybe I'll just tell people I'm having a mid-thirties crisis and going emo. If I start wearing black nail polish and wallowing in an imaginary quagmire of torment, someone intervene.

Day 1

I already broke the rules. I didn't mean to. It was less than sixty seconds. We were getting an assessment on our backyard for a garden (much more on this later in the month of our foray into green living), and it was 8:30 in the morning. It was cold and I hadn't had any coffee. I'd obediently dressed in my Haiti tee and jeans, so all started well.

But when gardener/activist Steven showed up to measure our yard and take soil samples, all I could see were the piles of dog poop my kids did *not* scoop. We appeared to be savages who couldn't be bothered to clean giant piles of feces from their living space. He acted like he didn't notice, but he drove himself here so he clearly wasn't blind. And I'm pretty sure his nose worked. As if on cue, my dog Lady walked right where he was digging and took a giant dump. I whisked the poop away, professing disdain, which sounded rather empty with the fourteen other mounds of excrement existing happily in our yard.

It was the poop's fault. It distracted me.

When I went inside to wash my hands, all I could think about was redeeming myself. I conjured up a story about how I'd been in Zimbabwe digging wells and just returned and found my family let everything run amok. I would reclaim our normally immaculate house, of course, but

I just hadn't had a chance yet. All I'd had time for since returning from Zimbabwe was preparing my typical vegetable frittata with freshly squeezed orange juice for my family's nourishment because I care about their health and stuff. That's how I am, Steven.

While inventing a detail about eco-friendly cleaning supplies, I snagged a jacket before rejoining him in the backyard. I slipped it on, tra la la. As Steven was talking about afternoon sun exposure, I realized I was wearing a non-7-sanctioned item. And it was 8:30 a.m. on Day 1. I'd managed a whole two hours of obedience. Strike up the band.

I ripped it off and threw it on the trampoline, and Steven looked up with what I recognized as alarm. Like maybe the skittish dog-poop lady lured him here to bury him in the backyard. I stammered through a quick explanation of 7, which did nothing to increase my normal quotient. I came across as an eccentric narcissist who lives in doo-doo and lies about global relief work. And by "came across as," I mean that I am.

So Month Two is off to a smashing success.

Day 2

"Make a coat one of your seven things."

"Aren't you going to have a coat?"

"Why didn't you include a coat on your list?"

"What about a coat or at least a jacket?"

"No coat?"

Yeah, I've been hearing this comment for the last two weeks. Maybe because this is February and my friends care about my discomfort. Or maybe these people are just extraordinarily bossy. Here's the deal: I'm not a coat wearer anyway (despite my jacket failure yesterday). I don't like to keep up with it. I'd rather be semicold from my car to the door of wherever I'm going.

Plus, I live in Austin. "Winter" is a loose term here. I habitually brag to my northern friends about our mild weather, and I'm certain to post pictures of us in T-shirts on Christmas morning. Winter in central Texas kisses and makes up with us for the brutal summer punishment it inflicts. Yesterday, yes, in February, my son wore shorts to school.

Today, however, it snowed all day.

In the last ten years, it has snowed a total of six days in Austin. The last recorded "snow accumulation" was one-tenth of an inch in 2007. This means that when there is a snow dusting, our schools close down, panicked Texans clear the stores, and some poor soul will wreck his car. The overreaction is apocalyptic.

My kids think a zip-up sweatshirt is a coat. They don't know about frozen snow toes. No one has gloves. They've never wiped out on an icy driveway. Snowmen are just something lucky children in books get to build. Their greatest seasonal hardship is packing away flip-flops for a couple of months, though that's a risky action since we often hit 70 degrees in the dead of winter.

So yesterday when our weathermen predicted snow, we
rolled our eyes. We know better. We've been their snow
pawns many times before. We know they are hogging
airtime with their "extreme weather warnings" only to
crush our little hearts with *rain*.

But low and behold, the thermometer hovered at 32
degrees, and it snowed for five straight hours in Austin,
Texas, today. It barely stuck since it was 54 degrees
yesterday and the ground is basically an oven, but still.
My second grader's teacher took the kids out to catch
snowflakes on their tongues. My daughter put seven
snowballs in our freezer. My middle schooler put on shorts
and jumped on the trampoline barefoot with his buddies to
see who could last the longest. (Sixth-grade boys. I'll say no
more.)

And I was seriously cold. I put my long-sleeved T-shirt
under my short-sleeved T-shirt and shivered. Jenny, the
most lenient member of The Council, sent this text: "I
think Jen gets a green light on a jacket and gloves so she
can play in the snow with her kids. Council?"

I declined and instead put my arms through my Capri
pants for reinforcement. I slipped my other T-shirt over my
head with my face peeking through the neck hole. I looked
like a nun with pants on my arms. With that, I headed
outside where my kids politely asked me to go back in
before anyone saw me.

As always, when the weather is frigid, I think of our friends
in the homeless community: Shoeshine, Red, Bridgette,
Mike, David, so many others. I was outside in inadequate
clothes for less than ten minutes, and I was chilled to
the bone. It took me an hour to warm up and I had a

roaring fire and 72-degree home. Our church has supplied the homeless with coats and gloves and scarves for two months, but that's putting a Band-Aid on a hemorrhage. No outerwear can protect against sleet and punishing wind for long. Austin has between thirty-eight and forty-five hundred homeless people, but only 803 shelter beds are regularly available. Additional beds are offered when the temperature drops below freezing and a few downtown churches open for emergency shelter, but thousands are still out in the cold.

More than one hundred people perished on the Austin streets last year; they died alone huddled in doorways and alleys. With one bed available for every five who need it, death by exposure is a certainty. For them, extreme weather goes far beyond inconvenience or thrill; it is perilous.

I'll never truly identify with those who lack sufficient clothing and shelter. 7 is temporary; I have 320 clothing items awaiting my return. When I got too cold today, I retreated inside the home I own. Problem solved.

I'm going to bed tonight grateful for warmth, an advantage so expected it barely registers. May my privileges continue to drive me downward to my brothers and sisters without. Greater yet, I'm tired of calling the suffering "brothers and sisters" when I'd *never* allow my biological siblings to suffer likewise. That's just hypocrisy veiled in altruism. I won't defile my blessings by imagining that I deserve them. Until every human receives the dignity I casually enjoy, I pray my heart aches with tension and my belly rumbles for injustice.

"The first question which the priest and the Levite asked was:
'If I stop to help this man, what will happen to me?'
But the good Samaritan reversed the question: 'If I do not stop
to help this man, what will happen to him?'"

—Martin Luther King Jr.

Day 5

I think it's worth mentioning that I'm developing a rather uncouth habit. Additionally, this habit confirms that I'm a lazy dresser who doesn't place nearly enough priority on decorum as is fitting for a thirty-five-year-old.

As you know, I have two pairs of shoes at my disposal— cowboy boots and tennis shoes. Both require two feats of Herculean effort: putting on socks and pulling on or tying shoes. Evidently I can't be bothered with this sort of exertion.

Anytime I'm not required to get out of the car, I'll choose to drive barefoot rather than put forth the effort to dress my feet. If I can't slip on flip-flops like usual, then I guess I'll slip on nothing. This habit is not thwarted by rain or freezing temperatures apparently. Zipping through the bank? Picking a kid up from school? Dropping someone at practice? Naked feet.

> My friend told me, "You know driving shoeless is illegal." Okay, really? Listen, I can't follow every law. I'm not a Pharisee. No shoes? No problem. At least not for me.

Day 6

So today was my first speaking engagement during clothes month. I was set up for success. It was a one-day, semi-local event, eliminating the need for two days worth of clothes. Not only that, but it was at a retreat center in the piney woods with ziplining and horseback riding and such, so I assumed the dress code was casual.

I wore my jeans, boots, and long-sleeved black shirt under my black Haiti tee. I couldn't accessorize with a scarf or jewelry or any of my usual tricks to make Target clothes passable as event wear. As I walked up to the lodge where the women were eating breakfast, I checked the wardrobe vibe, worried I was grossly underdressed and needed to start explaining myself. (I have *never* worn a T-shirt to an event, even a camp facility like this.)

I saw a sea of black T-shirts with white scrolly writing on the front. Just like mine. The graphics were nearly identical. It was the retreat shirt every registered woman received. On a quick glance, my event planner thought I'd snagged my retreat shirt early somehow. Ninety percent of us were wearing the exact same outfit. I was slightly fancier because of my cowboy boots; everyone else was in tennis shoes.

It was awesome.

We were a crowd of women in ponytails and old jeans, not trying to impress one another or paste on a Christian face. It was the feminine group dynamic at its simplest, and it appealed to the truest part of me that loves authenticity. I wish women could regularly enjoy this freedom together, liberated from competition and comparison. There is something so marvelous about women comfortable in their own skin.

As we worshipped and studied the Word and enjoyed good weather and even better company, God reminded me that gathering the saints is powerful not because we look our finest or make a big production of the details but because we unite to seek Jesus. *That's* the magic. I suspect God is more glorified in a humble room of earnest worshippers than a massive production designed to sound "relevant" to the listeners but no longer relevant to God. When the worship of God turns into a "worship experience," we have derailed as the body of Christ.

Scripture describes the people who drew Jesus' eye: the poor widow, lepers, the lost and hungry, adulterers, the outcast, the sick and dying. The already dead. Finery and opulence never impressed Jesus; quite the opposite. He lambasted religious leaders for their fancy robes, strutting around as if their ceremonial dress had any bearing on the condition of their hearts.

There is something noble about an assembly of believers in simple clothes, where the lobby isn't filled with people saying, "You look pretty" to one another. Maybe looking pretty isn't the catalyst for the Spirit's movement. Perhaps an obsessive occupation with dresses and hair and shoes detracts us from the point of the gathering: a fixation on Jesus. When the jars of clay remember they are jars of clay, the treasure within gets all the glory, which seems somehow more fitting.

Day 9

Council Member Becky patronized The Austin Women's Clothing Swap, benefitting Women for Women International, SafePlace (domestic violence intervention), The Center for Women and Gender Studies at the University of Texas, and of course, participating women who get free stuff. The concept: Contribute gently used clothes and accessories, and rummage through everyone else's junk and take what you want. It's a brilliant way to unload clothes you hate or that don't fit, get new-to-you things that don't require a rubberband around the button (if you don't know this trick, then you're too skinny to be my friend), and not feel like a wasteful glutton. All unclaimed items plus a $5 donation from each person go to the nonprofits. This was Becky's assessment:

> The idea really is genius . . . in theory. Clean out your junk, shop through other people's junk. It would have been great if I had no time constraints or went when it opened. As it was, it left me wondering if maybe I really have OCD.

> The Web site listed two drop-off sites, but as is often the case with well-meaning philanthropists, there was misinformation at both sites. So there I was, hauling my three bags of carefully selected castoffs, the ones that made the cut from the scrap pile and the Goodwill pile. This was the good stuff. Not everyone was so selective I found out.

> I hauled my bags to the "sorting zone," which is code for a beehive of women trying to find treasures before they hit the racks. I asked if there was any order to this, which almost brought the bedraggled volunteer to tears: "There was," she kept saying. "There WAS." God love her.

Here are some things you can always expect to find in a gaggle of women:

- An eighteen-month-old kid, strapped via sling to his mama, enjoying a little snack from her exposed boob.

- A totally chic outfit that appears to have started from a bath rug.

- Total cooperation: I can't even begin to count how many times I heard, "Wanna trade?" as we did the dance in the ten inches of space between racks.

- Stranger commentary: "That pink looks great on you!" or "You should rethink the high-waisted jeans." I love that we feel morally obligated to keep a perfect stranger from lookin' a fool.

Not only can you see why I love Becky, but her experience got me thinking: Why don't we do this among friends and neighbors? You know that scarf you hate because the color makes it appear your liver is failing? It looks awesome on me. These pants that fit until I discovered how to mix the buffalo sauce and blue cheese sauce at Chick-fil-A? They're the bomb on you. What is tired for you might be the piece I adore. My trash could be your treasure.

Unlike my sons who retire jeans with both knees blown out and bottom hem shredded, most women cast off clothes we're just tired of or outgrew. They're usually in great condition or could be reclaimed with one good dry cleaning. I have brand-new-looking clothes in my closet I haven't worn for three years. I say they're "old," but since they endured maybe a dozen wearings, let's call a spade a spade—they're practically still new.

Without spending a dime, we could freshen up our wardrobes and not feed the consumer machine more than it has already been fed. Clothes and accessories could be reincarnated into their second lives. Whatever isn't claimed can go to women's shelters and nonprofits.

I mean, seriously, do we really *need* more new clothes? When do we put the brakes on this runaway train? When I consider our resources, buying more clothes to add to the 327 I already own is positively stupid. That's just gross. My closet could easily clothe ten women with plenty of margin. Frankly, having thirty items sounds downright gluttonous to me, as I sit here in the same outfit I've worn three days straight.

You could host your own Clothing Swap with friends and neighbors and coworkers. Bring snacks, chill the drinks, put on the music, make a girls' night out of it. The more the merrier. Set up different stations: pants, purses, shoes, jewelry, shirts, accessories. Laugh and pretend you're kidding when you tell another woman if she touches that shirt, you'll cut her.

It's the smallest idea, but it suspends fashion spending that should bother us far more than it does. It's a start. Maybe once we slow the cash hemorrhaging, some buried issues could surface, interrupting our default settings and raising questions we've never asked.

And hey, at least someone would haul off the twenty items you've been waiting seven years to fit back into. Time to give up the dream, pretties.

Days 12-13

Pick the worst place imaginable to show up underdressed as a "professional Christian speaker," anchoring a two-day event for a bunch of women. Let me help you: Atlanta, Georgia—a city where little girls in $50 smocked dresses romp around on filthy playgrounds. Where every freshly birthed Southern baby gets two names and women wear pastel pantsuits to lunch. These ladies instinctively understand closed-toed shoes and slips and no-white-after-Labor-Day-unless-it-is-winter-white. It's places like Atlanta where Brandon's observation becomes starkly apparent: "It's so weird that God called you to women's ministry because you don't even speak the language of your own tribe."

Indeed.

In the south you dress right. Their customs run deeeeeeeep, and you don't mess with them. The house where I stayed for this event sported paintings of Confederate battles in every room. I didn't reference that pesky Yankee victory, old news to the tune of 145 years. Anyhow, if I were in laid-back California or no-nonsense Wisconsin, it would be a different story. But I was headed to a region where I once overheard this dialogue:

"So, are you a Christian?"

"No, I'm Southern Baptist."

Okay then.

I still hadn't decided if I should wear my nice shirt on Friday to make a good initial impression or wear it on

Saturday to make a lasting impression. (The fact that I was worried about my impression at all should tell you this month hasn't sunk in yet.)

In the end I wore my Haiti T-shirt on Friday night, and although I told The Council I wasn't going to explain myself, my first sentence was a description of 7 with a *What-was-I-supposed-to-do?* reference to my outfit. I couldn't help it. Okay, I could help it, but I had a social compulsion to defend myself, utterly vain and reminiscent of middle school.

Blame it on the Deep South.

Blame it on my need for approval.

I blamed it on "respect for my audience," but that may or may not be genuine.

I couldn't gauge their response. There was some polite nodding but definitely nothing to really put me at ease. Then I remembered that wearing seven items of clothes for a month on purpose sounds super weird.

But just as quickly as the insecurity wave crested, it receded, because we opened up God's Word and let it speak. The clothes and the project and making an impression just went away because we immersed in Isaiah 58. What I'm wearing and what you think of it pales next to loosening the chains of injustice and setting the prisoner free.

Interestingly, in Isaiah 58, God is describing the kind of fast He actually requires. Not unlike 7, they were abstaining. They were reducing. They were going without. The

Israelites were certainly uncomfortable, unmoored a bit.
And yet . . .

*"Why are we fasting and you have not seen it? Why have we
humbled ourselves and you have not noticed?" (Isa. 58:3)*

Don't you see our good behavior? Don't you notice all
we're forfeiting? Their spiritual house seemed in order,
stamped and certified by self-denial and physical sacrifice.
I mean, if we can't even feel smug about our abstinence,
what is the point? It was all there: the hunger, the heads
bowed low, the sackcloth, the ashes. All the external
signs of piety were in place (like pointing out my reduced
wardrobe to a room full of women).

"Is that what you call a fast, a day acceptable to the Lord?" asked
God. *(Isa. 58:5)*

Ouch.

Oh how we love our religious yokes, not for what they
communicate about God, but what they say about us. This
is the kind of people we are. We say "no" when everyone
else says "yes." We don't do *that*. We don't watch *that*. We
don't vote *that* way. We don't go *there*. We don't include
them.

But God's idea of a fast is less about what we're against
and more about what we are *for*.

*"Is not this the kind of fasting I have chosen: to loose the chains
of injustice and untie the cords of the yoke, to set the oppressed
free and break every yoke? Is it not to share your food with the
hungry and to provide the poor wanderer with shelter—when*

*you see the naked, to clothe him, and not to turn away from your
own flesh and blood?" (Isa. 58: 6–7)*

When we hear "fast," we put on a yoke of self-denial.
When God said "fast," He meant to take off the yoke of
oppression. The Isaiah 58 fast is not about the mechanics
of abstinence; it is a fast from self-obsession, greed, apathy,
and elitism. When it becomes more about me than the
marginalized I've been charged to serve, I become the
confused voice in this passage: "Why have I fasted and you
have not seen it?"

I don't want 7 to become a modern yoke because that'll
only result in useless self-obsession (and that from a girl
who wrote an entire book about myself already). While
fasting from futile things, I don't want to fixate on them,
missing the forest for the trees. The compulsion to defend
my clothes to a roomful of women reveals a heart that
isn't there yet.

In the yoke-on/yoke-off equation, I'm still on the wrong
side.

I hope one day clothes and appearance and everyone else's
assessment doesn't even occur to me. I would like to be so
focused on the valuable that what I am wearing doesn't
even warrant mental space. Not the fussy, concerned,
indulgent obsession with clothes; not the conspicuous,
public, distracting reduction where I am now . . . but the
zero balance of priority is where I hope to land.

Day 15

Conversation with Tray, Council Member Jenny's husband:

Tray: Hey, 7!

Jen: Hey.

Tray: Nice shirt.

Jen: Shut up.

Day 16

I wanted to say this earlier, but I gave it two weeks to see if it held. Sometimes you draw premature conclusions about something. You pledge your dying allegiance and make puffy-paint posters and get a tattoo declaring your loyalty, only to discover the meaning of the term "honeymoon phase" three weeks later. By then you've broadcast your opinion and made a fool of yourself, and you're either stuck in the bed you've made or eating a lot of crow.

But since my parents got engaged after two weeks of dating, I figure sixteen days is enough time to make a call with profoundly less consequences than sixty future years of monogamy. Here it is: I'm loving this month.

It's awesome. Month Two, how do I love thee? Let me count the ways: I love the zero wardrobe planning that graces every morning. I love the teeny tiny pile of laundry in our basket (Brandon is down to seven items, too, bless him). I love wearing jeans and a T-shirt every day. I love the simplicity and ease of it all.

Much junk took shelter under the "too many choices" umbrella: wasted time and energy, more pointless work, self-obsession, the ironic "the more I have, the more I want" cycle. It's helped that Brandon and The Council are participating since I see these people daily and no explanation is ever required, but still. I'm pretty down with seven clothes.

I obviously don't value clothes like food since Month One was ten billion times harder. To discover what matters to you, take it away and see where the chips actually fall. Before 7 started, I predicted Month Two would be one of my hardest. I was way off. I'm usually fairly self-aware, but I really miscalculated. I guess that's good news. While my closet reveals that I am still clearly caught in the machine, it's grip is looser than I imagined. I might untangle without severing a limb.

Then again, maybe it should bother me a tad to wear the same outfit four days in a row without washing it. I don't know. I don't know what balance is here. I'm not sure what appropriate attention looks like.

I will confess: I was working at a coffee shop yesterday and kept smelling mildew. I looked behind me for the offender and even leaned down and smelled my laptop (my kids spilled milk on it once, so a curdled computer is within the realm of possibility). Finally, I raised my leg up and smelled my knee; it was my jeans. Not only have I worn them every day this month, but also the last few days without a dunk in the washing machine.

So that's disgusting. I don't want to become a stinky girl with mildew jeans. I'll have to get dreadlocks. Maybe I should aim for "mildly concerned" instead of zero.

Day 19

Part of this month's restrictions is the no-jewelry clause.
I'm a jewelry minimalist, but I normally wear earrings
every day. My face looks disproportionate without earrings
framing it. My head is abnormally large, and big hoops
counterbalance my enormous noggin. It's like wearing
vertical stripes; earrings provide smoke and mirrors for my
cranial mass.

Outside of that I have a tackle box full of cheap jewelry,
mostly supplied by Target. I have a couple of long, funky
necklaces I enjoy, some chunky rings, a few big bracelets
to cover my wrist tattoos when I'm speaking at First (fill-
in-the-denomination) Church, USA. I have a few black and
silver pieces from my Brighton knockoff days and some
seriously flamboyant earrings. Nothing spectacular, but a
month without it has left me feeling quite unadorned. And
very big headed—physiologically, not egotistically.

So today I was in adoption dossier purgatory, on hold
with the police department trying to figure out how to get
fingerprinted. This, and three thousand other measures,
is to ensure the lovely children of Ethiopia don't get
adoptive parents who flash elementary school kids or
enjoy a larceny habit. Good practices, all, but believe me:
international adoption is not for the faint of heart. It's like
the first year of law school where the main objective is to
weed out the slackers.

What is a dossier, you ask? It sounds so pretty. *Doss-ee-ay*,
a beautiful French word, like *bourgeois* or *café au lait*.
France entices you with its lovely language, but *sabotage* is
also French, gentle reader. Dossier = doctor's clearances,
employment verification (oh so fuzzy for an author who

kind of works sometimes), police reports, reference letters, fire inspection, new birth certificates and marriage license, residential history from age eighteen (you can't understand how many houses we've lived in), a "rough sketch" of our floor plan, home study with a social worker, proof of pet vaccinations, health insurance documents, a picture album, passports, essays, fifty other forms . . . all notarized and less than six months old, or—you guessed it—redo.

This is where my head is.

Trying to determine if we needed a state background check or state *and* federal, the lady at the police department asked, "Do you have a fast pass?" which I've never once heard of; then she put me on hold. This was the crazy-eyed state of mind I was in when Brandon got home. Just as I was cut off after all that, Brandon redeemed the day.

What you need to understand is that my husband is an exceptional gift-giver. This is his thing. Everyone knows it. Giving is Brandon's love language; he waits for the actual day to give his present around 13 percent of the time. He tracks down the most meaningful, exactly right gifts for me all the time; it's almost embarrassing.

So he sat down with a big ol' grin, holding a cutesy bag, and said: "I've had the worst day, but this *finally* came in the mail, and my day turned around. I've been dying to give this to you."

I mean, seriously.

Out pops a gorgeous handcrafted silver necklace in the shape of Africa; "hope" engraved across the front, "Ethiopia" the back. People, he found it on *Etsy*, handmade vintage online marketplace. (After posting its picture on Facebook, Susana commented: "You got a man who knows 'bout Etsy? What?")

After a day of adoption labor and "Please hold" and phone calls and paperwork, Brandon reminded me why this is worth it with one beautiful necklace. I cried, of course, which is part of his reward. You better believe I slipped it on quick as greased lightning, rules shmules.

Completing "meaningful necklace day," two hours later Susana surprised me during Sewing Night (tomorrow's gem) with precious Etsy gift #2: A long necklace sporting an old-fashioned typewriter key. The chosen key?

7.

Slipped it on, quick as greased lightning. What dear people are in my life.

My Ethiopia necklace reminded me it's not about the maddening paperwork; it's about two babies waiting for a home. My 7 necklace reminded me it's not about adorning myself for attention; it's about simplifying for God's glory.

I plan on wearing them both every day, and if you don't like it, you can call me a Heinous Breaker of Rules. But they tell of the things that matter, that count, that are lasting and lovely. They represent people who love me and don't think I'm crazy for adopting children #4 and #5 from an impoverished country or wearing seven clothes for a month. Sometimes life feels lonely and radical; my necklaces remind me I am neither.

Rather, I belong to a husband and faith community who

embrace the grave challenges of the gospel and shore up my defenses. They inspire me. They travel with me. Remarkable, courageous people surround me. I am honored to be on mission with such extraordinary saints. While my stuff is decreasing, what matters is increasing in equal measure.

Plus, my necklaces are suuuuuper cute, so I'll just have that cake and eat it too. I can't help it if my husband and friend have great taste.

Day 20

Susana volunteered to host a sewing tutorial to demonstrate it is possible to buy fabric and run it through a serger and create something. We were below-average students, but oh did we laugh. Our evening kicked off with an honorary clip from Pretty in Pink, drawing inspiration from Molly Ringwald and reviving our crushes on Blaine. Then we laughed some more. In the end we were seamstresses I tell you.

Susana our muse captured the evening:

> Tables were set up, snacks laid out, fabric, scissors, pins, extra bobbins, and measuring tapes properly placed, and sewing machines ready. My kids were miraculously asleep by 7:45 p.m., fun music was streaming on the stereo, and my house gleamed from it's first professional housecleaning EVER. (Thanks Mom!)

> I had been wearing my handmade clothes all week but saved my favorite item for this day: an exactingly tailored khaki and cream a-line skirt with orange piping and beautifully

detailed exterior pockets, like a retro diner uniform. Oh, you know. Something I just threw together one day.

I patiently awaited my six pupils for the evening and checked my hair in the mirror. I made sure my phone was set to "loud" and checked e-mail to ensure no one needed directions.

Stop right here. Let me assure you I'm not a Type-A. I'm normally unpolished, unorganized, laid back, and easy. I like messy crafts, chaotic afternoons with children and dirt, and big kitchen messes. But if my biological makeup were faintly Type-A, that teeny tiny, anal-retentive chromosome would have teeny tiny letters that read "punctual."

And everyone was late.

Twenty minutes late.

"Susana, we're so sorry. We feel like total jerks."

"No. Come in! I'm just glad you're here!" (Jerks.)

But resentment lasted thirty seconds, because when you're with such amazing, hilarious women, well, it's hard to hold a grudge.

So we sewed. And laughed.

"Come here. Show me again."

"Fix it!"

"Hers looks better than mine."

"Susana, the thingie keeps getting stuck in the thingie!"

Wait, what?

Shonna wanted to give up first: "The machine keeps breaking." Jenny kept fixing it while Shonna went on to break the next machine. Then she'd go back to the first, and Jenny would fix the second. This cycle continued for some time.

And then there was quiet, confident Trina. Everyone insisted her purse wouldn't work. She had the wrong fabric. She cut her pieces askew. The seam didn't match up. What's this extra thing you've got hanging here? But Trina, quiet confident Trina, just kept pinning and stitching. And you know what? She didn't make a fold-over clutch. My dear friends, hers was an elegant evening bag. Just like she planned.

In fact, everyone finished the projects. Two "pillowcase" shirts and four fold-over clutches later (well, three clutches and an evening bag), they had enormous smiles and something to show off to husbands, "Honey, look what I made."

Remember that feeling from grade school? "Mom, look what I made!" It's that unadulterated sense of accomplishment. Visions of art galleries and coffee table books floating in your head. That is, until your older brother says, "What's that supposed to be? It looks like you pooped on it." And you run crying to your room swearing off future creativity.

Yeah. It's the same feeling when you're older. Exactly the same.

Day 22

I've spent half this month in wet clothes, and it's getting old.

When you only have seven clothes, and one is shoes, another is a dress shirt, the third is threadbare yoga pants, and the fourth is an irrelevant long-sleeved shirt as it's mid-March and summer has begun in central Texas, what you basically have are three items: a pair of jeans and two T-shirts.

Seven clothes is essentially three.

I don't have a dirty clothes pile to wash at leisure. I am literally wearing these daily. And to bed. This has created a washing dilemma. If I was a preplanner like Brandon who organizes every day in fifteen-minute blocks, creating short-term, mid-term, and long-term goals with corresponding to-do lists and relevant details in his synced iCalendar with reminder alarms and color-coded details (you think I'm kidding), then I might have clean clothes that I had the foresight to launder during the night.

Instead, I'm a spontaneous zero planner who has the Mac and iPhone but uses a paper calendar circa 1987 because I can't understand the Apple calendar feature and it won't obey when I try to enter a "New Event", so I have eleven "untitled" entries that never landed on the actual calendar. You might think the "+" sign under "New Event" would add a new event, but you would be wrong. So while my wireless gadgets were purchased to streamline travel, instead I call Brandon from airports to rummage on my computer for information.

He L-O-V-E-S this about me, and it never frustrates him.

I start thinking about my day right when it's happening. Which is why I remember not-more-than-but-possibly-less-than one hour before I need to be somewhere that my jeans smell like mildew (hence the unfortunate Day 16 entry).

So with my clothes on the shortest cycle, I walk around in a towel. Wearing other clothes is cheating. And I can't waste a wash/dry session without laundering *everything* because heaven knows it's all dirty.

You might have deduced, forty minutes is not enough to wash and dry a load of clothes. It is enough to get them somewhere between sopping wet and uncomfortably damp. At least six times this month, I've pulled soggy clothes from the dryer, struggled into them (wet jeans don't cooperate), and dashed out the door.

Listen lambs, wet jeans don't dry when they're on your body. Walking into Hill's Café with friends, I hollered, "My butt is wet!" while the husbands hid. Well, it was. I would feel sorry for them if their butts were wet. I sat in the front seat and pointed the air vents at my rear to dry out. This was not met with compassion so much as outright mockery.

Dear wet clothes, I won't miss you.

Day 25

I've slogged and underlined my way through *Consumed*, a remarkable book on the shifting nature of capitalism. After reading most paragraphs twice, the facts settled nicely in the brain space between the "Common Sense" and "Don't Be an Idiot" sections.

Like this obvious commentary:

> Once upon a time, in capitalism's more creative and successful period, a productivist capitalism prospered by meeting the real needs of real people. . . . Today, however, consumerist capitalism profits only when it can address those whose essential needs have already been satisfied but who have the means to assuage "new" and invented needs—Marx's "imaginary needs." The global majority still has extensive and real natural needs mirroring what psychologists T. Berry Brazelton and Stanley L. Greenspan have called "the irreducible needs of children." But it is without the means to address them, being cut off by the global market's inequality from the investment in capital and jobs that would allow them to become consumers.[1]

In other words, marketing used to represent basic needs of humans, without much embellishment or hyperbole. Certainly, the Third World still has these needs in spades— to the detriment of life and health and family—but no consumer power. Thus, Big Marketing turned to the wallet of the privileged, invented a bunch of fake needs (prepackaged sugar water, collagen moisturizer, Tide to Go pens, the slanket), and disregarded the people who were actually dying every day for lack of basics, exposed to the seductions of the consumer marketplace but without the means to participate in it.

> In this new epoch in which the needy are without income and the wealthy are without needs, radical

inequality is simply assumed. . . . Inequality leaves capitalism with a dilemma: the overproducing capitalist market must either grow or expire. If the poor cannot be enriched enough to become consumers, then grown-ups in the First World who are currently responsible for 60 percent of the world's consumption, and with vast disposable income but few needs, will have to be enticed into shopping.[2]

This is why I have 327 items of clothes in my closet.

With my genuine needs met but so many dollars yet unspent, shopping has become a stronger marker of freedom than voting, and what we spend in the mall matters more than what we're accomplishing together as the church. I am a part of the problem, a contributing member of inequality. Every time I buy another shirt I don't need or a seventh pair of shoes for my daughter, I redirect my powerful dollar to the pockets of consumerism, fueling my own greed and widening the gap. Why? Because I like it. Because those are cute. Because I want that.

These thoughts burden me holistically, but the trouble is, I can rationalize them individually. This one pair of shoes? Big deal. This little outfit? It was on sale. This micro-justification easily translates to nearly every purchase I've made. Alone, each item is reduced to an easy explanation, a harmless transaction. But all together, we've spent enough to irrevocably change the lives of a hundred thousand people. What did I get for that budgeting displacement? Closets full of clothes we barely wear and enough luxuries to outfit twenty families.

This is hard to process, so it helps to imagine standing in

front of the families of my Ethiopian children, who were too underresourced to raise their own beloved babies. As I gaze upon their hopelessness, I imagine them calculating what I've spent on clothing alone, realizing that same amount would've kept their family fed and healthy for thirty years.

What if all my silly little individual purchases *do* matter? What if I joined a different movement, one that was less enticed by luxuries and more interested in justice? What if I believed every dollar spent is vital, a potential soldier in the war on inequality?

When thirty-five years of choices overwhelm me, Jesus makes it simple again: "Love your neighbor as yourself." If you read the story, you'll see that Jesus takes a broad, global, interracial view of who our neighbor is. In other words, what standard is acceptable for my own life? My own family? This is the benchmark for everyone else, which necessitates a decrease in the definition of *necessary* (for us) and an increase in the definition of *acceptable* (for everyone else).

The average human gets around twenty-five thousand days on this earth, and most of us in the United States of America will get a few more. That's it. This life is a breath. Heaven is coming fast, and we live in that thin space where faith and obedience have relevance. We have this one life to offer; there is no second chance, no Plan B for the good news. We get one shot at living to expand the kingdom, fighting for justice. We'll stand before Jesus once, and none of our luxuries will accompany us. We'll have one moment to say, "This is how I lived."

More than thirteen thousand of those days are over for me.

I'm determined to make the rest count.

Day 30

Here we are, the end of the road for Month Two. Here are my observations:

First, wearing seven clothes was way easier than I expected. In my self-important mind, everyone would notice my repetitions and whisper about my wardrobe. People would obsess about my attire. You know what I discovered? Others aren't thinking about me nearly as much as I thought they were. Blending seamlessly into my environment, I brought up "my clothing situation" 100 percent more often than it was observed by anyone.

No one really cares. Shockingly, even I don't care as much as I thought. With the boundaries locked in, I lived this month unattached to "looking cute." And no one died. Ministry commenced untainted. Life carried on. I could live my real life on a fraction of my previous wardrobe, and nothing significant would be altered. In fact, the simplicity was a blessed relief.

In the grand scheme of things, "how I look to people" all of a sudden just seems ludicrous. Listen, if my influence is linked to my wardrobe, then my ministry is falsely inflated and built on sand. A well-known ministry leader pulled me aside after I received my first multibook contract and said: "Jen, stay especially connected to Jesus from here on out. With your age and persona, they will try to make a starlet out of you."

At the time that sounded ridiculous. I was a twenty-nine-year-old nobody with a vague notion of my mission. Yet that statement lodged deeply, and I was never able to shake it. In a culture that elevates beauty and style, the Christian community is at genuine risk for distraction, even deception. What do we truly admire in our leaders? Are we no different from the secular population, drawn to charisma and style above substance and integrity?

I hope not.

I want to belong to a Christian community known for a different kind of beauty, the kind that heals and inspires. I can't help but remember Jesus, and how God made sure to mention He was plain and simple by human standards:

He grew up before him like a tender shoot, and like a root out of dry ground. He had no beauty or majesty to attract us to him, nothing in his appearance that we should desire him. He was despised and rejected by men, a man of sorrows, and familiar with suffering. Like one from whom men hide their faces he was despised, and we esteemed him not. (Isa. 53:2–3)

There was nothing physically attractive about Jesus. He wasn't rich or notorious, well-dressed or handsome. At first glimpse Jesus was forgettable, neither standing out for beauty or charisma. Maybe this is why the widow and marginalized and sick and outcast flocked to Him. He was approachable in every way.

Jesus didn't garner esteem the conventional way, but make no mistake: He was noticed. He was loved by the outsider, hated by the religious elite, revered by His followers, and killed by His enemies. For a plain carpenter from Nazareth, Jesus sure found His way to the center ring; not through power or ruthlessness but subversion and truth.

His humility appeals to the unloveliness in us all. We are drawn in by His simplicity, then transformed by His magnificence.

Oh sure, there will always be people who want Jesus in the Oval Office, on Primetime, across from Oprah, on the Red Carpet, spruced up by a stylist and touched up for the cameras. They try to assign Him the power and public sway He always resisted; people want to make a starlet out of Jesus. But He insisted His power was activated in the margins. Jesus didn't redeem the world on the throne but through the cross.

I don't want to consume the redemption Jesus made possible then spurn the methods by which He achieved it. Jesus' kingdom continues in the same manner it was launched; through humility, subversion, love, sacrifice; through calling empty religion to reform and behaving like we believe the meek will indeed inherit the earth. We cannot carry the gospel to the poor and lowly while emulating the practices of the rich and powerful. We've been invited into a story that begins with humility and ends with glory; never the other way around. Let's align ourselves correctly, sharing in the humble ministry of Jesus, knowing one day we'll feast at His table in splendor.

After the suffering of his soul, he will see the light of life and be satisfied; by his knowledge my righteous servant will justify many, and he will bear their iniquities. Therefore I will give him a portion among the great, and he will divide the spoils with the strong, because he poured out his life unto death, and was numbered with the transgressors. For he bore the sin of many, and made intercession for the transgressors. (Isa. 53:11–12)

2,465 square feet.

Month 3

POSSESSIONS

Four bedrooms.

Two living rooms.

Two and a half bathrooms.

Nine closets.

Twenty-six cabinets.

Three bookshelves.

Ten dressers and armoires.

Every last one of them packed full. I invented an engineering trick to get them closed that I should patent. Some cabinets are stacked so high I have to remove forty pounds of stuff before I can retrieve the bottom dwellers. I don't even know what's in some of them.

About three times a year, I rant around the house, screaming at our stuff: "What is all this? How did this get here? Why do we have so much junk? How am I supposed to keep up with all this? Where did this all come from?" And then I remember:

I bought it all.

I suppose acting like someone snuck into my house while I was feeding the homeless and filled my shelves with more black shirts and a fourth set of Legos against my will is probably ignoble. To hear me fuss, you'd think I was a victim of drive-by consumerism. Guess what, doves?

I'm a part of this little game.

I see it (on you, on them, in their house, at Target, on TV). I manufacture a need for it. Then I buy it. I use it a little or not. I store it/shelve it/stack it/stuff it/get tired of it, then wage war against it one day when all my little things are strewn about as escapees from their shelves and drawers.

I could blame Big Marketing for selling me imagined needs. I could point a finger at culture for peer pressuring me into having nicer things. I might implicate modern parenting, which encourages endless purchases for the kids, ensuring they aren't the "have-nots" in a sea of "haves." I could just dismiss it all with a shrug and casual wave of the hand. Oh, you know me! Retail therapy!

But if I'm being truthful, this is a sickening cycle of consumerism that I perpetuate constantly. I used to pardon excess from the tension of the gospel by saying, "Oh, it doesn't matter how much you have; it's what you do with it." But that exemption is folding in on itself lately. Plus, let's be honest: what does "it's what you do with it" even mean? Are we really doing something honorable with our stuff other than consuming it? I'm not sure carting it all off after we're bored with those particular items is a helpful response since we just replace it with more.

Anyhow, I'm getting ahead of myself. So here's the word of the day: *giddy*. That's how I feel about this month. I originally planned on doing this as the fourth month, but I moved it up after the realizations from the last month horrified me. I am starving for reform. Here is the deal:

- One month.

- Give seven things away that we own.

• **Every day.**

Yes, I've done the math; 210 items out the door. This is a whole family project, and there won't be a drawer left untouched. I predict the first half of the month will be a cakewalk. I'm a purger by nature; ask anyone. Everything goes. When my friends keep sentimental baby clothes and old newspapers, I threaten to call "Hoarders" on them. Clutter stresses me out. I like clean counters and labels. I'll gladly purge the first round of stuff.

It's the second round I'm guessing will pinch. When the obvious things are gone and things move into the sacrificial zone, let's see what a peppy cheerleader I am. (My friends have gently skirted my treasures: "So, um, what about your books, Jen?" Back off or you're dead to me.)

This month will be executed with The Council and other participating friends. Some will be generic donations, and others will be specific; I'm looking for the perfect recipient. Donating everything through a third party removes the relational magic when one human connects with another. Donating to Goodwill is fine, but I read the following quote three years ago, and it changed my life:

> "I had come to see that the great tragedy in the church is not that rich Christians do not care about the poor but that rich Christians do not know the poor. . . . I long for the Calcutta slums to meet the Chicago suburbs, for lepers to meet landowners and for each to see God's image in the other. . . . I truly believe that when the poor meet the rich, riches will have no meaning. And when the rich meet the poor, we will see poverty come to an end."[1] (Thank you, Shane Claiborne,

for messing me up.)

So off we go. Seven things a day. Clearly missing the point, my friends asked to paw through my giveaways in case they want something before it gets to the poor. Nice. This reminds me of Caleb who asks *every single time* we feed the homeless if he can have a burger. One night when I refused, he mumbled: "The homeless get everything."

Well, this month they certainly will.

Day 1

I wanted for this first entry to be charming and hilarious like the others have been (and clearly humble). I thought I'd share a cute anecdote or let my freak flag fly, easing into Month Three, warming up for this monstrous giveaway. But here is what happened:

I cleaned out my closet and I am sick.

Sick to death.

I couldn't even count the items or get them organized. They are piled on my closet floor and spilling into my bedroom as we speak. I had to walk away and breathe and sort through my emotions, which are churning too fast to keep up with. So many issues surfaced, I don't know where to begin. They're all screaming, "Pick me! Pick me!"

Okay, here's one: I grossly underestimated how much I've spent on clothes. I pulled out clothes I haven't worn in three years: Limited, Express, BCBG Max Azria, Seven (hello irony), Banana Republic, Cache, Nordstroms, Lucky, Steve

Madden. These did not average $10 each, dear reader. And because I buy at the eleventh hour, moments before I need them, I mostly paid full price. No time for frugality when you're panic shopping.

Here's another reality check: I counted around forty items I've worn fewer than five times; four with tags on, never even worn. I might as well have sautéed that money in olive oil and eaten it. I think this bothered me most. *Forty items barely worn.* How indulgent and irresponsible and wasteful. Careless, that's the word. If I bought something that didn't warrant more than three wearings, I did not need it. That is thoughtless, default consumerism: see it, like it, buy it.

Cleaning out clothes that represented "my last life" kept me on a low simmer the whole morning. This was the bulk of all I purged, and I felt sad. These were beautiful clothes from another time, what I wore before we started Austin New Church—gorgeous, expensive clothes from a gorgeous, expensive season.

I don't know why I felt so sad. Maybe because these are the last reminders of a formative time. I wore these the first time I taught women, the first time I spoke, the first time I had a book signing, the first time I taught in church on a Sunday morning. These pretty clothes gave me confidence when I was terrified and uncertain. I'm looking at them and see Christmas brunches, women's conferences, memorable weddings, the church lobby. I lived my life in these clothes for seven years, and getting rid of them is a final farewell to our old life.

After this there is nothing left from "before."

Clothes used to define me when my genuine identity was fuzzy. When I didn't know who I was or what I was here for, I dressed like someone who did. I dolled up the container, but I'm learning that I'm really just a jar of clay. Because that was all I was ever supposed to be. It will be my pleasure to give these beautiful, well-crafted clothes to someone who needs them.

Because I don't need them anymore.

Day 2

125 things.

That's how many items survived the closet cut. It was easier to count what was left than what I donated, a 62 percent reduction. I came off the ledge and got to business. Yesterday was a mess, meaning I was. I left everything everywhere, and we stepped over/on it until this morning. My paralysis receded today, and I engineered a massive Sort and Organize. I had so many clothes that subcategories were required:

Trendy dressy   Dressy dressy   Out of style dressy

Ten-pounds-ago-clothes   Cute sleeveless

Ball diamond sleeveless

And on and on. Good grief. I could've opened a boutique with this inventory. There were two categories: business appropriate and everything else. "Everything else" was loaded into my car (seats laid down to accommodate the plunder), and off I went to SafePlace.

What is SafePlace, you may ask?

Well here you go. SafePlace's vision, as they report it is:

> Working toward a community free of rape, sexual
> abuse and domestic violence. SafePlace provides
> physical safety for women and families affected by
> sexual and domestic violence.[2]

The abused find immediate shelter at SafePlace; the
staff intervenes in the hospital and counsels children
through trauma. Working to break the cycle, SafePlace
provides community outreach, Expect Respect Program
for teens and youth, disability services, deaf services, and
community dialogue. Violent patterns won't be repeated
on their watch.

I thought about how my lovely clothes propped up the
outside while my inside was struggling to find its way. I
smile to think of a broken, abused woman slipping these
pretty things on and propping up the outside a bit during
her healing process. I pray they remind her that she is
beautiful, she is valuable, she is worth it.

In the giant pile was my second pair of cowboy boots. If
you read *Interrupted*, you've been here with me once, but
let's go again (the following is excerpted from *Interrupted*):

> Easter snuck up on us—the day that changed
> everything. Deeply moved by Shane Claiborne among
> others, evidently Brandon sent him an e-mail through
> dubious channels basically telling him *The Irresistible
> Revolution* was messing his wife up, and now he was
> reading it and didn't know what to do with it in
> his context. But we were wrestling and asking new

questions, so that was probably good. He just wanted
Shane to know that his message mattered to a pastor
in the suburbs, even if it was driving us crazy. Sent and
forgotten.

Ring-ring-ring. "Hi, is this Brandon? This is Shane
Claiborne . . . yes it is . . . oh, I got your number off
your e-mail . . . no your wife is not involved in this.
. . . Anyway, I'm going to be speaking at a small Asian
American church in Austin Easter night, and I thought
maybe we could have coffee afterward . . . no, you're
not being punked . . . okay, I'll see you in a couple of
days."

Seriously? Who does that? I get e-mails from strangers
all the time, and I was feeling good about responding
to them, much less pilfering their numbers off their
signature line and scheduling coffees with them when
I come to their cities. (As a traveling Bible teacher,
Shane also convinced me to imitate the hospitality
model of the New Testament and stay in homes when
I travel instead of hotels. Best decision I've ever made.
Guess what? There are people who actually have the
gift of hospitality and are really good at it! Who knew?
Paul and Jesus. And Shane.)

Anyhow, there was a 100 percent chance that coffee
was happening, so we cleared Easter evening to spend
with the members of Vox Vaniae and Shane. (Check
out this cool church at www.voxveniae.com—if I could,
I would eat their Web site.)

Easter weekend, we blew the six services out of
the water at our church: big, incredible, fantastic
production, guest musicians, "When the Saints Go

Marching In," trumpets, lights, gospel singers, rappers, sweet videography, killer. We herded approximately ten billion people in and out of there like cattle, clearing out as fast as possible for the next service. As far as wow-factors go, no one left disappointed. You got it, Jack. And Jackie.

Fast forward a few hours later, and we changed into jeans and drove downtown for Vox Veniae's one little Easter service with their guest speaker, Shane Claiborne. The church rented this crappy space on the University of Texas campus, and we parked in a ramshackle-looking parking lot a block away. As we walked up to the church, we saw a homeless-looking guy with weird hair, wearing what appeared to be a burlap sack in the shape of pants and a tunic. This was, of course, Shane. (He's been "escorted out" of several churches before they realized he was their guest speaker. Claiborne: Making Deacons Feel Awkward Since 1998.)

Maybe 150 people were at this Easter service, and it was simple and stripped down. There were candles, an unscripted welcome. The worship was so un-self-conscious and pure, maybe three or four guys in the band. It was completely unproduced and humble, all of it. It smacked of regular people and simple church; their only preoccupation was this obsession with Jesus. It was tangible. I loved every molecule of it. I wanted to sell my house and move into this room.

Toward the end of Shane's talk, he mentioned his time that morning with a large homeless community in San Antonio. He had asked their spokesman what their main needs were. Above all else, they needed good shoes. He explained how they were on their feet all day, and the shoes they got from shelters and Goodwill were everyone else's castoffs, worn down, worn out. (The homeless community has chronic leg and back pain from long days standing in inadequate shoes.)

As we were about to take communion, Shane said, "You are under no coercion, but if you want to, you can leave your shoes at the altar when you take communion. Oh! And leave your socks too. We'll wash them and deliver them all to the homeless community in San Antonio tomorrow."

Two significant particulars: One, Easter 2007 in Austin was unseasonably, crazy cold. Like 31 degrees that morning cold. Understand that in April in Austin, we would all typically be wearing shorts and flip flops. Guaranteed. From the youngest to the oldest. As it was, every person there had on real, substantial shoes because it was freezing outside.

Two, Brandon and I looked down at our shoes in unison and just started laughing. Why? We were both wearing our brand new cowboy boots we'd given each other for Christmas. By a huge margin, they were the most prized and expensive shoes we'd ever owned. I loved them so much, I gave them their own special box in my closet where moth and rust could not destroy.

Having thrown myself into this arena for a few months, I thought I would be thrilled to rip those boots off my rich feet and happily give them over to the homeless (who would promptly sell them since they are entirely impractical and worth a pretty penny—I've learned a few things). But I was discouraged to feel the twinge of selfishness rear its head first. Seriously? I'm going to make a deal over boots? Have I come only this far, God? I suck.

Jesus, unwilling to entertain my melodrama, cut to the chase: "Give them up. I have something to teach you." Evidently, this moment was not about me and my urban cowgirl boots. So I took them off, raised them to my lips for a farewell kiss, oh okay, and an embrace, and Brandon and I left them at the altar along with our socks and the last remaining thread of reluctance.

I'll not do the moment justice, but at the close of the service, I watched all these smiling people gladly walk barefooted out into the cold, and I heard Jesus whisper: This is how I want My church to look. I want her to rip the shoes off her feet for the least every single chance she gets. I want an altar full of socks and shoes right next to the communion table. I want to see solidarity with the poor. I want true community rallied around My gospel. I want a barefooted church.

A barefooted church.

Brandon replaced those boots on Mother's Day, and today I gave them away again. As we inventoried my things, I told this story to the SafePlace volunteer. He promised to personally ensure my boots found the right feet, someone who needed reminding that though she feels like the least, she is loved by a Savior whose eye is on the sparrow.

I pray for the woman who will literally walk in my shoes.

Jesus, embrace her with safety and healing. With every step she takes, wrapped in my clothes, may she know your faithfulness and experience your redemption. Take her to that sacred place with You where there is no more abuse, no more violence, only the sweet rescue of salvation.

Day 3

Since I gave away 202 items from just my closet, and Month Three requires 210 giveaways, we're going to adjust. The Council decided one week can involve clothes. The end. So even if we purge one thousand shirts, they will only count toward seven days.

Now I have to tell you something, and it's bad.

Three months ago I was cleaning out the kids' drawers as the season was changing from *warmer-cool* to *cooler-cool*. Out came shorts that didn't fit, T-shirts inching up their bellies, jeans from last year, and other outgrown items. I pulled at least twenty-five items per kid.

Every mom engages this purge twice a year. There is nothing noble about it. It's out with the old and outgrown, in with the new and shiny. It's not about reducing, simplifying, or sharing; it's really a function of our kids growing two sizes every three months while we research gland disorders and reswear off GMO products.

But I did something bad. I knew this month was coming, and I wasn't sure we'd have enough to purge so quickly after that cleanout. So I stored the piles to donate should our options become too slim. That's right, my trusting friends:

I prehoarded.

I'm sorry, okay? I won't count them. Sadly, I don't *need* to count them. We will exceed 210 items by a landslide. I told you I'm the type to cheat in advance, and now it's confirmed. Two hundred and ten sounded like a lot! I was scared we'd be leaning against the walls where our couches used to be by the end of the month.

But yet again, I underestimated how much we've bought.

Crimeny.

Day 6

I am a schizophrenic consumer.

I have an overabundance of certain items as unnecessary as diet pills for a supermodel. For instance, I have about a hundred books. On God. I have another sixty on women's issues. This doesn't include my fiction, memoires, essays, global issues, cookbooks, biographies, and reference books. Oh okay, and commentaries, mysteries, poetry anthologies, parenting books, and autobiographies. And history books. And maps and atlases. And humor essays. Books on tape. You get the picture.

Also, I have lots of movies. Like four drawers full of VHS tapes and no VHS player. Included is *Karate Kid 3*, a straight-to-video tragedy starring young Hillary Swank who was ridiculously annoying and also managed to seriously overact in said movie that I spent actual money on. That is an hour and a half and ten dollars I'll never get back.

And don't get me started on blankets. I am *uptohere* with

blankets. It's not like we live in the frozen tundra or don't enjoy a $250+ a month electric habit. We are not the Ingalls living in the Big Woods while our children, Caroline, Laura, and Mary, huddle together for warmth. I should invite Michael Jackson's son, Blanket, to live here among his own kind (and maybe Gwyneth's daughter Apple could live in our refrigerator and Frank Zappa's daughter Diva Thin Muffin can stay in my pantry).

However. I am downright destitute in other categories. Most black holes exist in my kitchen. For example, I have two potholders. Two. One is a Christmas-themed gem complete with mildew polka dots. It is as thin as a Kleenex, so it withstands actual heat for about three seconds then no longer protects my hands from burning metal. The other is a crocheted mini-potholder I bought from Trina's daughter. It is 1mm wide, so I've burned myself innumerable times as it doesn't cover the surface area of my hand (too bad for you, Bottom of Palm and Tips of Fingers).

My reaction to the potholder conundrum is nonsensical:

Scene: Jen suffers ninety-fourth burn, extracting dish from oven:

> "Aaaaaaghhhh! I burned the tips of my fingers again and now I won't have fingerprints! I can't be searing my hands all the time! I just ca-a-a-a-an't!" (Holding up hands dramatically, perhaps shaking them for effect.)

> "This is how I make a living! This is my livelihood! I'm a word surgeon. . . . I need my hands to execute my craft! These ten fingers are how the magic happens,

and without them I might as well cut out my voicebox too, because that's how useless I am on earth!"

Brandon, fantasizing about the missing voicebox, "Here's ten dollars. Go buy some."

I can't explain why I haven't bought new potholders. I guess its laziness. What else could it be?

The potholders aren't in that category by themselves. The same is true about bath towels (seven in the whole house), mixing bowls, cooking utensils (I have one half-melted spatula) and pots and pans. As a matter of fact, I still use a 1993 wedding shower pan that adds so much flaked Teflon into every dish, I'm certain I've seeded us all with cancer.

So evidently, I'm of the feast or famine variety.

Day 11

It's Easter.

Between ages zero and thirty-two, I celebrated Easter the fun way: with bunnies, baskets, and expensive clothes. What better way to say "Jesus reigns" than dressing my preschooler in a $45 dress to show her off in the church lobby? (You're welcome, Jesus. Be blessed.)

Now let's be clear: if you had asked me what my Easter priorities were as I stood all fancy in the lobby, I'd become grave and mention the resurrection. For crying out loud, I'm a Christian. But truthfully, between the outfit shopping, the Easter baskets, the egg _____ (dying, stuffing, hiding, hunting), the pictures, the lunch menu, and the gift buying, Jesus was flat last. I started thinking about Him as the band started at church, and I thought about Him for a whole hour.

That's just true.

But for the last three years Jesus has messed with me. Frankly, He's hijacked all my holiday endeavors. I've always celebrated holidays with a cultural major and a spiritual minor. Take Christmas, for example. I endlessly spent on garbage no one needed and worked myself into a December frenzy and oh well. La de da. Now I'm overwhelmed by the poor and the disgusting consumerism cycle and the heinous neglect of Jesus and the appalling nature of it all.

Then we got to Easter, or as God called it, Passover. *Easter* is a little name picked up from the Anglo-Saxon fertility goddess of spring, *Eostre,* who saved a frozen bird from the harsh winter by turning it into a magical rabbit who could lay eggs. Hence: "Easter" bunnies and eggs. Why are elements of a pagan religion associated with the highest holy day of the Christian faith? Oh bother. Can't we just carry on and dye our Eostre eggs in peace?

Assessing the typical American Easter, on one side I see Jesus on the cross, humiliated and mutilated, bearing the failures of every person past and present, rescuing humanity through an astonishing miracle of divine redemption, splitting history in two and transforming the human experience for eternity. On the other side I see us celebrating this monumental heroism with chocolate bunnies and boiled eggs, with Jesus as an afterthought. It doesn't make sense. (Insert some of you tossing this book in the garbage. *Don't mess with my Easter fun, you hippie chick*.)

This year, Austin New Church decided to rethink "The Traditional Easter Service That Brings In More People Than Any Other Day of the Year." It is our church's two-year anniversary, and certainly we could stand more foot traffic, but I'm not sure Passover is best celebrated by a high-attendance Sunday of people who won't be back until Christmas Eve.

We literally asked ourselves . . . What would Jesus do? Would He drop a bunch of cash on fancy clothes? Buy out the chocolate and plastic egg supply? Find the biggest church in town and spend twenty minutes posturing in the lobby?

Who in Austin might want to celebrate the astonishing hope of resurrected Jesus but might feel uncomfortable surrounded by beautiful people dressed to the nines? Who needs the gospel spoken into their brokenness but might not be welcomed by the saints in the sanctuaries? It came quickly to us:

The homeless.

If Jesus came to proclaim freedom for the captives and good news to the poor, then Passover uniquely belongs to the bottom dwellers. So we cancelled service and took church downtown to the corner of 7th and Neches, where our homeless community is concentrated. We grilled thirteen hundred burgers and ate together. Our band led worship; then in a powerful moment of solidarity, we shared Communion. It was a beautiful mess of dancing, tears, singing, and sharing. It wasn't an *us* and *them* moment; it was just the church, remembering the Passover Lamb and celebrating our liberation together.

Now, if we get one repetitive request when serving our homeless friends, it's this: "Do you have a bag?" (Could also be: Can I have that bag? Can I take that trash bag? Do you have a bag I can put this bag in?) So this was the perfect moment to give away seven of my nine purses, which were nice and roomy, just like the ladies want.

When the gals had a perfect view for maximum impact, I hollered:

"Hey girls! Anyone want one of . . . these?"

Cranberry red leather.

Green with gold buckles.

Chocolate brown bohemian bag.

Turquoise with short handles.

Burnt orange across-the-shoulder.

Shiny black backpack bag.

And one little purse I debated on bringing. It was a tiny thing, hot pink crocodile by Gianni Bini, functionally useless but fashionably magnificent. Our street girls want the biggest bags possible, since they carry everything they own. A wheelbarrow would be a huge hit. So my little vanity purse was a wildcard, but at the last second with a conspiratorial nudge from the Spirit, I threw it in.

Not surprisingly, it was the last purse left. What self-respecting homeless woman picks a hot pink purse that would barely carry her bus pass? Glamour handbags are only for women who have eight others and a house in which to stash them. So I stood there with my one little purse, when it's rightful owner, the one for whom I daresay that purse was stitched together, made a beeline for me.

She had on her Easter finest, tights included, though it was ninety degrees. Flouncy dress with—what else?—hot pink flowers. Hair done in sections with matching beads, pink floppy hat on standby. Leather dress shoes polished to a sheen. Dainty ribbon necklace and rings on four fingers.

She was six-years-old. Her name was NeNe.

Never has a purse better matched its owner. She slipped that hot pink number over her arm and never put it down, not even to eat. Her mom looked at me and no words were necessary; mothers speak a silent language. I took her picture and fussed over her beauty and breathed a thank you to Jesus for the nudge.

I serve a Savior who finds a way to get pink purses to homeless six-year-old girls.

Jesus is a redeemer, a restorer in every way. His day on the cross looked like a colossal failure, but it was His finest moment. He launched a kingdom where the least will be the greatest and the last will be first, where the poor will be comforted and the meek will inherit the earth. Jesus brought together the homeless with the privileged and said, "You're all poor, and you're all beautiful." The cross leveled the playing field, and no earthly distinction is valid anymore. There is a new "us"—people rescued by the

Passover Lamb, adopted into the family and transformed into saints. It is the most epic miracle in history.

That is why we celebrate. May we never become so enamored by the substitutions of this world that we forget.

"It was just before the Passover Feast. Jesus knew that the time had come for him to leave this world and go to the Father. Having loved his own who were in the world, he now showed them the full extent of his love." (John 13:1)

Day 13

I have a growing number of friends joining 7. I casually mentioned it on Facebook, which started a firestorm of questions. Which begat more e-mails. Which led to rogue groups joining the fray. Which led to one group in Nashville demanding the outline because they couldn't wait for 7 to become a book.

Our ANC friend circle is joining, and I get e-mails from all over the country telling me their 7 moments and following along. God is rewriting so many of our stories at once.

My girlfriend Amanda discovered "The Prom Project," which collects formals and all the fixins for underprivileged girls to wear to prom. If you only understood how perfectly this nonprofit fits Amanda. She donated not one, not two, but *twelve* formals complete with gloves, heels, jewelry, and shiny hair ornamentation.

Me: Amanda! Twelve?? Have you been attending the local proms on the prowl? Does Ryan know? Why on earth do you have twelve formals?

Amanda: I used to do a lot of fancy things!

Me: I do a few fancy things, and I've worn the same dress for seven years, making me a social tragedy. No long silk gloves or bejeweled heels either. Explain.

Amanda: I'm from the Valley, okay! We learned to be gaudy at a young age. I grew up with a "more is more" mentality. Between everyone's Quinceaneras and Los Dias de los Muertos and Cotillion and all my real estate cocktail parties and Renaissance fairs, I have a bunch of costumes, I mean, formals.

Me: Wait, Renaissance fairs?

Amanda: The Dark Ages are done. Fiat Lux.

Thanks to Amanda, twelve skinny high school girls will attend their proms in the highest fashion without spending a penny. She made a prom memory possible, a rite of passage for the American teenager but impossible for girls in poverty.

This is why the body of Christ is so essential. I could no more meet the needs of impoverished teenagers attending prom than I could recount the basic years of the Renaissance. (1500s? 1700s? I vaguely recall the word *mutton* and a movie with Heath Ledger.)

But this is Amanda's offering. She's doing her part. We each meet unique needs in our cities and our world. If we all raised others up instead of raising ourselves a little higher, there would be few needs left on earth. I marvel at what God accomplishes with the generosity of his sons and daughters. I'm proud they are brothers and sisters.

What a family.

And hey, if you need any elbow-length satin gloves or chandelier rhinestone earrings . . . I know a girl.

Day 17

Were it not for the intervention of the Holy Spirit, my girlfriends and I would end up on Jerry Springer. We are loud and silly (Brandon would say obnoxious). When one friend volunteered to move in with me so that together she and I might make one whole wife, Brandon said, "Oh yeah, that's exactly what I need. One more woman in this house who thinks she's hilarious."

Admittedly, we skirt the edges of inappropriate and hold some pictures as leverage against one another, but let me tell you: If you're ever in a crisis, we're as effective as the Red Cross. We can mobilize in four minutes.

This month of 7 created plenty of opportunities to team up. Susana sent an SOS e-mail about her single-mom friend, Staci, and her two daughters who'd lived with someone for a year, all three in the same room. Staci left a destructive marriage with whatever fit into the car. She was working, putting herself through college, and trying to rebuild a healthy life for her girls. She'd saved for a small apartment—a thrill—but she literally had nothing. No beds, no furniture, no silverware.

The working poor get lost in the shuffle. Susana and Staci were friends for six months before she realized Staci was struggling. Their girls were in a club together; there was plenty of laughing and banter. By all appearances Staci's station seemed "normal." The usual clues that point to poverty are ambiguous for those in the gap.

The working poor are one missed shift from homelessness, one lost paycheck from hunger, one overdue bill from repossession. However, they learn to camouflage nicely into society. They laugh at the right jokes and deflect questions with sarcasm or silence. The children are ashamed to admit they haven't eaten all weekend or can't afford to play soccer, so you'd never know. In many ways they are invisible.

Had Susana not asked for a plate at Staci's house, and had Staci not pointed to the two plates holding snacks and said, "You're looking at them," she wouldn't have known the family was hanging on by a thread. Susana urged (read: bullied) Staci into making a list, and she rocketed the needs out to our friend tribe.

We had her apartment furnished, stocked, filled, and decorated in four days. Because of 7, we'd liquidated tons of items, awaiting the right recipient. Beds, linens, microwave, couches, TVs, table and chairs, dishes, pictures, all of it.

Staci sent Susana this e-mail on Monday:

> We were so overwhelmed yesterday that I am not sure I even said thank you. Thank you for listening to that still small voice from God. Thank you for inviting your prayer group into your vision. Thank you for setting such a wonderful example of Christian service and womanhood. Dylan notices EVERYTHING and she told me, "Those people are Christians." Yes, honey, they are. And God said we will be known by the love we show

one another. How nice to lay in that bed and sit at that table and stare at those groceries in the cabinet. This is the best vacuum cleaner I have ever had. The microwave and the trash can and bowl of apples (my favorite red delicious apples) and the brown smooth sheets all scream GOD LOVES YOU AND YOU ARE NOT ALONE. Who knew apples could say so much? I have an overwhelming feeling that everything will be fine for the first time since I moved back to Austin.

This was one of those moments when my mission became very clear, very concentrated, very unambiguous. Static has always surrounded the Christian life; so much threatens to distract us from the main point. People have always preferred details and complications and rules, but when Jesus was pressed, He said (Jen translation), "Love God and love people. That's pretty much it." Staci's story reminds me:

This is what we do, and this is why we do it.

Sometimes the best way to bring good news to the poor is to bring actual good news to the poor. It appears a good way to bring relief to the oppressed is to bring real relief to the oppressed. It's almost like Jesus meant what He said. When you're desperate, usually the best news you can receive is food, water, shelter. These provisions communicate God's presence infinitely more than a tract or Christian performance in the local park. They convey, "God loves you so dearly, He sent people to your rescue."

I guess that's why *"love people"* is the second command next to *"love God."* And since God's reputation is hopelessly linked to His followers' behavior, I suspect He wouldn't be stuck with His current rap if we spent our time loving others and stocking their cabinets.

But there I go, off on another tangent, imagining apples can be part of the gospel.

Next I'm going to tell you *the last will be first* or something crazy.

Day 18

I'm two and a half months into 7, and I'm noticing some things. God historically moves epically in my life. I don't have subtle seasons of change. Our rhythm works like this: I experience a maddening tension I can or can't exactly put my finger on, and then BAM. God kicks me in the teeth and things change.

7 is becoming epically transformative. Tension led me here; now God is making a mess of things. I sense God preparing us for change. My sensitivity is peaking; noteworthy, because I have the sensitivity of a thirteen-year-old boy. I feel raw and less and less attached to my stuff. Scripture is pouncing on my brain like a panther. It's like when I first got glasses and couldn't get over how clear everything was. And I walked weird because my perception was altered. I kept shouting, "Look at all the leaves! I can see every leaf on the tree!" like it was a miracle after having been impaired so long.

I have no idea what this means, but my hands are opening. I know my next phase of life is not going to look the same.

I'm scared. Hmm. When I first typed that, I accidentally spelled *sacred*.

Perhaps those have always been flip sides of a coin. Like my friend says, "Obedience isn't a lack of fear. It's just doing it scared."

Day 20

"God? Connect us with people who need our stuff."

"Okay. Hey? How about these refugees?"

Refugees are an invisible population, marginalized by language barriers and ethnic stereotypes. They disappear into society, unseen as they clean our hotel rooms, flip our burgers, and sweep our airports. We look right past them, unaware of the trauma they've endured or the countries they've left behind. Their stories are lost to people who only see their function—Please leave us extra towels. Take us to 5th and Broadway. One Coke and the paper.

Austin New Church is learning about refugees the way we do: stalking experts and attaching like barnacles. The Refugee Services of Texas is teaching us how to empower this forgotten group. Typically, RST is understaffed and overworked, the plight of the average nonprofit. So we jumped from, "Hi! We'd like to learn about refugees, please," to "Good! A Burmese family is flying in Friday with the clothes on their backs. Can you furnish their apartment and pick them up at the airport?"

Oh lawd.

Insert: e-mail frenzy, harried administrating, and a massive cancellation of calendars. Off the list I spotted some items I'd been waiting to give away, one in particular: bedding.

This Burmese couple and their two teenage daughters needed everything, and this was something I had to share. In addition to one full-sized bed, out went:

Seven sheet sets and the fixins.

We supplied furniture, dishes, toiletries, groceries, clothes, and accessories. Obviously, that is only the beginning of this family's journey. The true obstacles are yet to come: financial independence, language acquisition, education, empowerment, community—an overwhelming transition in an unfamiliar country. They'll need us more in the coming months, but for tonight they'll sleep on their own sheets in their own beds at their own apartment for the first time in years.

So once again, we pray God is evident in every pillowcase, each fork, all the simple comforts we take for granted. While they've known violence and fear, we hope tonight they'll experience safety and love.

Day 25

For the last three years, God used Easter to mess me up. I've mentioned the Easter I gave my boots away and life was forever altered. The next Easter we launched Austin New Church, and my story divided in half: before ANC and after. The following Easter was our church's one-year anniversary as God delivered on His promise, and ANC was legit, a monumental lesson on His faithfulness.

So let me finish the story about this Easter; there was more than NeNe and her little pink purse. When you bring your entire church downtown to feed eight hundred homeless people including a band, worship, a message, Communion, and resource stations, it gets . . . messy. The sanitized version of church goes out the window. The rules to maintain an organized service simply don't apply to an outdoor service dominated by the homeless.

So during Brandon's brief message, one very sad, very lost woman screamed, "Where were all of you when these men were violating me?! Where were you??" There was more, none printable. It was raw and desperate, littered with expletives and sorrow. If we came to proclaim freedom for the oppressed like Jesus said, then we needn't look further than this broken woman.

What did I do? How did her grief move me? Well, I motioned for Tray to "take care of her."

My instinct was to protect the service, keep everything decent. I mean, a shattered woman screaming during church is just too messy to indulge. My church family, however, responded with grace befitting the Bride. Brandon spoke gently to her, Christi tried to embrace her, Ryan held out his hand, others interceded for this prodigal daughter. If Jesus really meant the church was a hospital for the sick, not a showcase of the healthy, then we were seriously having church.

Cut to the next day.

I was preparing to be the keynote speaker at a monstrous event two weeks away, the Ladies' Retreat for the Baptist General Convention of Oklahoma, around three thousand women. I was locked into Mark 10, where Jesus engaged blind Bartimaeus a week before He went to the cross. I got down to business studying.

I had so much to teach. Other people.

Ahem.

Bartimaeus: poor, blind, beggar. Probably looked like every homeless person I know. Outcast, shunned from the temple, unclean, discarded in every way—a true societal reject. And here comes Jesus with His entourage, headed to Jerusalem to be "king" (oops, they had a little misunderstanding about what that meant—their bad). Everyone is excited, everyone is cheering. Yay, Jesus! We're getting our king and we'll be free!

As Jesus and his disciples, together with a large crowd, were leaving the city, a blind man, Bartimaeus (that is, the Son of Timaeus), was sitting by the roadside begging. When he heard that it was Jesus of Nazareth, he began to shout, "Jesus, Son of David, have mercy on me!" (Mark 10:46–47)

Whoa up. Yikes. This is awkward. This is embarrassing actually. There is nothing dignified here. This reeks of desperation. I mean, Bartimaeus? Poor, blind Bartimaeus screaming at Jesus? Sheesh. What a mess, Jesus surrounded by normal, decent followers, forced to deal with this sad, sorry homeless guy screaming bloody murder.

Many rebuked him and told him to be quiet, but he shouted all the more, "Son of David, have mercy on me!" Jesus stopped and said, "Call him." So they called to the blind man, "Cheer up! On your feet! He's calling you." Throwing his cloak aside, he jumped to his feet and came to Jesus. "What do you want me to do for you?" Jesus asked him. The blind man said, "Rabbi, I want to see." "Go," said Jesus, "your faith has healed you." Immediately he received his sight and followed Jesus along the road. (Mark 10:48–52)

And bam, right in the middle of my important studying to teach others how to follow Jesus, the Holy Spirit leveled me. Who was I in this scenario? Not Jesus, mercifully pausing for a blind beggar *on His way to the cross*, but the embarrassed "Christ followers" who scorned this humiliating interruption during their Christ-following and sanitized this awkward confrontation to get on with their holiness.

I cried for an hour.

I have so far to go.

"Rabbi, I want to see." Bartimaeus asked for the most basic human need. In biblical times blindness meant he was considered cursed by God, which made him unclean, which made him an outcast, which made him a beggar. Unlike James and John who nine verses earlier asked to sit at Jesus' right and left hand in glory (predicated by the awesome demand, "Teacher, we want You to do for us whatever we ask"), Bartimaeus only asked for mercy.

This is like the starving asking for food, the orphan asking for parents, the homeless asking for shelter, the sick asking for medicine; basic human needs—food, shelter, care, love. These aren't tangled up in power or position; they aren't born out of entitlement or greed. They are a plea for mercy, the cry of every human heart.

Decorum has no relevance for the mother who prostitutes to feed her children or the nine-year-old who eats trash to survive the streets. The "rules on how to behave" are meaningless for the sixty-six children infected with HIV in the last hour or the twenty-five thousand people who died *today* from starvation.

The poor world is begging for mercy like Bartimaus, while the rich world is asking for more favor like James and John.

I taught this mess at the BGCO Ladies' Retreat, including my dismal failure on Easter two weeks ago. I wondered if the American church was like well-mannered nice-talkers, sitting in a living room sipping coffee, talking about choir practice, while the world burns down outside our windows. While the richest people on earth pray to get richer, the rest of the world begs for intervention with their faces pressed to the window, watching us drink our coffee, unruffled by their suffering.

It's just not right.

So I blubbered in front of three thousand women, bawling for the anguish of others and my own heinous disinterest, worried we were missing the point. I told the story about giving away my boots and asked if a similar moment wasn't in order—not that shoes will change anyone's life, but there is something spiritual and submissive about offering the shoes on your feet, the sweater off your back. It tells Jesus: I'm in.

It's the engine behind this month of 7: giving away is somehow sacred, connecting to the sacrificial heartbeat of Jesus. It's as transformative for the giver as a blessing to the receiver. When God told us to give, I suspect he had spiritual formation in mind as much as meeting needs.

You might want to sit down.

Before I formalized this or offered any structure, women

started pouring down the aisles, pulling their shoes off.
They left jackets, Bibles, purses, diamond necklaces,
wedding rings, cameras, iPhones, bags—I have never
seen anything like it. Eventually, I just turned off my
microphone as hundreds of women lay face down, sobbing,
barefoot. The stage was covered in their offerings, falling
onto the ground and taking over the room.

It filled seventy large moving boxes.

It was the greatest possible giveaway of Month Three.

I learned something: There is much hope for the American
church. It's too soon to declare the Bride hopelessly selfish
or irrelevant. The fear my message would be received
poorly was so debilitating I hadn't slept for a week.
When women are accustomed to beauty and happiness
messages, discussing a crumbling world caused me no end
of anxiety.

I'll repeat: seventy moving boxes full of offerings,
thousands of women going home in the pouring rain
barefooted. The church is not beyond the movement
of Jesus. A stirring is happening within the Bride. God
is awakening the church from her slumber, initiating a
profound advancement of the kingdom.

Please, don't miss it because the American Dream seems a
reasonable substitute, countering the apparent downside
to living simply so others can live at all. Do not be fooled
by the luxuries of this world; they cripple our faith. As
Jesus explained, the right things have to die so the right
things can live—we die to selfishness, greed, power,
accumulation, prestige, and self-preservation, giving life to
community, generosity, compassion, mercy, brotherhood,
kindness, and love.

The gospel will die in the toxic soil of self. Paul wrote, "We were therefore buried with Him through baptism into death in order that, just as Christ was raised from the dead through the glory of the Father, *we too may live a new life.* If we have been united with Him like this in His death, we will certainly also be united with Him in His resurrection." We want the life part without being united with Jesus in the death part, but that version of Christianity doesn't exist—that is a false gospel, void of sacrifice.

The fertile soil of death is where the gospel forms roots and actually bears fruit. We have to die to live; we have to die so others can live. It almost sounds like Jesus' mission. This is the church He was willing to die for, a Bride that inspires and changes the world. This vision is worthy of radical obedience. Don't give up on the church.

There is hope for her yet.

Day 27

Connie: I know you're giving stuff away, and I have some really underresourced kids at the school where I teach.

Jen: What do you need?

Connie: One of my boys wears his sister's old jeans every day. They are so small he can't button them, so he pulls his shirt down.

Jen: Bring him to me. I'll be his mother.

Connie: That's one idea, but maybe just give him clothes.

Jen: Perhaps.

Connie: We also need girls' clothes. And boys' clothes. In basically every size.

I delivered three boxes of my kids' clothes and shoes. There is no reason for any boy to wear his sister's jeans when we dump kids' clothes at Goodwill twice a year. Calling the counselor of an underresourced school about felt needs takes three minutes. Meeting a need directly is a guaranteed solution, getting nothing lost in the shuffle.

Day 30

After a month of liquidating, my friends and I still have stuff to give away. I am not even kidding. Our closets, drawers, cabinets, garages, attics, and shelves have been purged, and the volume created a pit in my stomach I can't shake.

When did this lose relevance for me?

Do not store up for yourselves treasure on earth, where moth and rust destroy, and where thieves break in and steal. But store up for yourselves treasures in heaven, where moth and rust do not destroy, and where thieves do not break in and steal. For where your treasure is, there your heart will be also. (Matt. 6:19–21)

I've creatively distanced myself from this, namely, a strategic focus on the "treasures in heaven" with a blind eye to the contrary "treasures on earth," addressing the spiritual list, ignoring the tangible list. But Jesus set these two in opposition, much like:

You can't serve God and money.

You're either a sheep or a goat.

There is only a wide road and a narrow road.

You either love your brother in Christ, or you're a liar.

We've invented a thousand shades of gray, devising a comfortable Christian existence we can all live with—super awesome, except the Bible doesn't support it. According to Scripture, no real disciple serves God while addicted to the dollar. There is no sheep/goat hybrid. There is no middle road. There is no true believer who hates his brother.

Grayed-down discipleship is an easier sell, but it created pretend Christians, obsessing over Scriptures we like while conspicuously ignoring the rest. Until God asks for everything and we answer, "It's yours," we don't yet have ears to hear or eyes to see. We're still deaf to the truth, blind to freedom, deceived by the treasures of the world, imagining them to be the key when they are actually the lock.

Nothing like handing over a big pile of your stuff to drive this point home! After giving away one thousand items this month, there is still more. Ditto for my friends. (Insert pit in stomach.) So Molly, with her "bonus storage room" that would make packrats weep with envy, devised a plan: Let's organize her space and use it as a supply room for streamlined giveaways from here on out.

The storage room was solitary confinement for Molly's junk, so everything had to come out first. Fortuitous, since we found a trunk packed with high school memorabilia. The six of us plopped down and roared with laughter for an hour. We summoned her husband Chris and demanded an explanation for his long, middle-parted hair from 1996.

We returned his stored pager; I've told him to "page me" seventy times since. He pretends to keep laughing.

We purged and organized and rearranged and categorized, and now Molly's storage room houses home accessories, toiletries, jeans and shoes, kitchen appliances, linens, and toys. No more scrambling when someone needs our stuff; we can go from phone call to delivery in ten minutes.

But now here's the real issue: Will I just replace all this? Will I purge another one thousand items three years from now? Will I slowly refill the empty spaces? Or will my family disconnect from the machine, creating a more courageous legacy than simply consuming? I want to confront the big part that says "more" with the smaller part that says "enough."

Believers, let's oppose the powers that manipulate us, lying about our needs, our responsibilities, our neighbor. Let's challenge the laissez-faire response that dismisses our consumerism with a casual shrug. But be prepared for the upstream struggle. The keepers of the market want us to spend. In a typical year the United States spends about $16 billion in foreign aid and $276 billion on advertising. Like Barber wrote in *Consumed*, "How much easier it is for the keepers when their task is to let Peter Pan fly free and keep Wendy cartwheeling under Peter's careless gaze rather than contain narcissism and help children grow up. For the keepers know the risk that comes with helping children grow up: they do not necessarily grow up into consumers. They sometimes become citizens."[3]

Paul put it this way: "When I was a child, I talked like a child, I thought like a child, I reasoned like a child. When I became a man, I put childish ways behind me. Now we see but a poor reflection as in a mirror; then we shall see face to face. Now I know in part; then I shall know fully, even as I am fully known" (1 Cor. 13:11–12).

A child says "me." An adult says "us." Maturity deciphers need from want, wisdom from foolishness. Growing up means curbing appetites, shifting from "me" to "we," understanding private choices have social consequences and public outcomes. Let's be consumers who silence the screaming voice that yells, "I WANT!" and instead listens to the quiet "we need," the marginalized voice of the worldwide community we belong to.

We top the global food chain through no fault or credit of our own. I've asked God a billion times why I have so much while others have so little. Why do my kids get full bellies? Why does water flow freely from my faucets? Why do we get to go the doctor when we're sick? There is no easy answer. The *why* definitely matters, but so does the *what*. What do we do with our riches? What do we do with our privileges? What should we keep? What should we share? I better address this inequality since Jesus clearly identified the poor as His brothers and sisters and my neighbor.

What if we tried together? What if a bunch of Christians wrote a new story, becoming consumers the earth is groaning for? I suspect we'd find that elusive contentment, storing up treasures in heaven like Jesus told us to. I'm betting our stuff would lose its grip and we'd discover riches contained in a simpler life, a communal responsibility. *Money* is the most frequent theme in Scripture; perhaps the secret to happiness is right under our noses. Maybe we don't recognize satisfaction because it is disguised as radical generosity, a strange misnomer in a consumer culture.

Richard Rohr described American Christians in *Simplicity*:

"We're just about to become adults, to honestly let the Gospel speak to us, to listen to what Jesus says, in no uncertain terms, about poverty and about leading a simple life in this world, a life that shows trust in God and not in our own power and weapons. God never promised us security in this world. God promised us only truth and freedom in our hearts. What does all this mean for us? It means that we're on the way."[4]

Let's prove that theory correct.

Month 4

MEDIA

Excerpted car conversation:

Caleb: I wonder what it feels like to die?

Gavin: I wouldn't want to die of constipation like Elvis did.

Me: Wait, what?

Gavin: Dad told me Elvis died on the toilet.

Caleb: Gavin, Elvis isn't even real!

Gavin: I thought he was the King of Rock?

Caleb: Gavin, do you really think someone would name their baby "Elvis"?

These used to be funny stories to tell grandparents; now they are sound bites for Facebook (this one generated fifty-two responses). Spam and Jesus forwards hijacked regular e-mail: *"Blah blah blah . . . forward this to all your friends. Remember, if you deny Jesus before man, He will deny you before the Father! PASS THIS ON OR ELSE! DON'T MAKE THE BABY JESUS CRY!"* Three years ago we had four channels; now we literally have thousands with the dumbest shows ever conceived. (I'm talking about you, Lifetime, featuring *Mother May I Sleep With Danger?* starring Tori Spelling.)

TV was innocent when our kids watched *Dora the Explorer* on Nick Jr. But now it's the Disney channel, where you can bet the farm those little overactors will turn straight crazy the second they turn eighteen and start their "music careers." It's awesome when the *High School Musical* stars post naked pictures on social media; thank you, Vanessa Hudgens! I was short on teaching moments for my daughter until you came to the rescue with your online boobies.

Don't get me started on gaming. This, I know, is ironic, since "someone" bought these systems then waged Mortal Kombat against her kids' Xbox 360, Nintendo DS Lites, Wii, and computer games. Listen, the son who can't muster an initiative to wear clean socks can attend to complicated war games for two hours. It's a miracle.

We have:

- Four gaming systems

- Two MacBooks and one desktop computer

- Five TVs

- Three cell phones (two of the "i" variety)

- A DVR

- Two DVD players

- Three handheld Nintendo DSs

- Three stereos

Stunning, since I didn't have a computer, e-mail address, or cable until 2005. We went from zero to full-blown addiction in five years. Our family is now owned by The Man (Time Warner Cable), and we're paying the piper, too (Hello, Apple, we're talking to you.) I don't know how we lived before Al Gore invented the Internet.

What the heck? I don't know how this happened; we hedged on boundaries one careless degree at a time, and now I hardly recognize our family rhythm. We have our own little screen worlds to immerse in; actual human contact seems optional.

Time to stop the madness.

So this month we're going radio silent. We're shutting down seven screens and muting the chatter. No:

TV Gaming Facebook/Twitter

iPhone apps Radio Texting* Internet*

The double asterisk involved much discussion with The Council and the hubs. Texting is a double-edged sword. Sometimes it is a time-saver; I can get an answer without talking for twenty-five minutes about hair products. So sometimes, it *adds* minutes instead of subtracting them.

On the other hand, sometimes texting is extraneous, even ridiculous. When I text this to a friend: "Friendship is like peeing in your pants. Everyone can see it, but only you can feel the warmth. Thanks for being the pee in my pants . . ." then I have too much time on my hands. And also I need to grow up.

Asterisk 1: our texting rule: If it is a time-saver and/ or necessary, then text away. If it's to be sarcastic, silly, or inappropriate, then pass. We're deferring to our own discernment, so someone should check my texts weekly because heaven knows I need accountability.

Asterisk 2: The Internet is a necessary tool for our jobs and life. Event planners, the kids' teachers, our adoption agency, my Restore Group, agent and publisher, and my neighbors correspond through e-mail. Additionally, I research for my books and messages online. I can't ditch Internet for a month. Neither can Brandon for all the same reasons, except for "corresponding with the kids' teachers" who I'm 90 percent sure he couldn't name.

But we *can* go without Facebook, Twitter, Sportcenter.com, adoption blogs, iPhoto, StuffChristiansLike.net (make sure you've emptied your bladder first), Hulu, scanwiches.com (recall my sandwich fixation), Amazon, twitter.com/xianity (i.e., "Dispensational republican audience turns on Christian comedian after one joke too many about red heifers."), thepioneerwoman.com, and YouTube (I'll miss you most, Annoying Orange). Good-bye.

The Council is in various levels of participation. Becky and Susana are going Full Monty. Shonna and Jenny are limiting screens to seven hours a week. Trina is contemplating giving up her cell phone. Dear Molly is still traumatized—recall the three DVRs loaded with "her stories." She begged me to move media month out of May. Because of sweeps. Because of season finales. Oh, the humanity! I suggested reducing to seven shows, and she gave me the look that predicates an assault and battery charge.

So remote controls are stashed, Facebook notifications turned off and corresponding iPhone app dumped, gaming controllers locked up, and the kids' computer unplugged. I've certainly received an earful on this:

"This month is going to be terrible! What are we going to do? I don't even like to read! What else is there? I think *some* TV would be fine! No texting?! All my friends text me! You're going to have your nose in a book while I'm bored with nothing to do! How many weeks? *Four??*"

And that was just Brandon.

Day 1

E-mail banter with The Council on our Facebook withdrawals:

Becky: This Facebook-sized hole is causing me to send e-mails like this: Chatted up AGAIN by the creepy preschool dad! Eeewww! (Only have a small case of the shakes today.)

Susana: Dude, I so get it. I have all this hilarious, self-aggrandizing drivel wasting away while I'm abstaining from the hive of Facebook. Like that statement I just gave. That's brilliant Facebook fodder. Wasted.

Jen: How will anyone manage without knowing Sydney and I made calzones tonight and that I have a fruit fly problem? What is the point of living if you don't get to hear that we took our first trip to the snow cone stand today? This is public FB material, and without posting it, it's like living our lives in privacy with no purpose.

Shonna: What are we supposed to do with our witty one-liners? How is anyone going to know how funny we are?

Jenny: I had decided not to give FB up, but my Bible reading today was terrible: "Dear children, keep yourselves from idols." I decided FB is an idol of mine since it steals my attention and affections away from God. But then I thought: maybe He wasn't talking to me. It did say "DEAR children." I'm not dear.

Molly: I've been trying to figure out my contribution to media month, and I will definitely be signing off FB. I'm struggling with the rest, well not the rest, just one thing:... TV. You know how much I love TV. It's what my degree is in. I make a spreadsheet every fall with all my shows and new ones I want to try (check my kitchen cabinet where it's taped). I have three DVRs and have to watch two shows a day so my main DVR doesn't exceed 97 percent full. Clearly I need professional help. It's May, and that means all the season finales. (Thanks, Jen.) Who will be my next "American Idol"? Will the *Glee* kids win regionals? Will Meredith and Derrick have a baby, thus ending one of their careers on *Grey's Anatomy*? And for the love of the land, I MUST know what that island on *Lost* is about! That's a five-year commitment I intend to see through. These are the questions that keep me up at night.

Trina: Sent from your iPad. Clearly you love technology. I also am pondering our commitment. I'm considering ditching my cell phone for the month. The biggest worrier here is my husband—he calls Jen when he can't find me.

Susana: There's freedom from addiction. Trust me. I gave up my shows for no good reason other than to be obedient and see what happens. And so, after eight seasons of never missing an episode, I have not seen *American Idol* this year. And I'm still alive. Except *Glee*. I still watch *Glee*. Umm . . . (plastered smile, eyes shifting) I have no excuse for this.

Jen: I love you, *Glee*.

Day 4

Okay, it's Thursday. We started Monday. No one has died. With love and affection for this person, and devotion and respect, and tenderness and esteem, the only complaints are Brandon's. This morning:

Brandon: (reading off open laptop) Jen! Avery Bradley is going into the NBA draft. Can you believe it? He only averaged eleven points this year! He needed another season with us, and he would've been clutch. But we recruited another stud point guard from Nevada of all places, and he's a shooter.

Jen: Um, what Web site are you on?

Brandon: Rivals.com. Why? What? What?? This is off limits?? How am I supposed to get my news?!

Brandon gets his news from college sports sites and I get mine from Facebook, so I don't know how two news junkies like us will manage. What if something monumental happens, like preseason football polls drop or *The Voice* gets a new judge? How can we live in such ignorance? I suggested buying a newspaper, and Brandon said, "Do they still make those?"

Anyway, the kids are doing surprisingly well. In four days I've not heard one word. The boys organized air-soft gun wars, so eight sweaty, stinky boys are running through my house wielding semiautomatic pellet guns dressed in sweatshirts though it was 97 degrees yesterday. My rule on this boy business: "Don't cry if you get pinged, and if one stray pellet hits me, I will run over your guns with my car." This is life with sons, people.

Sydney and I tackled ambitious recipes from my Pioneer Woman cookbook. We've rolled out crusts, made homemade calzones, chopped and diced, sautéed and baked. Report: homemade mac and cheese—FAIL. (I hate you, separated cheddar cheese that ruined my creamy sauce. Why are you so temperamental about heat? Velveeta would never treat me like this.)

We've played Pictureka with our (cheating) kids, and Brandon and the boys trash talked through HORSE on our "basketball court." The gang built a massive fort in the playroom (imagine overturned couches and stacked chairs). I even mopped and dusted because I wasn't spending time on Web surfing and the Food Network.

Maybe this month won't mean the end of the universe, after all.

Day 5

I take back everything I said about my kids behaving.

From 3:00 to 4:00 today, my house was a war zone. Gavin and Caleb were "kickbox fighting" on the trampoline. I can't imagine why this ended in tears and yelling, but it did, the little one accusing the big one of "fighting him too hard." I made matters worse by laughing because Caleb's Six Stages of Anger are so funny (get hurt > lay on the ground > cry eyes out > transition to "red rage" > come up swinging > shout something that includes the word *revenge*). The red rage—also known as Going Mad Dog—certainly hints of anger issues but is hilarious nonetheless.

Sydney started a puppetry project, transforming a

cardboard box into a stage with a pillowcase that sacrificed its life to become a curtain. It should've been sturdy held together with blue painting tape and wood glue (sarcasm intended), but it was rickety. This set her off and she became . . . difficult. All my suggestions were pure drivel. It was also my fault when she couldn't see the line I drew on the pillowcase and cut the opening too big. "Mom! You just don't get it!"

Between the fighting, crying, whining, and blaming, I hit a metaphorical wall. I wanted to turn on a movie and silence their little mouths. A nice screen trance would settle the tumultuous waters. Instead, I sent everyone to bedrooms until I gave the word.

We have to deal with rather than anesthetizing tension with TV or video games. It's easier to bypass relational snags with a convenient distraction, forfeiting the chance to improve problem solving and listening skills. I don't want my kids to be more comfortable interacting with a computer screen than a human being. We stay the course until we've resolved an issue, not allowing "Phineas & Ferb" to fill the space instead. This is harder and requires more time, but my kids will marry people and have bosses and children. Learning healthy relational skills is now or never.

Thirty minutes later we pressed the reset button. Perspectives were shared and apologies offered. All reengaged the puppetry project. The day was recovered: we collaborated on homemade pizza, and the puppet show was a smashing success. The kids reenacted "The Three Little Pigs" with some questionable alterations to the plot. Why did the boys' puppets have machetes? We don't ask these questions in the Hatmaker house. They just do. Thank you for understanding.

Day 8

Take something away, and your habits become clear. Parts of my day I don't miss media because I'm working or running errands or meeting with people. But I can easily identify the sections when media is a habit, a faithful companion to that time slot or task:

- Morning coffee + *The Today Show*

- Prewriting procrastination = Facebook and adoption blogs

- Folding laundry + *LA Ink*

- Mental writing break = cooking blogs and www. failblog.org

- Lunch at the table + Food Network

- Post kid bedtime = TV shows

These are the wrench in the media fast machine. Folding laundry today, I called Trina on speakerphone because I couldn't handle the silence. She commiserated, as our morning ritual includes a few segments of *The Today Show*. Unanchored this morning without Matt and Savannah's company, she stood in the bathroom, watching her hubby Andrew shave.

Andrew: I'm guessing you're bored.

Trina: I don't know what to do.

Andrew: Start tackling your tasks?

Trina: I can't yet. I'm suffering *Today Show* withdrawal.

Andrew: Would it help if I gave a tech script overview of the likely programming?

Trina: Yes, but don't make fun of my soft journalism.

Andrew: Let's see, cheery good morning, one belly laugh and show summary, then cut to serious-faced anchor, most likely ethnic.

> News: Somewhere in the U.S. a child is either missing or was horrifically harmed. Straight outta the trailer park, her grandmother will be interviewed with an attorney on one side, a T-shirt with the child's image on it, feather earrings and bad dental work.

> The oil spill is still a massive catastrophe, according to the individual in the live shot standing in front of distinctly coastal Louisiana scenery (shrimp boats are nice). We'll see images of oil-soaked birds struggling to escape caring hands and dead sea life on the beach.

> The President will say something about something.

> Then, in the weather, it will either rain or not rain locally, and we'll see footage of someone somewhere picking through the wreckage of a tornado-flattened house or being plucked from the rooftop of a flooded home by a helicopter or johnboat.

> In celebrity news a much prettier person than we will ever meet in real life either did or did not have sex with someone, meaning there is either a scandal or a child on the way/newly born.

Cut to commercials, most likely Clorox, diaper, or menstrual related.

Back for a cooking segment, probably a summer-themed recipe, which means there will be fresh tomatoes in it. Pray the second-tier talent doesn't sever a tendon while clumsily chopping ingredients.

Cut to witty banter between the show's personalities either at the desk, in a faux living room setting, or outside where regular people holding up signs are kept at arm's length by rope barriers and the veiled threat of tasering.

Repeat every half hour until *Ellen* comes on.

In a similar substitution Jenny's husband Tray sent me three pictures from www.awkwardfamilyphotos.com to view via e-mail, *technically* following the rules to abstain from time-wasting Web sites. (He sent me two, but I begged for a third to satisfy my sophomoric, inappropriate humor.) There is nothing better than a family of eight, dressed in *Star Wars* regalia, posing at Olan Mills.

I am really, really immature.

Day 12

This silence has been awesome. Our house feels peaceful—well, as peaceful as a house with three kids and all their homies can feel. I *like* the missing white noise of media. I *like* the silence during the day. I *like* the alternative rhythms we're discovering. Like:

- Cooking together

- Walks after dinner

- Porch time with our friends

- Sydney's endless craft projects at the table

- Dinner with neighbors

- Actual phone calls

- Four books read, a fifth in queue

- Caleb's new obsession with fishing

These are emerging out of the black hole of media. It's not rocket science; there's just space for them now. With the TV off, we ask, "What else can we do?" With the Wii packed away, the kids invent their own games. With an hour to kill after dinner, we grab Lady and hit the sidewalk. Some of this is out of boredom, some out of desperation, but still.

Several times, as I realized I was caught up on correspondence, done with laundry, and finished with my to-do list, God whispered:

"Hi there."

My communion with God suffers not for lack of desire but time. And let's be honest: I say I don't have time, yet I found thirty-five minutes for Facebook and an hour for my shows. I found half an hour for YouTube videos on how to fix black hair. I found fifteen minutes for the radio and twenty-four minutes for a missed *30 Rock* episode. So when

I say I don't have time, I'm a gigantic liar.

I have time. I just spend it elsewhere.

God hasn't made a nuisance of himself or given tasks for my newfound time. He's just been . . . extra there. Sort of like, "Remember I'm here with you all the time? And I can help you choose kindness and patience during the day?" (Could also insert: gentleness, meekness, self-control, love, selflessness, forgiveness . . . you know, all the things that come so easily to us humans.)

God is using 7 to transform the ease of my communion with Him. It's intimacy like a comfortable sweatshirt, beyond dressed up Sunday wear—past the formality, past the spiritual tasks. More like, "Let's just live this life together." I'm not transferring this extra time to hard-core Bible study and theology formation. Honestly, that's already my bread and butter. I study God's Word for a living.

This is something different. Something more relational and daily. Something in the gaps of spiritual activities, in between the stuff on a calendar. It's just simple communion, the natural kind between people who spend a lot of time together. I'm pondering this:

He has showed you, O man, what is good. And what does the Lord require of you? To act justly and to love mercy and to walk humbly with your God. (Mic. 6:8)

Without the noise and static, I'm learning about that *walk humbly* part. Frankly, justice and mercy are my first languages; I'm a doer. Acting justly satisfies the deep part of me that so wants a happier, safer, kinder earth. I feel productive with a task, a list, a project, a mission. I like the word "act" in this verse. (Gotta be honest, I've been trying to earn my salvation for some time.)

But God is teaching me *walk humbly*—daily, simply, quietly. It's in the walking humbly that God trains me for acting justly and loving mercy. Being aware of God's presence is a powerful catalyst for courage later. Acting on the latter without the former is just charity, not worship. Plenty of people enact justice without devotion to Jesus. There is no salvation in that, no devotion. That well of mercy will run dry without replenishment, without supernatural motivation.

If more of us took the "walk humbly with your God" part seriously, we might become agents of justice and mercy without even meaning to.

Day 14

Straight up: I dreamed about TV shows last night.

I saw the *So You Think You Can Dance* premier. Epic. There was an Animal Planet piece about an alligator I can't recall, but I remember thinking, *See? This is the kind of important science I'm missing. I'm getting dumber during this media fast.* I watched a sewing show (?). My REM mind was grasping at TV straws. It's very deprived. Lastly, I enjoyed *Law and Order* specifically starring Mariska Hargitay as Detective Olivia Benson and Sam Waterston as Executive Assistant District Attorney Jack McCoy; yes, I know they are on different *Law and Order* dramas, but the sleeping mind will have what it wants, and mine wants those two on the same show. (Can you imagine the snappy dialogue?)

The last thing I recall was the sharp realization I was doing something naughty. I was a TV watching fraud. 7 had been compromised. I swear to you, I was already making excuses in my dream ("Brandon turned it on." "I thought 7 was over." "I didn't take my gingko biloba.").

I apologize to my readers for watching TV in my dreams.

Day 15

Between 7 tunnel vision and this media vacuum, my eighth book released today and I thought it was next month. My in-box started blowing up with preorder messages: *I got my copy! Guess what I got in the mail today?! Got my hot little hands on your book! I've already read half! The cover looks awesome, Jen!*

Me: Really? I can't believe you got it a month early!

Friend: It came out today, stupid. Don't you know your own release dates?

Me: Um, evidently not.

This is helping make sense of the Blog Tour I start next week. I *thought* it was dumb to promote a book that wasn't available yet.

7 will be my ninth book. As I type that, I am stunned. After my fifth book, I said I was done writing because I didn't know anything else. I'd mined everything in my brain, and there was nothing left. So God changed our lives. Then I had more to say apparently, although from book six on, my writing sounds like a girl who has clearly come

undone and cannot communicate without an avalanche of emotion. I've bawled through the writing process on my last four books.

When I think about the girl who wrote *A Modern Girl's Guide to Bible Study*, my first book, I can hardly remember her. Recalling what I cared about, how I acted, how I spent money, what mattered to me, what I misunderstood about my mission, what I thought I knew, how I loved, how I lived . . . it's like describing another person.

If I could go back to the Jen of 2004, surrounded by babies and banging out that first book on a borrowed laptop, I would tell her a few things:

First, I would stroke her hair and tell her I knew how hard she was trying. I know she genuinely loves Jesus and is trying to be obedient. I would be far more gentle with her than she was with herself during those years. I would remind her she is only twenty-nine, and managing three kids under five with a husband logging seventy-hour workweeks is ridiculously hard. It's okay to cry sometimes. This will pass. The kids will grow up and wipe their own butts soon. You're doing a good job. (Why is the current me so much kinder to me than the 2004 me was to me?)

Second, I would drive myself around the extravagant neighborhoods in west Austin, the houses I dined in and met with women in and brutally coveted while we baptized people in their multimillion-dollar backyards. I would note the meticulous landscaping and four car garages and the beautifully groomed women with killer wardrobes and perfect bodies. Then I would gently tell myself: "This is all meaningless; substitute happiness. This vicious trap will capture you with no mercy if you get too close." I would describe the liberation of living below your means, something the 2004 me has never experienced. I would assure her that this affluent lifestyle is a horrible goal—go ahead and stop trying, stop dreaming, stop striving. You will be stunned where true happiness actually comes from soon.

Then I would link arms with myself and walk down the street we lived on. I would kindly explain that our neighbor to the left, the one who never mows and lets her house fall down around her, junking out the neighborhood, is actually a widow whose grown son and friends take advantage of her. I would go on to explain that she is all alone with a pastor's family next door who has never lifted a finger to serve her but only complains about her messy yard. I'd show 2004 Jen that the gospel is neutered until it grows hands and feet and actually becomes good news to someone, like someone whose only label was "irresponsible neighbor" when it should've been "widow in distress."

I would tell Jen:

It's okay to admit your worst struggles. To actual people.

You don't have to be awesome. You can be ordinary.

You can trust the Spirit when He challenges your interpretation of Scripture.

You can ask, "Why do we do this? Why do we think this? Why do we say this?"

Pastors aren't always right. God is your authority.

Jesus warned against wealth for a reason. Stop chasing it.

Next, with affection, I would ask 2004 Jen if she knew where Ethiopia is. She would lie and say yes because she hasn't discovered the freedom in admitting ignorance about anything yet. I would describe this beautiful, tragic country and the others like it. To her shock, I'd reveal that she would become so burdened by its poverty and enamored with its beauty that she would adopt two of its children. (2004 Jen tells me to get out at this point, as she had a one-year-old on her hip, a three-year-old on her leg, and a five-year-old whose exact location was unknown.) I'd kiss her overwhelmed cheek and assure her better days were coming, days that weren't so self-absorbed and lost and frustrating.

I'd tell 2004 Jen that one day she would garden. We'd laugh our heads off together.

Then I would call forth the best in her, and I would say: Guess what? Soon your whole life will be centered on justice. You're going to walk away from power and reputation, and you'll break bread with the homeless and give away the shoes off your feet. It will be awesome. You'll be free soon. This nagging tension that things aren't right, that life is more than blessing extremely blessed people . . . that's all true. A torrent of believers are demanding more from the indulged American life, daring to imagine that discipleship is adventurous and risky and sacrificial and powerful. You won't believe how many of them there are. You'll be drawn into a thrilling chapter God is writing in the church, with new and ancient themes.

Finally, I would hug 2004 Jen, understanding that discipleship is a journey, and each stage is a necessary precursor to the following one. God was right in Proverbs: our light is the dimmest at the beginning of salvation, but it grows brighter and brighter as we go. There is no wasted scene, no futile season. God gives us what we can handle, when we can handle it. We are drawn more and more deeply into the knowledge of Jesus. A baby can't handle a steak before she has teeth. The steak will come, but for today milk is on the menu. That's not an insult; it's biology. The baby will get there. Be patient. Do the best with what you know. When you know more, adjust the trajectory.

Self-hatred is not appropriate when God reveals a new angle. That is not the way of Christ, who abolished condemnation under the banner of grace. The wise responder humbly receives truth, allows it to supersede the version he or she is holding, and adjusts. This progression is not cause for shame but gratitude; thankful God never leaves us where we are but draws us into a richer faith. I giggle to imagine what 2017 Jen would come back to teach me; I don't even know what I don't know.

So for now I'll continue to reduce and simplify, fight and engage until I know what else to do. What I know now is this: less. I don't need to have the most, be the best, or reach the top. It is okay to pursue a life marked by obscurity and simplicity. It doesn't matter what I own or how I'm perceived. Whether I succeed in the market or land hopelessly in the middle is irrelevant, although this used to keep me up at night.

I'm just beginning to embrace the liberation that only exists at the bottom, where I have nothing to defend, nothing to protect. Where it doesn't matter if I'm right or esteemed or positioned well. I wonder if that's the freedom Jesus meant when He said, "Blessed are the poor in spirit, for theirs is the kingdom of heaven" (Matt. 5:3). In order for Jesus' kingdom to come, my kingdom will have to go, and for the first time I think I'm okay with that.

Day 18

Last year our husbands left Jenny and Shonna and me unsupervised for too long, and we planned a Disney World Christmas surprise. My kids had never been, and after wasting colossal amounts on Christmas crap, I decided this was superior holiday spending. We got past the hotel-booking-stage, even beyond the five-day-fast-pass investment, when Brandon and I said, "We're morons. We have a $40,000 double adoption. What kind of idiots spend their adoption money on Space Mountain?"

So with no small amount of disappointment, we pulled out.

Jenny and Shonna—best friends that they are—must have decided never to mention the trip again, as I was like the senior girl who didn't get to go to prom because she got mono. Being good friends, all her BFFs said prom was stupid anyway, the band was going to be lame, and they were only going because their moms were living out their unrealized dreams vicariously through them.

Jenny and Shonna were so tight-lipped that I forgot they were going. I'm certain this was intentional because we exchange 438 e-mails and initiate 762 conversations about every trip we take together. Our husbands beg us to stop talking about it two months before our plane leaves. The anticipation is half our fun, but I didn't hear one solitary predetail about their *five days at Disney*. I mean, come on.

This same emotional preservation is happening right now. I'm sure of it.

I know this because my favorite show is currently on its fourth week—*So You Think You Can Dance*—and I haven't heard boo about it from my friends. They are acting like they aren't watching. I mentioned it to my girlfriend Christi, and she shrugged it off, "Oh, it's just tryouts. Super boring. Who cares, right?" AS IF we haven't organized watch parties, dance contests (true story), show trivia quizzes, season soundtracks, and attended SYTYCD Live in Austin for the last three years.

The same friends who call me to *watch a show together on the phone* are acting like they've lost interest in reality TV. I know they're reminding one another not to mention anything and to act like TV is for losers, pretending to wish *they* were on a media fast because there is nothing good on and they could spend more time in Bible study and meditation like I was getting to.

This is an elaborate conspiracy, and I'm onto them.

And I love them.

Day 21

Is it really ground breaking news that too much media is bad for us? Is anyone thinking, *You know what my kids need? More TV.* I see couples having dinner in silence, checking their phones, as if *anything* cannot wait one hour. Don't get me started on the Bluetooth guy; it makes me want to ask, "Have you always been a jerk?" Wear it in the car, dude; do not wear it into Jason's Deli and have a loud conversation while making the cashier wait for your order. If I am close enough, I will pinch you, and I don't even know you.

Lots of experts are weighing in. It turns out, all this input isn't just annoying; it's troubling. A recent *New York Times* article, citing dozens of sources, reported that *this is your brain on computers*:

> Scientists say juggling e-mail, phone calls and other incoming information can change how people think and behave. They say our ability to focus is being undermined by bursts of information.
>
> These play to a primitive impulse to respond to immediate opportunities and threats. The stimulation provokes excitement—a dopamine squirt—that researchers say can be addictive. In its absence, people feel bored. The resulting distractions can have deadly consequences, as when cell phone-wielding drivers and train engineers cause wrecks. And for millions of people these urges can inflict nicks and cuts on creativity and deep thought, interrupting work and family life.[1]
>
> Even after this multitasking ends, fractured thinking persists because evidently *this is also your brain off computers.*

In 2008, people consumed three times more information each day than they did in 1960. Computer users at work change windows, check e-mail, or switch programs nearly thirty-seven times an hour, new research shows. I am completely guilty of this, and it gives me ping-pong brain. It is increasingly hard to focus on one task for longer than twenty minutes without succumbing to an alternate source: Hey look, my in-box says "6," my favorite blogger posted something new, let me just send this quick text, what's the daily recipe on cooks.com?

Researchers at Stanford found that media multitaskers seem more sensitive to incoming information than nonmultitaskers, and that is not necessary good:

> A portion of the brain acts as a control tower, helping a person focus and set priorities. More primitive parts of the brain, like those that process sight and sound, demand that it pay attention to new information, bombarding the control tower when they are stimulated.

> Researchers say there is an evolutionary rationale for the pressure this barrage puts on the brain. The lower-brain functions alert humans to danger, like a nearby lion, overriding goals like building a hut. In the modern world, the chime of incoming e-mail can override the goal of writing a business plan or playing catch with the children.

> "Throughout evolutionary history, a big surprise would get everyone's brain thinking," said Clifford Nass, a communications professor at Stanford. "But we've got a large and growing group of people who think the slightest hint that something interesting might be going on is like catnip. They can't ignore it."[2]

I think these people have been spying on me. I've developed an addiction to input, and I'm not sure how to turn it off. It is worsened because I work on the computer. If my career involved art or labor or customer service or raising babies again, I'd naturally find myself unplugged more. But writing books and developing messages and corresponding with readers and event planners is all right here on my handy laptop, and oh, there's an iPhone alert, and oh, there's my in-box, and oh, here's Facebook, and oh, let me click on this article real fast, and oh, here's a sidebar link, and oh, I meant to check that Web site, and oh . . .

Do you remember when we used to mail letters and read the paper and leave messages on answering machines? We were not available every second, and my gosh, I miss that. I cannot be unplugged for three hours without someone asking, "Where are you? I've e-mailed you and sent you three texts." My time no longer belongs to me, and if I disconnect for a few hours, people take it as a personal affront.

This month has been heaven on a biscuit. 7 gave me permission to say, "Don't text me, don't Facebook me, and don't e-mail me unless it's an emergency because I won't answer." And then everything went silent. As it turns out, I can set media boundaries and everyone will live. The instinct to check all my accounts and programs went dormant, knowing nothing would be there, and I was like an addict taking my first deep breath of unpoisoned air in awhile.

I don't want to be addicted anymore, and I certainly don't want my kids slaves to these compulsions. "Researchers worry that constant digital stimulation like this creates attention problems for children with brains that are still developing, who already struggle to set priorities and resist impulses," the *New York Times* article reported.

Do all these screens sabotage the neurological maturity

our kids are already struggling to achieve? Well, I for one have given my son instructions while he was on the Xbox, found zero progress on said instruction fifteen minutes later, while he swears I never said anything. Really? What about when I stood twelve inches away and said in plain English, "Go pooper-scoop the yard." He's making a good case for that lower brain-function theory.

Now the question is: How do we remain unplugged after next week?

Day 26

I pulled up Hulu.com, clicked on *Modern Family*, then turned it off.

There. I said it.

Brandon has been out of town for three days, I've been wrangling these out-of-school kids who have no media to occupy their little minds (read: mouths), and it was 10:00 p.m. and everyone finally went to bed. I didn't want to read. I didn't want to write. I didn't want to tackle my e-mails. I didn't want to be productive.

I wanted to laugh at Phil and Cam and Gloria.

I stopped short of actually watching it. I know the universe wouldn't have imploded if I had. One thirty-minute episode of TV couldn't ruin the whole experiment. But my DNA won out (first born, Type-A, selective rule follower). The principle of the thing fought its way to the top, shoving down the lesser players like boredom and entitlement.

So let's review the months thus far:

I ate Ethiopian food on the fifth day of 7.

I wore a nonsanctioned jacket during Day 1 of the clothes fast.

I prehoarded piles of clothes for giveaway month, just in case.

I came this close to watching TV during media fast.

I warned you about these tendencies. I never pretended I had a will of iron, people. That I'm still doing this is a miracle. The threat of public humiliation keeps the wheels on 7, since waaaay too many people know about this thing. While drive and determination might fail me, people pleasing will never let me down as an excellent motivator.

Is there something similar in biblical community? Does the collective will and watch of like-minded people keep us from derailing sometimes? Innumerable times I've grown weary, but the powerful backing of my faith community lit the extinguishing fire, and I carried on.

Maybe "letting down my fellow journeymen" isn't such a bad reason for pushing through either. In my circle of Christ followers, we take turns being strong. While one of us is down, the rest rally. Later, we'll trade. The equation always balances in the end. Sometimes a second surge of effort affects another believer in profound ways. I can't count how many times I've thought:

If she can do it, then I can too.

If he can hold steady, then I should try.

If God is keeping them afloat, then he'll do the same for me.

Our stories affect one another whether we know it or not. Sometimes obedience isn't for us at all, but for another. We don't know how God holds the kingdom in balance or why He moves a chess piece at a crucial time; we might never see the results of his sovereignty. But we can trust Him when He says press on, cling to hope, stay the course. He is always at work, even if the entire thread is hidden. I might just be one shade of one color of one strand, but I'm a part of an elaborate tapestry that goes beyond my perception.

The power of the church has always been in its many, many parts. In a culture of hero worship and conspicuous rainmakers, this concept struggles to emerge, but the story of God's people comprises a billion little moments when an average believer pressed on, carried through, stepped up. In the quantity of ordinary obedience, the kingdom truly advances. So that one area you where you are fatigued and considering surrender, remember this:

Therefore, since we are surrounded by such a great cloud of witnesses, let us throw off everything that hinders and the sin that so easily entangles. And let us run with perseverance the race marked out for us, fixing our eyes on Jesus, the pioneer and perfecter of faith. For the joy set before him he endured the cross, scorning its shame, and sat down at the right hand of the throne of God. Consider him who endured such opposition from sinners, so that you will not grow weary and lose heart. (Heb. 12:1–3)

Day 30

Whew! What a month. I know in the big scheme of things, a media fast is not headlining news, but I gotta tell you, we had to dig deep this last week. For me, it wasn't so much the media I was missing but the knowledge that I was the only one missing it. The party was going on outside my window, and I uninvited myself.

But the wiser (read: smaller) part of my brain interrupted this pity party with a question: What are you really missing? Asinine television programming? Web sites that suck you in then waste your time? The Facebook knowledge that someone "is going to the store" or her "son went big boy poopy in the big boy potty today"? These don't enrich my life in the slightest. They do, however, steal energy from my home and family, substituting face-to-face time with screens. We're all losing on this exchange, and we won't revert to the plugged-in family we were before.

Enjoy this end-of-month summary by Brandon, of www. rivals.com fame:

> One of Peter's early leadership lessons from Jesus was about letting go. He said the things we hold loosely are more likely to have eternal impact than the things we bind. When we hold too tightly to things, we lose perspective as well. While Jesus was talking about the kingdom in this passage, His words certainly give us insight to our created nature.
>
> We like our stuff. We need our things. Usually the things we think we need become the very things we need a break from. This was the case for me with media.

I remember when you wouldn't expect a return phone call for a day or two; now if it's not within minutes, people fear you're "screening" them. A letter response that might have taken weeks has morphed into an e-mail with an expected turnaround of hours. Media has changed the way we interact with one another and what we spend our time doing. Our social norms have changed. The pressure is on. We are being held at gunpoint by our technological expectations.

What began as advances in the ease of communication has become something that clutters and consumes. Media "noise" is everywhere, and some perspective would do us all some good.

This month came with a surprisingly high level of prep work: Updates on social media warning my peeps I was taking a break, scouting the month for any critical sporting events, and getting any necessary projects or anticipated recreational media out of the way before we started. In hindsight, this was feasible because I knew it was only a month. Truth is, most of us could do anything for a month, but very few of us could do without media for much longer. Like my dad refusing to learn e-mail or own a cell phone, it's unrealistic to expect society to reorient their norms around any of us.

That said, while beginning this month of 7 was harder for me than the others (and I gave Jen a harder time about it), it became a refreshing break from the norm. Everyone was respectable—if not envious—of my Twitter and Facebook "fast," few cared whether or not I watched TV, and surfing the Internet had already lost its flair for me. Honestly, my biggest fear going into media month was that the world might stop turning until I was done, but I discovered others didn't need me to be as wired as I thought. Most of my media involvement is simply about me (blah).

This is rarely a good thing.

All told, media month offered some pretty good perspective. Someone once said, "Think about the things you'd most hate to lose (outside of your family), and you'll identify your idols." These are not only the things we treasure too much but what we've likely lost perspective on. We place this stuff on a pedestal that wasn't built for it. If we're not careful, TV can become this. Facebook and Twitter can become this. Even the unreasonable pressure to respond to every e-mail immediately can become this.

The dangerous part of our social media and technologically saturated world is not it's existence but what it distracts us from. We found quality time with family, focused attention to conversation and creativity in planning our weeknights and weekends— all refreshing additions to our month. And while the Hatmaker clan resumed a very abridged schedule of TV and Internet and gaming, we certainly gained a new perspective on them all.

Month 5

WASTE

The motto of my city is "Keep Austin Weird." Austin is superbly bizarre because of our musicians, granolas, foodies, intellectuals, exercise enthusiasts, liberals, crazies, and environmentalists. Our nicest five-star restaurant would feature a couple dressed to the hilt next to five college frat boys in backwards hats. No one thinks this is strange. Ask any local about Leslie—our cross-dressing homeless transvestite who once ran for mayor. I love it here. Brandon and I plan to live here forever and bury each other in the backyard. When we moved to Austin ten years ago, I asked two questions:

Do I have to start running?

Do we need to start recycling?

Part of Austin's charm is its green obsession, I mean, consciousness. Our impervious cover law forbids residents or corporations from building on more than 20 percent of their land—you know, to save the trees. (A visiting friend as we drove down the highway: "Where is the city?" Me: "Under all these trees. Look hard.") Austin is inhabited by recyclers, refurbishers, and repurposers.

And then there is me.

I'm less Mother Earth and more Mother Load, as in GAH, I can't be fussing with recycling bins and rainwater collection and remembering my reusable grocery bags and tree-hugging. I mean, it's just the earth. If we use it up and trash it into oblivion, it will regenerate, right? Plus, I'm a Christian author, so my deal is to write Bible stuff, and the hippies can worry with creation.

Wait a minute.

Does "creation" have anything to do with God whom I call "Creator"? Oh, pish posh. Surely God isn't worried about how we handle His creation that He created. His main concern is making His followers happy and prosperous, yes? And if we need to consume the rest of His creation to make us happy, then I'm sure God doesn't mind. I bet "creation" mainly refers to us humans, and the soil and rivers and animals and forests and oceans and wildflowers and air and vegetation and resources and lakes and mountains and streams are purely secondary, if not inconsequential.

If I'm taking cues from many mainstream evangelicals, then only Democrats and loosey-goosey liberals care about the earth. It's a giant conspiracy to distract us from the abortion and gay issues, which evidently are the only subjects worth worrying about. Ecology is for alarmists who want to ruin our lives and obsess about acid rain.

I'm beginning to wonder if the unprecedented consumption of the earth's resources and the cavalier destruction of its natural assets is a spiritual issue as much as environmental. Like Wendell Berry wrote: "The ecological teaching of the Bible is simply inescapable: God made the world because He wanted it made. He thinks the world is good, and He loves it. It is His world; He has never relinquished title to it. And He has never revoked the conditions, bearing on His gift to us of the use of it, that obliges us to take excellent care of it. If God loves the world, then how might any person of faith be excused for not loving it or justified in destroying it?"[1]

He might have a point.

This month the Hatmakers are doing their part, setting

aside apathy and respecting the earth God made and loves,
trying to care for it in a way that makes sense for our kids
and their kids and everyone's kids. Because let me tell
you something: We are wasters. We are consumers. We
are definitely a part of the problem. I no more think about
how my consumption affects the earth or anyone else
living on it than I think about becoming a personal trainer;
there is just no category for it in my mind. (Please revisit
my introduction to 7 where I declared *repentance* the first
motivation. Thank you.)

So, Month Five = seven habits for a greener life, a fast
from assuming I am not a part of an integrated earth but
somehow above it all, expecting that sacrifices necessary
to accommodate humanity should be made by species
other than me.

- Gardening

- Composting

- Conserving energy and water

- Recycling (everything, all of it)

- Driving only one car (for the love of the land)

- Shopping thrift and second-hand

- Buying only local

If you've implemented these habits for years, forgive
me if I ever called you *earthy crunchy*. We currently do
none of these, so this is a giant departure from careless
consumption that requires nothing of me. God's earth is

like my kids' artwork:

Rather than briefly admiring it then throwing it away
when they turn their backs because MY GOSH where
am I going to put these handmade treasures that
seem to have no end, instead I'll treat their creations
respectfully. I'll carefully display their work and declare
it all a masterpiece while realizing that though it seems
production will last forever, it will run out as my kids grow
older, and my days of enjoying the work of their hands will
be over, and if I don't preserve their creations right now,
one day I'll have bare walls because I squandered these
beautiful offerings when they seemed plentiful.

I've got to separate myself from this astute observation by
the writers of twitter.com/xianity: "Today is Earth Day, or
as conservative evangelicals call it, Thursday."

Ouch.

Day 1

My fingers are raw.

My back is aching.

My feet are throbbing.

My shoulders are burning.

As I sit in filthy clothes past the "wring the sweat out"
phase but damp enough to chill me to the bone and also
gross me out, I'm ruminating on the first day of Green
Month/Waste Fast.

It started with a trip to the Sunset Valley Farmer's Market with my produce sherpas, Gavin and Sydney. We brought the necessary tools: reusable cloth grocery bags and cold hard cash. (You want to draw scorn from the Austin local foodie community? Exit the Farmer's Market with fifteen plastic bags. Might as well dump oil into Lake Austin and drive a Hummer through the Earth Day parade.)

Austin is a very green city, so plenty of patrons at the Farmer's Market looked like average 9–5'ers. However, there was an exciting contingency of granola people, which made for excellent people watching ("Mom! That lady's nursing her baby *while she's walking around!*").

It's July, so the Farmer's Market is in lovely form: tomatoes, English cucumbers, blackberries, melons, peaches, beautiful squash, green beans galore. Other local vendors bring artisan breads, gourmet olive oil, freshly ground flour, handmade hummus/salsa/pesto/pico, fresh eggs, organic meats and cheeses, fresh tamales (bliss). We devoured homemade tacos and hand-squeezed lemonade while a sweet little Birkenstock band played us some bluegrass.

I was in foodie heaven.

My perfect children improved this nirvana by freaking out over every eggplant and heirloom tomato. Whether this was sincere or satirical, I'm not certain, but still. We carried bags packed with produce picked in the last day or two, smudged with dirt, all delightfully messy and unpackaged.

With vendors like this, how could we go wrong? Acadian Family Farm, Fruitful Hill Farm, Full Quiver Farm, Engle

Orchards, It's About Thyme Garden Center, Johnson's Backyard Garden, Kitchen Pride Mushrooms, Rocking B Ranch, Sandy Creek Farms—the farthest farm is an hour away, most within city limits or just outside.

We brought our bounty home and ate half immediately. It's peach season in central Texas, reader. Our Fredericksburg peaches lasted three hours. I sliced up cucumbers, onions, and tomatoes and immersed them in vinegar, sugar, fresh dill, salt, and pepper, which will be gone tomorrow. Everything else got chopped, peeled, diced, or rinsed, ready for quick consumption.

So I'll discuss this in detail tomorrow, but we planted a garden two months ago for this phase of 7.

I have so much to say about this.

Again, tomorrow.

Anyhow, today Brandon and I edged our garden with two by fours. This involved a lot of digging, scooping, grunting, and lifting. The fingers on my right hand are so sore, I keep choosing words that are left-keyboard dominant. (My nemesis? The letters I, K, and M. *-y --ddle f-nger -s ach-ng!*) I'm such a garden virgin that I don't have proper tools; hence, ungloved hands that act as shovel, hoe, wheelbarrow, and vice.

The garden properly contained, I went inside to construct my first composting bin. Piece A to Piece B, snap in, snap down, slide on top . . . voila! An overpriced plastic box. Considering my mom's compost is a huge pile of rot on the ground (this has a good connotation here), no one need overspend on a plastic box with "ventilation outlets" (holes) to contain it all.

Brandon: Are you putting that together inside?

Jen: No, I just spread the parts all over the floor because I wanted more things to pick up around this house.

Brandon: I'm picking up on your sarcasm. Are you sure it will fit through the back door?

Jen: Uh, I think I can accurately eyeball the basic width of a box and determine if it can fit through the door.

So I'm in the living room typing next to my compost bin that won't fit through the door. Whatever. (My husband made sure I included that wee detail in the day's retelling.) I've spent hours researching composting, and even though every Web site says, "This is the easiest thing in the world!" the next line includes formulas for the necessary carbon/ nitrogen balance lest your compost turn into a slimy, stinky, rotten mess and attract every rodent and fruit fly in a ten-mile radius.

"Leaves = 60:1, Legume Hay = 15:1, Non-Legume Hay = 30:1, Sawdust = 400:1. A moisture content between 50 to 60 percent is desirable in an active compost pile." *What the what??* How do I know if hay has lost its leguminess? What does 60 percent moisture content look like? Somewhere between putrefied decay and damp rot? There is clear room for this project to turn nasty.

So for now, I'll just kick my feet up on my compost bin and watch a little Food Network (thank heavens media month is over).

Day 2

I'm smart about a few things. I've managed my kids' math homework all the way to seventh grade with only a couple of meltdowns. I can talk pretty confidently about Gilmore Girls. I am now an expert on international adoption (I-600A? USCIS? DTE and RR? I know what all that means). Thanks to my girlfriend Laura, I can now "turtle down" with my head and make my face look skinnier in pictures. So clearly I've got some skills.

Gardening is not one of them.

Rarely have I encountered a subject I am more ignorant about. For three-quarters of all produce, I have no idea how it grows. I don't understand life cycles or know where anything is found in nature.

Sydney: Mom? Can we plant watermelon?

Me: Honey, I don't know if we have room for a watermelon . . . bush?

I've never plucked an eggplant off its vine/stem/root (please circle whichever system gives eggplants their life). Until now, my produce originated from the same place where it is all in season, all the time: the grocery store. Whether it is a hot-weather vegetable or a fruit that requires sandy soil, I haven't a clue. It doesn't matter because it can be prematurely picked, artificially ripened, and shipped from anywhere on earth if I need it for my cobbler that day. I've never picked something from my backyard and fed it to my family.

Thinking ahead to this month, I couldn't shake the idea

of gardening, cultivating respect for the earth and the miraculous way it sustains humanity. I don't want to raise ignorant little consumers who think food is from the fridge where produce angels magically deposit it. Appreciating creation means learning what it is capable of producing. I want to initiate the seed > plant > harvest cycle, like every generation in history has done until mine.

Here is the appropriate place to mention I kill all plants.

My mother-in-law gave me a cactus, which needs water once every two months, and it perished under my sustained neglect. Every plant in my home is plastic. Somehow I gave life to actual human children, but I cannot remember to splash water on a bougainvillea. I have a dismal history growing anything other than Homo sapiens. To be honest, while considering a garden, the voices in my head said, "You won't actually do this" and I was 95 percent sure they were right.

Enter the best thing that ever happened to Month Five. E-mail from my friend Amy:

Amy: Hey Jen! Your mom said you were researching garden stuff but you were probably too garden stupid to pull it off. I am similarly inept but interested and just found a nonprofit that is the answer for remedial bleeding-heart gardeners.

It's called the *Karpophoreō* Project (pronounced car-puh-fuh-RAY-oh), a Greek word that means "to bear fruit in every good work." The KP Project bears genuine fruit, from the soil and in the lives of real people. This is their mission:

> The Karpophoreō Project bears real fruit (and

vegetables and farm-fresh products!) in the truly good work of reclaiming our barren and underutilized landscapes. We aim to be a blessing to the environment, to the social fabric, and to the lives of beautiful people across the city of Austin.

KP and the HOW program work with a community of men, women, and families that once suffered from chronic homelessness, most having experienced at least one year on the street. The marks of such homelessness go much deeper than can be solved solely by the acquisition of a home. KP is a community environment, fostering an environment for healthy interactions with each other and a positive contributor to the city.

Every person has a voice with a distinctive story and specific skills they can offer the world. Every person plays a necessary part for someone in the world. How does a formerly homeless person get in position to play the role of their lifetime? That's where KP comes in. We provide a basic set of skills and employment opportunities that can help take the financial edge off societal reintroduction.[2]

Willing partners offer KP their land for a backyard garden and/or backyard farm (the farm involves chickens, and I'm sorry, but I can only handle so much, ya'll), and the KP folks BUILD AND PLANT THE WHOLE GARDEN. Their team includes regular volunteers as well as formerly homeless men and women.

Then, they come out weekly and prune, treat, and harvest. Half the produce stays with the homeowner, and the other half is sold at the farmer's market or in CSA boxes. The formerly homeless who work the gardens keep 70 percent of the profit. Bam. Sustainable income from locally grown organic produce with nearly zero overhead.

Genius.

What a creative use of privately owned land in lieu of costly public property! What vision to connect privileged landowners with the chronically homeless, building relationships and making something beautiful together. KP just planted a huge garden at the Travis County Correctional Center, continuing their inventive mission of bearing good fruit in unlikely places with unlikely farmers.

Speaking of unlikely farmers, I have a garden, thanks to the KP team. I'll write about the garden inauguration tomorrow, but if you've paid attention, you realize I managed to mix local organic food (Months One and Five) with intervention for the poor (months all) where other people do the heavy lifting and I get to feel good about that instead of guilty.

And you should see my tomatoes.

Day 3

You might recall from Month Two that in the midst of dog excrement, a legitimate gardener assessed our backyard: Steven, founder of the KP Project. There was some digging, some looking at the sun, some staring at dirt. Outside of the obvious poo-poo situation, our space passed, and a date was set to install our garden.

Our backyard is pretty small, so we planned a 15 x 15 garden. We bought $200 of rich composted soil, which was unceremoniously dumped by our back gate. Twenty wheelbarrows full and a minor hernia later, we moved it *twenty feet* to the actual garden site. (Really, dirt guy?) We staked out the garden, which felt very farmerish and awesome.

"Mississippi" was one of the formerly homeless assigned to the Hatmaker garden, and he could've easily passed for James Earl Jones's brother. In the marathon dirt relocation process, he had a mantra for the females:

"Use your legs, girls. Use your legs. Easy. Eeeeeasy . . ."

I wanted to use my legs, Mississippi, but my arms were required in shoveling seven hundred thousand scoops of compost into wheelbarrows. (These arms could not be lifted the next day. Thanks for nothing, legs.)

About this time Steven busts out the tiller, and it had its way with him for twenty minutes. It was like watching an out-of-control bull rider hanging on for dear life. Thus, the sod we lovingly installed was churned into oblivion, reincarnated into its next life where it will produce more than beautiful blades of Bermuda.

Hearing a low hum, I looked for a swarm of locusts or approaching tractor. The hum grew louder, picking up volume and definition. Our heads popped up as we attempted to identify the crescendo and conceal our alarm. The sound became chattery and high-pitched, causing a fight-or-flight response in me, left over from ten years in student ministry. Then they descended:

Twenty-five teenagers on a mission trip from Arlington.

Steven failed to mention they were coming to "help."

Jen, the KP liaison (not me, Jen, as in the author, a second Jen, KP Jen), escorted them with what can only be described as wild eyes. With a frozen smile and post-traumatic stress, she said, "Yeah, I'm not as good with teenagers as I thought." Evidently, ours was the third garden install of the day, and this church group was assigned the heavy labor to provide a superior spring break option other than starring roles in *Girls Gone Wild South Padre.*

Let me sum up their involvement: Twenty-three of them flirted with each other while the other two sporadically tossed grass clods aside (which I retrieved and put in trash bags). The event also included: water poured on heads, cheerleading moves practiced on trampoline, and one girl who sat in my living room with sweet tea because she was *overcome.*

I fully remember why we quit youth ministry.

They left after thirty minutes, and the rest of us burst out laughing. (Is this at all like Americans who take international mission trips and make a giant mess of things and leave feeling good about themselves while the locals shake their heads and clean up the wake? Oh, surely not. We know what's best for everyone in the world, right?)

Anywho, Steven, Jen, Mississippi, my mom, and a handful of volunteers planted the goodies, and with Steven's careful instruction, in went squash, tomatoes, bell peppers, corn, basil, zucchini, green beans, arugula, and watermelon. Seeds the size of atoms stuck two inches under dirt. Yeah, I was 100 percent convinced this was so not going to work. I predicted crop failure immediately. I instantly became a farmer—tipped my hat back, looked to the skies, scratched my head. Like washing my car is the impetus for a downpour, planting a garden guaranteed a drought. I expected it to commence at once.

When the team left, it was exactly like the moment I was alone the first time with my baby. When the experienced mothers vacated, I was left with an infant no one was sure I could raise. (Ironically, we practically have to be sainted to get through the adoption process, but any fool can spawn and have a baby, tra la la.)

So I had a little come to Jesus meeting with my new garden:

"Garden? I'm really going to try here. I promise to care about you and feed you water and fight off your enemies. I can't make too many promises, Garden, because I once (allegedly) killed a cactus, but I'm turning over a new vine. I'll be there for you. These five words I swear to you. When you breathe, I want to be the air for you."

Garden just sat there looking rather embryonic, but I picked up on the signal it sent out. It said:

"I feel very scared."

Day 5

Garden update: My melons won't grow.

The last time I said this was seventh grade, with an eerily similar angst.

If I understand this problem like I think I do, Watermelon Vine is sick with envy, wondering why Tomato is ripe with plump, round fruits while she is still flat as a Kansas highway, developing gawky, awkward shoots everywhere, but no freaking melons. I bet she does a self-examination every morning hoping, *hoping* for development, a promising bud at least, only to discover a lengthening of her skinny vine in another clumsy direction, impossible to maneuver with any grace.

I keep telling my melon vine that her day will come; we develop differently, that's all. It's basic biology, nothing to fret about. Some vines sprout early, requiring wires and string to hold up their bulging fruits sooner than others. Not to worry, Watermelon Vine, soon you'll need your own wire and string, and your melons are going to be waaaay bigger than Tomato's. Trust me.

I know she looks smug, what with her perfectly rounded bounty that everyone admires while you're just a skinny vine without so much as a bud, but believe me, Tomato will be yesterday's news once your sweet fruits develop. I've seen the gene pool you came from; the future looks bright for you, WV. Your kind grows them big. (If you want, we can get you a wire and string like your more developed garden friends so Basil will quit mocking you; like he's so awesome—he's just a bunch of leaves.)

Parenting my garden requires way more emotional energy than I expected. It was easier when they were just little seeds and all they needed was water. Sure, I worried about them in their infancy, but at least it was *simple*. Now there's all this drama and competition: who's sprouted, who hasn't, who is independent, who is more—how shall I say it nicely?—*needy?* Wow. It's a good thing we don't know all that is involved in raising a garden when we first conceive it, or none of us would bear any fruit.

Day 8

So, one car.

I realize 86 percent of the world does not even own one car to squabble over, but we have been a two-car union since our dating years when my hair took over the entire cab of my bad-to-the-bone RX-7.

When my friends and I were in Manhattan last year on a girlcation, we took public transportation everywhere, and it was both invigorating and slightly stinky. I like the idea of public transportation, the efficiency of it, the urban lure. Next to our mortgage, cars and their upkeep comprise the biggest slice of the budget pie. I'd gladly kiss gas stations, Jiffy Lube, and the DMV good-bye forever. If I never drove on I-35 in bumper-to-bumper traffic again, you could color me happy and maybe declare a moratorium on my little road rage problem.

But those urban transit alternatives do not transfer well to suburbia. We've made our Master Planned Community bed, and now we have to drive to it. Our suburb is not concentrated with little bodegas and boutiques within walking distance. We have big-box grocery chains. We have landscaping. We have a Cracker Barrel. We drive eight hundred yards to our neighborhood pool, for the love of the land. The American urban exodus came at a cost, and commuting was certainly on that bill.

Brandon and I technically work from home, so you would think a one-car system would work, but you would be wrong. Especially since it's summer and I am in full mom mode. I'm neck deep in waterparks, movies, swimming pools, camps, and "Kids Eat Free" destinations. Perhaps this is obvious, but none of these are next door. The car has seen a lot of action.

Additionally, and again, perhaps this is obvious, but the working from home thing suffers with the offspring up in our grill every day. Every summer, I bid farewell to productivity. But because Sunday sermons and book deadlines are fairly inflexible, Brandon and I vacate the house so we can keep our little jobs by actually doing them. We do this by driving away from home. In our cars.

Our first upset came courtesy of my travel schedule. I spend a decent amount of time flying somewhere to speak. I'm no stranger to the airport or its little cousin, Parking Garage, who babysits my car for $10 a day. So when packing for a convention in Orlando, I said, "Oh my gosh. You have to take me to the airport. This is so awesome for me! Uh, sorry for you." No parking garage, no smoldering walk to the terminal, no $20 exit fee, no "where did I park?" dilemma, one husband and three little faces waiting for me at the curb when I deplane.

Yes, please.

Less driving is theoretically marvelous for me, albeit practically challenging. To reduce our dependence on two cars, we would need to reconsider how and where we live. We'd have to think like my friend Carson who lives downtown with her little family, riding their bikes everywhere. (I ran into Carson at Target around Christmas with my basket burgeoning with presents. I asked her what she was giving her daughter, and she replied: "An apron." I just blinked at her dumbly, like a pigeon.)

Or we'd need to reconsider our availability, driving all over Austin for lunches, meetings, coffees, and sessions. Come to you? Yes. Drive to your part of town? Sure. Meet for coffee instead of talk on the phone? No problem. You need me? On my way. This has rendered us slaves to two cars. Leary of letting someone down or substituting a two-hour lunch with a twenty-minute phone call, we pass out our time like Halloween candy, traversing the city and feeding the odometer.

What if we said, "Wednesdays are for meetings, and the other days are off-limits"? If we stopped letting the tail wag the dog, could a one-car scenario work for us? It seems like simple planning, and a proactive stance could revolutionize the way we drive, maybe even the way we live.

Which reminds me, I need to text Brandon; I fly home tomorrow at 2:35, and he's picking me up. I'll be the girl on the passenger pick-up curb casually checking e-mails and waiting leisurely for my driver.

Day 10

The Council is split on green habits; five really try, and one doesn't at all (I shan't name names, but said person not only employs zero green efforts; she lies about it). The rest of us waffle between zeal and guilt, diligence and hypocrisy. Here are Becky's ruminations on going green:

> Before I moved to Austin, I was in no way green. I wasn't even teal. Since then I have tried to live more responsibly. I keep shopping bags in the car, I recycle, I take old batteries to Radio Shack (meaning I keep a pile of batteries so long that my husband gets sick of it and takes it for me), and I send away my empty ink cartridges. Recently I joined the KP Project that tends my garden for half the produce. Therefore, I garden.

Since I garden (chuckling), I decided to compost. I feel very
Ma Ingalls sending my daughters out to dump the countertop
compost bin—an ice bucket I got at Goodwill—into the
backyard "compost bin," (i.e., a trash can with holes punched
in the side). I laugh every time the girls do the heebie-jeebie
dance at the sight of God's little creatures doing their work.

Although I recycle so much more, there are four thousand
ways I can live more green. One thing is sure: my carbon
footprint will always lead back to Sonic until some tree-
hugging hippie discovers a non-Styrofoam vehicle to deliver
the icy perfection that is the Sonic soda.

Sorry, planet.

Day 11

You know what's a layup for buying local in Austin? Dining
out. No hay problema. Austin is a jackpot of locally owned,
independent restaurants. This is a foodie town, so choosing
Olive Garden instead of Carmelo's is like skipping a Jonny
Lang concert for the Jonas Brothers; cause for great scorn.
When discussing a good steak, a friend of ours asserted
with absolute seriousness: "Well, you can't beat Chili's,"
and we have repeated that line behind his back one million
times since.

Like music, we take food seriously here in the capital city.
Plenty of remarkable chefs call Austin home. You're more
likely to drive past Salt Lick, Magnolia Cafe, Iron Cactus, or
Matt's El Rancho than an Applebee's around here. This gives
us plenty of opportunities to eat creative, innovative food
and act superior. (Notable exceptions to the chain aversion:
Chick-fil-A, P.F. Chang's, and Whole Foods. I'm comfortable
with some hypocrisy.)

So although Sonic and Starbucks are off the menu, I can still drive my (one) little car to Leaf, Moonshine, and Eastside Café. (Please come to Austin immediately and eat at these restaurants.) Circulating my money back into Austin's economy is thinly veiled as noble, barely disguised as purely preferential.

Day 12

Why buy local?

Food:

- Most produce is shipped an average of fifteen hundred miles to your grocery store, and that's just domestic produce. International mileage is substantially higher.

- We can only afford this because of artificially low energy prices we currently enjoy and by externalizing the environmental costs of such a wasteful food system.

  ○ Cheap oil will not last forever though. World oil production has already peaked, and while demand for energy continues to grow, supply will soon start dwindling, sending the price of energy through the roof. We'll be forced then to reevaluate our food systems.

- By subsidizing large-scale agriculture with government handouts, we:

  ○ Expedite the extinction of small farmers and diversified crops.

  ○ Facilitate agriculture that is destroying and polluting our soils and water, weakening our communities,

and concentrating wealth and power into a few
hands.

- Industrial food production is entirely dependent
  on fossil fuels, which create greenhouse gases that
  are significant contributors to climate change.
  The biggest fossil fuel use in industrial farming
  is not transporting food or fueling machinery; it's
  chemicals. As much as 40 percent of the energy used
  in the food system goes toward the production of
  chemical fertilizers and pesticides.

- Food processors use large amounts of paper and
  plastic packaging to keep food from spoiling as it
  is transported and stored for long periods of time.
  This packaging is difficult or impossible to reuse or
  recycle.[3]

- These large-scale, agribusiness-oriented food
  systems are bound to fail on the long term, sunk by
  their own unsustainability.

- Only 18 cents of every dollar, when buying at a
  supermarket, go to the grower. 82 cents go to various
  unnecessary middlemen.[4]

  - Farmers' markets enable farmers to keep 80 to 90
    cents of each dollar spent by the consumer.

Goods and Services:

- When you buy from an independent, locally owned
  business, twice the money recirculates through the
  community, doubling the positive impact on the local
  economy.[5]

- Nonprofit organizations receive on average 250 percent more support from smaller business owners than they do from large businesses.

- Help keep our communities unique; our one-of-a-kind businesses are integral to the distinctive character of our cities.

- Reduce environmental impact.
  - Locally owned businesses generally make more local purchases requiring less transportation.

- Small local businesses are the largest employer nationally and provide the most jobs to residents in our community.

- A marketplace of tens of thousands of small businesses ensures innovation and low prices over the long term. A multitude of small businesses, each selecting products based not on a national sales plan but on their own interests and the needs of their local customers, guarantees a much broader range of product choices.

- Local businesses owned by people who live in the community are less likely to leave and are more invested in the community's future.[6]

Day 13

We had our first cognizant 7 fail. Okay, we actually had two. In the same day.

The first came courtesy of back-to-school shopping. Like all children, mine are mutants growing at unnatural rates. Overnight, their jeans become capris, and their big toes emerge from their shoes. It's ridiculous. Although we test the feasibility of last year's shoes at the end of every summer, it's like Cinderella's stepsisters jamming their hammertoes into the tiny crystal slippers that look like they were made for Cabbage Patch dolls. No dice.

This created quite a conundrum for "buying local."

I researched, I hunted, I made phone calls, I googled, but I couldn't find a local tennis shoe that wasn't made out of hemp or straw. The only option was RunTex, a local high-end runners' store, but the day I spend $110 dollars on a pair of shoes for my eight-year-old is the day someone needs to slap the tarnation out of me. Sorry. Not even for 7 will I turn into an imbecile.

I waited until the last second hoping to solve the dilemma, but with school starting in four days, I went to Academy and bought them Nike's. _Just do it?_ I did.

Failure 2 was a result of poor planning. I signed up to bring not one but two people dinner this evening. Somehow I imagined that back-to-school shopping, sour cream chicken enchilada creation, and food delivery could fit into a four-hour window. They might have were it not for that stinkin' recipe; www.cooks.com is a liar. Those enchiladas take "30 minutes to prep" only if Rachael Ray and Bobby Flay are my sous chefs chopping, pureeing, sautéing, and shredding while I'm executing the other forty-nine steps.

An hour behind, I realized I wouldn't make it home in time to hand the car off so Brandon could bring Caleb to his first football practice. Preparing them for this conundrum, I threw out an asinine question: "Can you go twenty minutes late?"

Three seconds of stunned silence followed while one thirty-eight-year old and one third-grader tried to comprehend the blasphemy I'd just uttered. Then their brains recovered and the crap hit the fan:

"It's my first practice!"

"He's getting his uniform!"

"I wouldn't even miss five minutes!"

"I want to stake his place on defense!"

"The coach will think I'm a slacker!"

"We're not going to be that family who traipses in late!"

"This is football, Mom! It's not like school!"

"This is football, Jen! It's not like church!"

Reader, allow me to explain the seriousness that is football in Texas. There are things we take lightly here, like education and soccer. Texas ranked 48th on SAT scores, but who cares when UT has the number one college football recruiting class in the nation? So what if he can't read; our incoming offensive lineman ran a 5.10 40 at the combine. In Texas, football is first. Decrease the enthusiasm by 86 percent, and you'll find every other sport.

Of course I know this, even subscribe to it. We have season tickets on the front row at Darrell K. Royal Texas Memorial Stadium where we get on TV every other game, due largely to our grizzly seatmate to the left who holds signs like "Bob Stoops drives a minivan" and rings a cowbell after every play. I once turned down a conference because it was during the Red River Shootout. I love football like most girls love shopping.

So I owned my temporary insanity, blaming my faux pas on the Nike's and the stress they caused me. I promised to drive like Danica Patrick to get back on time. Midway through my second delivery, I called and told them to take the other car to practice; I wouldn't make it unless my car turned into a flying DeLorean.

And the one-car family became two.

You could argue that pee wee football practice wasn't a sufficient reason to breach 7, but I'd like you to come down here and say that to our faces. Do you think Vince Young's mom made him late for practice while he finished his English homework? Clearly she did not. And the whole state is grateful. Some things are more important than others. When my son is employed by the NFL as a tight end, anchoring the strong side and developing a sturdier pocket, he will point back to his upbringing, extolling the factors that led to his success, and among them will be this:

"My mom made sure I was never late for practice."

Day 15

I realize the novelty of recycling wore off around 1992, but somewhat late to the party, please indulge my enthusiasm. We decided to recycle every possible item this month: glass, tin, cardboard, plastic, batteries, ink cartridges, paper, and cans. Even our food scraps are recycled into compost, and leftover water goes to Lady's bowl. I have

bins for every category just inside the garage door.
Breaking news:

We have like zero trash.

We used to roll our trash bin out with the lid propped
halfway open, thanks to eight bags of waste crammed
inside. Our family was keeping the landfill business in top
working order. That big trash swirl in the ocean Oprah did
a show on? I think I recognized the cereal boxes I cut Box
Tops out of before promoting them to their second career
as pollution.

But after the spaghetti boxes and jelly jars and coffee tins
and detergent bottles relocate to the recycling bins, there
is almost nothing left. We put out one small trash bag for
the whole week.

This has become an obsession for me. I inspect the trash
can every day to see if something can be rescued for
recycling. Every time I find a plastic container or cardboard
box, the family gets another rendition of "Why This Does
Not Go into the Trash Anymore," which they LOVE. I study
my recycling bins once a day, marveling at how much
trash we generate. I will *not* do the math on how much
we've tossed that could've been repurposed.

Speaking of, the U.S. has 3,091 active landfills and
more than ten thousand old municipal landfills. The
environmental issues these generate run the gamut from
hazardous waste, toxic gas emissions, low-level radioactive
waste, and leakage into ground and surface water. The
health hazards posed cause much protestation and
controversy.

Then there is the issue of volume, which even the most sophisticated system can handle for only so long. Americans generate trash at an astonishing rate of 4.6 pounds per day per person, 251 million tons per year.[7] This is twice as much trash per person as most other developed countries. Trash production has almost tripled since 1960, thanks to the onslaught of prepackaged everything-under-the-sun.

Trash in a landfill will stay there, as is, for a super long time. Trash is dumped in sections (called cells), compacted, and covered with dirt before the next round. With little oxygen and moisture, trash does not decompose rapidly, as landfills aren't meant to break down trash, only bury it. When a landfill closes—because no site can bury trash indefinitely—it must be monitored for thirty years because of the contamination threat.

This is an unprecedented problem as ours is the first society to generate disposable material by the millions of tons annually. Plastic bottles, containers and packaging, technology waste . . . these are the byproducts of "modern progress." Cheese didn't always come packaged in plastic with paper dividers; people used to just make their own and then eat it. Twenty-five years ago you'd be hard pressed to find a bottle of water for sale, but thanks to a clever industry who repackaged basic tap water and sold it to a society of convenience as a superior option, as if they collected it from the runoff of the Colorado Rockies, we now consume 8.6 million gallons of bottled water a year, at only a wee cost increase of 240 to 10,000 times the price of tap water.[8] Then into the trash, la de da. For the bargain price of a dollar, I receive sixteen ounces of tap water and contribute to the waste crisis.

But just when I was feeling tickled pink about recycling, I read this:

> The most effective way to stop this trend is by preventing waste in the first place. Waste is not just created when consumers throw items away. Throughout the life cycle of a product, from extraction of raw materials to transportation to processing and manufacturing facilities to manufacture and use, waste is generated. Reusing items or making them with less material decreases waste dramatically. Ultimately, less materials will need to be recycled or sent to landfills or waste combustion facilities.[9]

In other words, by the time I put my glass in the recycling bin, it has already caused the lion's share of damage via processing and shipping. I'm not sure we should throw a party over a recycled wine bottle that was commercially mold-blown in a factory with its little friends, and then burned up 11,884 nautical miles getting from the processing plant in Brazil to Italy then back to my pantry. Recycling at that point is like ordering a super-sized Big Mac Value Meal then adding, "With a Diet Coke, please." Nice try, sister.

True reform involves purchasing fewer disposable materials in the first place, like bulk products, produce from the farmer's market, and second-hand goods that have already shed their packaging. Best practices include reusing containers over and over, lowering the consumption of single-use materials. Recycling is probably a third-tier tactic toward genuinely reducing waste for maximum impact.

Society was much kinder to the planet before this century. Granted, earth gave society minor problems like the

plague and smallpox, but we got the last laugh with
deforestation and global warming. Can we unlearn our
destructive habits and reimagine a way to live lighter on
this earth? What if we changed our label from "consumers"
to "stewards"? Would it change the way we shop? The way
we think?

My luxuries come at the expense of some of God's
best handiwork: forests, petroleum, clean air, healthy
ecosystems. We also ravage the lands of vulnerable
countries, stripping their resources for consumption.
The wealthy world has a sordid history of colonization,
ruling by force over indigenous people and profiting from
their natural resources and local labor. Yes Africa, we'll
take your diamonds, gold, and oil, but you can keep your
crushing poverty and disease.

What does it mean to be a godly consumer? What if
God's creation is more than just a commodity? If we
acknowledged the sacredness of creation, I suspect it
would alter the way we treated it. I agree with Tracey
Bianchi, author of *Green Mama*:

> There are a limited number of resources in this
> world, and when we take more than we need, simply
> put, we are stealing from others. By pillaging the
> earth for more than our share, we break the eighth
> commandment. To my dismay, I realized that even
> in my own, sort-of-green world, I was stealing from
> people, present and future. Turns out I constantly steal
> from my kids (and yours). I'm snatching up goodies
> like clean air and water while millions of families
> clamor for a drink and struggle with disease. I'm
> throwing away excess paper and packaging while rain
> forests disappear. I'm a kleptomaniac. But I am

determined to address my failings.[10]

I am too.

Day 17

The following account by Molly is true. I've seen the recovered bottles lined up by her trash can, and I literally have a picture of her hubby Chris wading through their flooded street to retrieve the recycling box as it floated away like Noah's ark. Perhaps media month made her feel violent, but Molly is the Queen of Green.

It all started four years ago when my daughter was two and my son was a couple of months old. We were the most consumption-driven family in America. The teeny tiny two hundred gallon trash can the city gave us wasn't enough to hold all the diaper boxes, baby toy packaging, wine bottles (clearly the neighbors were sneaking those in), soda cans, junk, and whatever else we just used up and tossed.

I was sneaking our trash into the can next door when I realized those people had a small green bin for their plastic, glass, cardboard, and cans. If I got rid of that stuff from my microscopic trash can, I would have tons of room! That's when I found our city-issued green bin in the garage holding a busted water hose and some garden lights. I cleaned it out and started our Family Recycling Initiative of 2006.

I needed more room for trash so I started to recycle.

Fast-forward four years. My husband has weekly poker games in which everyone brings their own drinks. At the end of every poker night, I dig through the trash for rogue bottles or cans that were tossed instead of placed neatly on the counter to be recycled.

A couple of weeks ago, I crept to my new neighbor's curb, took some huge boxes out of their trash can, and broke them down for my recycling bin. I think I may have a problem at this point.

It started as a selfish act and has turned into a way of life. I can't stand to watch someone throw anything away that belongs in my green bin. I take my own bags to the grocery store, I rarely use a disposable baggie in my kids lunches, and I helped plant a huge garden this spring. I grew up in a house always set at 67 degrees; we leave ours on 73. I know that's still cool, but I'm making progress. Maybe next year I can stand 74.

There are areas we can improve upon, but those small changes have our families calling us hippies. I wonder where we got our disregard for the earth?

Day 18

Good news, everyone.

My melons grew.

Sydney, our resident gardening enthusiast, came running inside breathless, dragging me out to inspect our late bloomer. As I live and breathe, we had six preadolescent fruits exhibiting the firm, round blossoming of youth. Oh sure, they're only a handful right now, but those babies haven't seen the end of their girth. I told you, Watermelon Vine. Mama knew your buds would grow. (Who's laughing now, Tomato?)

As her rite of passage, we outfitted WV with wires and string to hold up her new developments. She perked right up, thrilled with her admission into the fruit club.

Watermelon was the last of our garden babies to sprout. We have green beans, yellow squash, zucchini, peppers, tomatoes, two different kinds of melons, and enough basil to supply the greater Austin area. Our garden is producing despite our profound ignorance. It's a miracle. Treat the earth with care, and it will give you food.

Sydney deserves the credit for the general maintenance of our little plot. She has become a ten-year-old farmer, inspecting her plants and reporting their progress. She plucks the day's ripened produce, proclaiming over every vegetable with the same manic enthusiasm her peers direct at Justin Bieber. Sydney and Steven—our KP partner—are totally in cahoots. ("Steven taught me how to detect squash bores." "Steven says to cut basil at least five segments from the top." "Steven says the cherry tomatoes are ready when they are bright orange.")

The KP team harvests once a week, and we've delightfully worked alongside the volunteers and formerly homeless. The residents who benefit from the KP project live in an RV community in east Austin, relocated through an initiative called Community First. CF works with chronically homeless men and women, providing recreational vehicle housing and empowering them with support, community, and income to help effect positive change in their lives.

The KP project is an arm of Community First; the residents have several community gardens in the RV park in addition to the backyard gardens they help maintain. They enjoy "Stone Soup Breakfast" every Friday morning at the community trailer in the RV park, bringing fresh produce from their gardens and cooking together. KP partners and residents meet once a month for dinner, supplied by our own produce. Steven and Jen, the oh-so-passionate innovators of the KP project, moved into the park themselves, making that rare transition from *advocates* to *neighbors*.

The KP project has kinks to work out, of course. Like any start-up, some things are just trial and error. But I'm so grateful to be a part of its inaugural year. I've learned so much; about soil, about produce, about loving my neighbor. There is something so healthy about working the ground together, moving beyond the cultural boundaries that normally divide us. Bearing good fruit has many facets—in agriculture, in hearts, in the community. It's as much about the human being as it is the zucchini.

Some of us were on the streets three months ago, some of us have master's degrees, lots of us are battling addictions, and all of us have failed, but the ground is leveled when together we turn the soil, plant the seeds, cut back the leaves, pluck a perfectly gorgeous tomato, each learning the same ancient practices that have sustained humanity since Eden. The earth brings us together. It is common ground that is becoming holy ground.

Day 22

When I was ten, I watched *Sybil* at a sleepover and didn't tell my parents. That movie was certainly prohibited, but my friend had HBO *and* MTV, two forbidden fruits I devoured with reckless abandon since we had one console television with manual knobs to flip through all four channels. Oh, Cable, you elusive siren!

Sybil freaked me out. This was the true story of a woman who developed multiple personalities to deal with psychological trauma inflicted by her schizophrenic mom, who abused her in ways that made zero sense to my fourth-grade mind. The emergence of Sybil's sixteen different selves caused me no end of grief.

For months I feared my alternate personalities were preparing to assert themselves. I self-inspected my brain daily, watching for signs of a split or clues of impending pathology. If my preadolescence succumbed to a moment of hysteria, I'd sit cross-legged on my floor and chant a mantra: "Sybil, you cannot take me over." (I merged the concepts of "multiple personality disorder" and "demon possession." I was a Southern Baptist GA who watched HBO. Thank you for understanding.) Anytime a renegade thought passed through, I wondered: *Is that me? Or my alter ego Savannah?*

Friends, my fear of dissociative disorder appears to be manifesting now that I am comfortably in my thirties. And it was triggered not by abuse but by 7, a creation of my own making. After five months of retraining my thoughts, I now have competing voices in my head, struggling for domination as I attempt to shop like a responsible human.

Sometimes my organic personality, Sage Moonjava, emerges; and my top priority is to buy real food with wholesome ingredients. Sage Moonjava doesn't blink at spending $11.99/lb for bulk organic cashews, because they were harvested responsibly and not doused in partially hydrogenated oil. Grocery chains are the bane of Sage Moonjava's existence; the produce is covered in vegetable petroleum, beeswax, and lac resin; the aisles contain ten thousand combinations of high fructose corn syrup, refined grains, and chemicals; and the meats are genetically modified and pumped full of antibiotics.

I've abandoned a half-filled cart and walked out in utter defeat.

But at other times my "buy local" personality, Ryvre, materializes. Attempting to support the local economy and diminish the high ecological impact of importing goods, this seems like the winning approach. Buying from corporate chains is paying The Man; I like the little guy, the Mom and Pop store, the imaginative small-business owner. I'd rather subsidize local vendors who retain creative ownership and feed back into our local economy. Ryvre is into "Live here, give here," and shopping at Wal-Mart solidifies my place in the flock, contributing to a questionable supply chain and putting thousands of locally owned stores out of business every year.

However, my third alter ego, Freedom Shakra, whom you'll meet more next month, is trying to unhook from the consumer machine, and all this buying is not helping. Freedom Shakra is just trying to spend less, *way* less. This is a numbers game, and the winners are off-brands, generic products, knockoffs, and used goods. F. Shakra understands that name brands and chic labels are the marketing brainchildren of The People Who Sell Us Stuff We Don't Need. There is no good reason to buy designer water, over-priced spaghetti, or two sprigs of basil for $3.99 when it enjoys prolific growth in my own backyard from a $.25 cut. Addressing our embarrassing overconsumption is practically the whole point of 7, and Freedom Shakra is knocking the budget down by purchasing cheaper things, fewer things, smaller things.

Here's the rub.

Ryvre spots an adorable chocolate brown wrap sweater at local boutique The Red Door right here in our little town.

Talk about spending local! It's five minutes away in historic Downtown Buda, and the owner lives up the street. Adios, mall. No Gap for Ryvre! She's supporting the local gal.

But Freedom Shakra emerges and says, "Wait just a minute, Ryvre!" (And she rolls her eyes and pronounces *Ryvre* sarcastically to make it clear she is mentally spelling it "River.") Because that wrap sweater is $45, and my bank account couldn't care less whether it goes to The Red Door or straight into the pockets of Sam Walton. All Freedom Shakra knows is she's down fifty large for a sweater with a two-year shelf life, and I don't care where it came from, that's lame. Buying local is often synonymous with *overspending*.

FS is winning the day, so off she goes to the grocery store where she spies a carton of eggs for $.99. Hooray! At nine cents per egg, that is a purchasing victory for this Thrifty Mama. Add the $2.99 package of bacon and $1.69 can of biscuits, and we're talking about breakfast for five for $5.00. Beat that, Dave Ramsey!

But out pops Sage Moonjava, who gravely reads the biscuit ingredients. All twenty-nine of them. She recalls the dreadful farming practices that produced those hormone-injected, antibiotic laden-eggs. SMJ scolds Freedom Shakra for skipping after this processed, additive-packed bacon like it was the Pied Piper:

Fiddle-dee-dee I sing,

Cheap processed food is king!

Who needs organic?

Such ridiculous panic!

GMO products ain't nothing but a thing . . .

Sage Moonjava would buy the $3.50 eggs from grass-fed, free-roaming chickens, the $5.99 organic bacon from responsibly raised pigs; and the day she feeds canned processed biscuits to her family is the day she turns herself over to the local authorities.

Sprouts is an organic grocery store, but it's not local.

Central Market is a local gourmet grocery store, but it's not economical.

HEB is the most economical grocery store, but it's not organic.

So Ryvre is horrified by Freedom Shakra's priority to buy cheap, and Freedom Shakra outright mocks Sage Moonjava and Ryvre for spending more on "local" and "organic" (she uses finger air quotes when she says this). The competing voices confuse me, and I'm not sure which personality should dominate. This leaves me in a mess half the time, and I manage to feel guilty one way or another, no matter which purchasing priority wins the day. I've either spent too much, bought cheap processed junk, or I've subsidized the sweatshop industry. Evidently simplifying can be complicated. GAH!

Sybil, you cannot take me over!

Day 23

This month of 7 has really gotten into my bloodstream. I think about my choices constantly, rescuing recyclable items and second-guessing pretty much everything we consume. All my default habits are up for debate.

The latest matter to enjoy an awkward solo dance in the spotlight of Month Five is school lunches. As school just started, I'm confronted with my dependence on plastic baggies and prepackaged food, two thorns in the flesh of green living. These cause me at least one rock-and-a-hard-place moment every morning. Susana may have discovered the solution:

> Never mind the frozen, sodium-filled, processed garbage the school lunch system is feeding our kids. It turns out even those of us feeding our kids the good stuff are doing some serious environmental damage. Between the organic juice and the individual edamame packs with SpongeBob on the front, not to mention the plastic bags filled with carrot sticks and almonds (I know! Yeah me!), my three kids are discarding about two hundred pounds of packaging waste per year. (Oh, wait. Boo, me.)
>
> Great, now I have guilt.
>
> So, like I overhauled their lunch menu from sugar-water and Cheetos to the current healthy choices, this year I decided to overhaul the packaging situation.
>
> First step, no more zipper bags. I went through these things like water. I vowed a zipper-bag-free school year for my kids. I took a $20 plunge at The Container Store and bought three super-cool lunch boxes with what my freakish six-year old calls "a center protective barrier" and what I call a flappy-thingie, that allows for three separate compartments you can fill with food without any intermingling. The whole thing snaps shut nearly airtight and—get this—is dishwasher safe. Sold. Even Adrian Monk would approve.

The next step: prepackaged foods. I'm a sucker for string cheese and juice boxes. As it happens, my kids like Colby-jack just as much as mozzarella. So now I buy the two-pound block, whip out the cheese cutter, and voila! Problem solved. I'm still working on the juice box problem. I just like juice boxes so much. (It's a childhood deprivation issue. Don't ask.) It's silly, because my kids got BPA-free water bottles with their lunch boxes, so really all I need to do is fill them. Okay, fine. I'll do it. And then, the final step . . . cloth napkins. Yeah. Ahem. So . . . I hate laundry. We'll just have to see about this last one.

The bonus is, this system is way cheaper. Buying in bulk is saving my family money. Big food corporations are making a killing off lunch-sized packaging. Individually wrapped string cheese averages $9/pound and I get my Colby-jack for about $4/pound. A no-brainer. Juice boxes are about $.50 to $.75 each, and water is—oh yeah—free. Seems to be adding up quite nicely.

If waste-free school lunches were a hassle, as some environmentally friendly things can be, I might complain. But this is pretty easy. It is also a lesson I'm passing to my kids, the future generation. And that might be the most important part of this equation.

Day 25

Okey dokey.

I need to hem and haw a bit before I say what I need to say. Sooo, hey everyone! Thank you for making it this far with me. Wow! Five months of this business. Um. My kids are back in school, so if my writing seems more coherent lately, that's why. If not, disregard the previous sentence.

What else? Oh! This is actually relevant. We just submitted
our dossier to Ethiopia! Hooray! We are officially in line
for our referral now, and I've started dreaming about
our African kids like I did during pregnancy. Last week I
dreamed we brought our baby (?) back from Ethiopia, but
we had to pick her up at baggage claim. Another mama
was waiting for her baby, too, and I was petrified she was
going to take mine so I kept edging her out. Finally my
baby came around the turnstile, and she had a giant afro. I
named her Kyla.

We bought a used Suburban during green month.

Okay there. I've said it, but better news is coming, so
keep reading. You might remember we only drove one car
this month, which was not as challenging as expected.
However, we are now on official adoption notice, meaning
shortly we will have five children. This will require a big
vehicle. The end. I've pulled my hair out, wrung my hands,
and shaken my head from side to side, but there is no
getting around it. A family of seven doesn't *arrive* at their
destinations so much as they *invade*.

We looked at minivans.

We looked at hybrids.

We looked at conversion vans.

We looked at station wagons.

Activating my multiple personalities, we juggled
competing priorities: space, price, gas mileage, fuel
consumption, and emissions. Prioritizing fuel consumption
cancels out space. Choosing emissions can utterly inflate
the price. Selecting price can wreck gas mileage. Since

space was nonnegotiable for our family, I would have loved a big hybrid Tahoe, but if we spent $45,000 on a car, Freedom Shakra would've killed me in my sleep.

We did the math.

We crunched the numbers.

We googled our hearts out.

We bought an eight-year-old Suburban that runs on . . . flex fuel!

Comfortably priced in four digits, it was the best option to appease all the voices. Let me condense the alternative fuel research for you: Rather than running on straight gasoline, flexible fuel vehicles (FFVs) are powered by an 85 percent ethanol/15 percent gasoline blend, which is considered an alternative fuel by the EPA. Ethanol is produced domestically from corn, reducing our dependence on foreign oil and producing less greenhouse gas emissions.[11] Yay for alternative fuel! We're getting closer to Doc's DeLorean from the future.

Downside: FFVs gets fewer miles to the gallon. Upside: Flex fuel is about $.30 cheaper per gallon so cost per mile isn't a massive increase. It will cost an additional $400 a year to run our Suburban on flex fuel. Ouch. Freedom Shakra is not too happy, but Ryvre and Sage Moonjava are thrilled because at 85 percent ethanol it uses a fraction of the gasoline, and we will conserve roughly 735 gallons of gas a year, seventeen fewer barrels of gas. Comparing an FFV Suburban to a regular one, its carbon footprint (which measures a vehicle's impact on climate change in tons of carbon dioxide emitted annually) drops from 13.3 to 9.6;

greenhouse gases *not* emitted = 4,820 pounds a year.[12]

It's no Prius to be sure, but using only 15 percent of the gas otherwise required is quite an improvement. Like this FFV Suburban owner calculated: "The price of E85 in my area doesn't justify E85 on price alone, but lowering dependence on oil and cleaner air does justify it for me. Look at the mileage for gasoline consumption alone: At 360 miles per tank using only 4.8 gallons of gasoline (85 percent ethanol and 15 percent gasoline), my gasoline mileage is greater than 75 mpg. That's better than the hybrids."[13]

Following all these numbers? Here's what it boils down to: a little pricier to run but remarkably better for the earth. It's a start, people. And how is this for providence? Austin has only *three* ethanol filling stations: one is just south of us in Kyle, 6.7 miles doorstep to doorstep, and another is in my zip code in Buda, 3.8 miles from my driveway. When God shuts a door, He opens a window. Or something.

Bad sound bite: Jen bought a Suburban during green month.

Good sound bite: It uses less gas than an economy car.

Day 27

Hey? How fun is www.Groupon.com for local buying?? Specializing in local businesses, you enter your zip code, and Groupon sends a daily e-mail coupon for some service or restaurant or product. You have to purchase (not use) the Groupon that day, but I just got $20 worth of food from Mama Fu's for $10. That's free money from a local restaurant I patron once a week anyway.

Groupon takes the sting out of some pricier local shopping options:

- $12 for $25 worth of food from Hyde Park Grill (Their French fries and "special sauce" will change your life.)

- $8 for a $24 one-year subscription to *Austin Monthly*

- $69 for four-week unlimited workouts at Boot Camp 512, valued at $150 (I'll pass on this one and eat the fries from Hyde Park Grill instead, thank you.)

- $65 for a one-hour photo session and image DVD from Silver Bee Photography, normally $320

This is a great way to keep your money local while not busting the bank. Brandon and I couldn't eat at a Pizza Hut for less than $12, but thanks to Groupon, we get a highbrow date night on a fast-food budget. And believe me, we're highbrow people. I call as my witness the cutoff sweatpants and "Beach Week 2002" T-shirt I'm wearing. That I also wore yesterday. And to bed.

Day 28

I drove by a neighbor's house on trash day today. I do not know these people. I saw a huge cardboard diaper box sticking out of their bin. I stopped. I reversed. I pulled it out of their trash can, broke it down, and put it in our recycling bin. It might be the creepiest thing I have ever done.

Day 29

In many ways, I'm more like a dude than a chick. Oh sure, I straighten my hair and wear scarves and earrings, but I don't want to talk about it when I'm mad. I'm a terrible gift-giver, and I love stupid humor and dumb movies.

Also excluded from my not-so-feminine DNA is the shopping gene. I would rather have my saliva permanently transmuted to urine than spend extended time at the mall. I just don't like to shop. It's fun for like zero seconds. This is why my clothes come from Target; I'm there for Sharpies, so I guess I'll buy this shirt facing the aisle. If it doesn't fit I'll return it never.

So for this month of 7, "buy only local or thrift" wasn't as hard as it might have been for a real girl. Not going to Express or Kohl's or wherever is not so much a tenet for 7 as it is for my entire life. Well, it is challenging when we legitimately need something not readily available through local and thrift outlets, but as you might recall, we busted straight through that boundary for backpacks and tennis shoes. (My girlfriend: "You could've sewed their backpacks out of reclaimed sweatshirts." Me: "What do you mean, *sew*? I don't understand the words coming out of your mouth.")

That said, I strolled through Goodwill to honor green month. I'm not an accomplished thrift shopper, meaning I never thrift shop. I'm easily overwhelmed in a *regular* store organized by genre, color, and price point, so throw a little chaos and fifty crammed racks together, and I might start maniacally humming and hitting myself in the head.

Here was my assessment of Goodwill: In the category of organization, I give it a 90 percent approval rating. (The other 10 percent was its consequence for still being a store.) Items were even grouped by color, which is helpful for an antishopper like me. Sizing had taken a fairly severe hit by entropy, but still. Shoes on the back wall. Furniture to the right. All very clean and orderly. Kudos, Goodwill.

Thanks to the color and genre subcategories, even a skeptic like me scored. My sophisticated thought process went something like this:

Too many things.

Can't breathe!

(TRYING NOT TO MAKE HYSTERICAL MONKEY SOUNDS!)

Breathe.

I like shirts.

I like brown.

I like yellow.

Here are brown shirts.

Here are yellow shirts.

I bought a cable-knit brown sweater and a buttery yellow v-neck tee that will make the perfect backdrop for my long Africa necklace. Both styles hit the scene just this year; I saw them everywhere, and by everywhere I mean on commercials. $8.45 out the door.

Plus the staff at Goodwill has a nice, laid-back, *whatevah* attitude I'm totally into. No perky sweater folders, no annoying "I'm on commission" sales reps, no judgmental cashiers following me around because my outfit communicates, "I put things in my purse." In fact, as I approached the register with my two little treasures mined from the masses, the cashiers finished up a good fifteen seconds of their conversation before attending to my purchase:

"He a fool."

"I told you."

"His Mama didn't raise him like that."

"He stopped going to church five years ago. Thatta tell you somethin'."

"He ain't going back to church unless they get a smoking section."

"Just leave him. Rhonda can have your sorry leftovers."

[Noticing me.]

"Oh hey, sugar. Sorry about that. We're just talking 'bout how men are dogs."

Me: "No please, by all means, carry on. Any man who quits church is up to no good. One day he stops going to church, the next day he's glued to the Barcalounger barking for a beer."

"Girl, you ain't never told a lie. Come a little earlier next time, sugar. You can sit on the counter and enjoy ALL our gossip."

I just might.

Day 30

Oh my stars, has this month ever lodged deeply!

I keep thinking about our obsession with health. Our
kids have been immunized, checked, prodded, measured,
tested, and examined since the day they were born. Cuts
get antibacterial crème and Band-Aids. Twisted ankles
get ice. Strep throats get antibiotics. We fuel our bodies
with good food, drinking enough water and milk to keep
the wheels on. Brandon and I make sure our parents get
annual checkups, and we visit the dentist twice a year. I'm
watching for tricky moles and checking for lumps. I inspect
my kids' lymph nodes and keep us all sunscreened. We
have a cabinet of pills if something veers off course, and I
can pick up a prescription one hour after a diagnosis.

Why?

Because God gave us spectacular bodies, and we value
them.

But as certainly as God created man in His image, He
first created the earth. With the same care He designed
sixty thousand miles of blood vessels in the human
body, He also crafted hydrangeas and freshwater rapids
and hummingbirds. He balanced healthy ecosystems
with precision and established climates and beauty. He
integrated colors and smells and sounds that would
astound humanity. The details He included while
designing the earth are so extraordinary, it is no wonder
He spent five of the six days of creation on it.

So why don't we care for the earth anywhere near to
the degree we do our bodies? Why don't we fuss and

examine and steward creation with the same tenacity? Why aren't we refusing complicity in the ravaging of our planet? Why aren't we determined to stop pillaging the earth's resources like savages? Why do we mock environmentalists and undermine their passion for conservation? Do we think ourselves so superior to the rest of creation that we are willing to deplete the earth to supply our luxuries? If so, we may very well be the last generation who gets that prerogative.

"There is not always more," explained Steven Bouma-Prediger in *For the Beauty of the Earth.* "Except for our energy income from the sun, the world is finite. Numbers of individual organisms may seem limitless, but they are not. Species may appear to be beyond counting, but they are finite in number. Our life support systems may seem beyond abuse, but there are limits to what they can bear. Like it or not, we are finite creatures living in a finite world."[14]

I've been gobbling up the goodies, making a huge mess and assuming someone else would clean it up and foot the bill. But let me tell you, this month put the brakes on that. I cannot believe how God has captured me for creation care. All of it: recycling, using less, gardening, composting, conserving, buying local, repurposing instead of replacing; I'm in. From the nearly empty garbage bin to the lower electric bill, the immediate effects of a greener lifestyle are obvious.

My land, do we have far to go! My hypocrisies are too numerous to count, but this month birthed something unmistakable: I'm done separating ecology from theology, pretending they don't originate from the same source.

The earth is the Lord's, and everything in it, the world, and all who live in it; for he founded it on the seas and established it on the waters." (Ps. 24:1–2)

A friend said, "I don't know why you're trying. It won't matter. No one else cares." To that, I'll close with this bit of wisdom:

> If God is really at the center of things and God's good future is the most certain reality, then the truly realistic course of action is to buck the dominant consequentialist ethic of our age—which says that we should act only if our action will most likely bring about good consequences—and simply, because we are people who embody the virtue of hope, do the right thing. If we believe it is part of our task as earthkeepers to recycle, then we ought to recycle, whether or not it will change the world. Do the right thing. If we think it part and parcel of our ecological obedience to drive less and walk more, then that is what we ought to do. Do the right thing. We should fulfill our calling to be caretakers of the earth regardless of whether global warming is real or there are holes in the ozone layer or three nonhuman species become extinct each day. Our vocation is not contingent on results or the state of the planet. Our calling simply depends on our identity as God's response-able human image-bearers.[15]

Let's do the right thing.

Month 6

SPENDING

Spending

Once upon a time, a girl averaged how many different places per month her little family spent money. She tallied bank statements for the previous year, and they averaged sixty-six vendors a month, not counting repeat expenditures. She wanted to throw up. The end.

When Brandon and I married in college, our joint income was $11,270. We were so poor, people on welfare gave us cheese and peanut butter. This trend continued through the early days of youth ministry and into the lean days of one income, babies, and toddlers. I remember Brandon handing me a twenty-dollar bill to feed us for a week. The refrigerator and pantry were empty, I had a preschooler at the table, a toddler on my leg, and a baby on my hip. I sat in the middle of our kitchen and bawled my eyes out.

Back then we didn't just watch each penny; we scrutinized, counted, shuffled, and squeezed every last one. Sonic was an outrageous extravagance. Staying true to our generation, we dug a deep, dark debt hole to purchase the lifestyle we couldn't afford but for some reason felt entitled to. Unwilling to live within our means, we lived paycheck to paycheck, floating checks and nodding politely as the wealthy people at church talked about their vacations and new cars, wondering who we had to make out with to acquire these luxuries (Chase and Capital One were happy to oblige).

Fast-forward a few years and here we are. I no longer fill my gas tank half full or feed my tribe on twenty dollars a week. We've conquered that debt and—brace yourself—we even have a savings account. I assure you, we don't wipe our behinds with Benjamins or anything. "Rich Christian author" is an oxymoron, trust me. Ditto for my hubby's income as "senior pastor." SPs are like farmers—only a few are heavily subsidized into obscene wealth while the little organic guys are just praying for a harvest and trying to keep the lights on.

Anyhow, once I finally quit panicking my debit card would be declined (which took *years* in the black to overcome), the pendulum swung to the other side. Now I am completely careless. And clueless. Anyone who spends money in sixty-six places a month is the most heinous kind of consumer. Had you asked me to estimate, I would've guessed less than half of what we actually fritter away.

I am the consumer the poor world and the responsible world and the world itself can't stand or sustain any longer. How will I answer for my choices when God confronts them one day? With this much expendable income funding restaurants, shoe stores, and movie theaters, I doubt Jesus will accept my excuses for neglecting the poor on account of cash flow.

Speaking of cash flow, we're only spending money in seven places this month—a slight decrease in consuming (sarcasm): 89 percent fewer vendors in a month, for the love of Moses. These are the vendors getting our dough:

- The Sunset Valley Farmer's Market

- HEB gas station (flex fuel!)

- Online bill pay

- Kids' school

- Limited travel fund

- Emergency medical

- Target

Target is the all-purpose back on my roster because there is a (slight) chance the weather will turn and my kids' jeans will neither button nor cover their shins. And for the dozen other glitches (like toilet paper and detergent), Target is there for me, ensuring I don't send my son to a birthday party with kale from the Farmer's Market. However, we'll attempt to meet our needs any other way before traipsing off to Target, as I could sustain our entire life there without missing a step.

This means no restaurants, movie theaters, Chick-fil-A, no Coke and nachos at the UT/UCLA game (or parking), no Kindle/Barnes and Noble /amazon.com/Borders/Half Price Books to feed my habit, no lunch after church, no Hays High School football games unless my Mom The Principal scores us free tickets, no hunting paraphernalia (Brandon), *Call of Duty 4* (Gavin), iTunes (Sydney), fishing worms (Caleb), and Mama Fu's Spicy Mongolian Beef over Brown Rice with a Beef Curry Roll (moi).

The Council is giving me the proverbial "we'll see" (or its Christian cousin "Let me pray about it") when I ask about their participation. Let's face it: Month Six bites. Boiling down even moderate spending to seven options is so very un-American. Becky summed it up nicely in this e-mail:

> I thought about this while sitting in the Chick-fil-A parking lot eating dinner by myself. I'd gotten off work early, and I was only going home. But I thought, "Do I really want to partake in whatever nachos-and-applesauce dinner Marcus made for the girls?" No. "Do I

want to cook dinner just for myself?" No. Spending money unnecessarily is fun and I like it. I'm just sorry.

She's *really* going to be sorry if she mentions Chick-fil-A to me again this month.

Day 2

Let me begin with a caveat since I already spent nonapproved money.

Ahem.

So let's make a distinction between *spending* and *giving*. The beast we are battling is consumerism, defined as "the fact or practice of an increasing consumption of goods."[1] We are severely limiting the purchase of goods or services for ourselves. The stuff *we* eat, *we* buy, *we* use, *we* like. This consumerism has become ordinary to the point of being imperceptible.

Giving, however, floats down a separate river. We're still sponsoring Arun and Aruna, orphans in India; we're still sponsoring Givemore, a fifteen-year-old orphan in Zimbabwe, and we're still tithing, without labeling these as reform worthy. We're hedging with the spirit of the law instead of the letter here. This prompted the "giving clause" via the Council, which exempted charitable spending.

Okay? So I happily funded two events this week: a grill-out for the homeless with our Restore Group, and a fund-raiser for our church ABBA Fund for adoption. This is Jesus-approved spending, people. The recipients are not just my belly, my feet, or my indulged life but the ones Jesus told us to care for. Like ten thousand times.

If you don't like us spending on the poor this month, take it up with Jesus Christ and His dad, God.

Day 2

Molly let herself into my house and left a tub of Central Market pimento cheese in my refrigerator. If I ever say another sarcastic word about her three DVRs or TV-watching spreadsheet organized by network and day with twenty-four weekly color-coded shows and room for additional mid-season premiers, may a pox fall upon my house.

Day 3

Molly offered to bring over a FREE CHICKEN BISCUIT from Chick-fil-A. (Our new CFA is giving away free breakfast every Wednesday morning this month.) If this is a campaign to become Top Friend, she is clearly winning. *Clearly.*

Day 5

I have two outlets for shopping at the farmer's market: Saturday mornings on site and my weekly CSA box from Johnson's Backyard Garden, a seventy-acre organic farm five miles east of Austin. Buying this produce makes me deliriously happy. It is so solidly out of the industrialized food system and so deliciously local I put the smudged, unpackaged produce to my nose and deeply breathe its delightfulness every week.

CSA? Community-supported agriculture, a popular way for consumers to buy local, seasonal food directly from a farmer. Basically, a farmer offers "shares" for a monthly, weekly, or yearly fee. The share is a box of produce picked that week, and you get what you get. This sends me to the interwebbings to scrounge recipes for eggplant, bok choy, swiss chard, and other delectable veggies I never bought because I didn't know what they were. My box includes a dozen eggs from their happy chickens and a pound of organic, free-trade coffee.

Johnson's Backyard Garden literally started as a backyard garden in urban Austin, supplying thirty families with weekly organic produce. Then it became a backyard, side-yard, and front-yard garden, thanks to word of mouth from thrilled customers. With growing community support, the Johnson's bought twenty, then forty, then another ten acres just east of Austin, and they now run a thousand-member CSA operation. I actually know my farmers' names. People, their kids are running behind the tractor on the Web site. I mean, come on.

I cannot explain how happy I am to direct my consumer dollar to this food supply. Yes, it is more expensive than inferior grocery store produce. No, it isn't conveniently available 24/7. Yes, my kids complain we don't have any food. Yes, I get produce I might not buy otherwise, but I'm down with this food adventure! CSA members post recipes online, and we've discovered some treasures (I'm looking at you, kabocha squash and beef coconut curry).

We have less food, but what we have is nutritious and local and marvelous and perfect. I sent the kids to school today with homemade soup in their thermoses, English cucumbers, the last of the Texas peaches, and the most scrumptious yellow peppers you have ever eaten in the history of the world. There is a big empty pantry shelf where the individual servings of Pringles and 100-calorie packs used to be, but let's call that a good step, no matter what my kids have told you.

As Michael Pollan explained, I'm voting three times a day with my fork for a wholesome food supply. I know my dollar is a spit in the wind, but enough of us start spitting, and the Suits that control our food supply will listen—not because they care about our health, but they certainly care about money. Big Food Business will follow the dollar, enticed by a burgeoning organic market that netted 26.6 billion dollars last year, up 5.3 percent from the previous year.[2]

And when I get a teeny bit discouraged that my little rage against the machine is silly, I remember that I'm making healthier choices for my family and rediscovering the farm-to-table system God created, and that counts. When I look at our earth's resources and all the humans it needs to sustain, I have to adopt an "as for me and my house" perspective on responsibility.

Stewardship is like that. I won't answer for the way another Christian managed money. I won't be charged with another person's irresponsible consumption. Nor will I get credit for how another faith community shared or sacrificed luxuries for the marginalized.

I'll answer for my choices.

It won't work to say, "But the church . . ." or "But they . . ." or "What about them . . ." for how we managed our money, our share of the earth. The "my vote doesn't really count so why bother?" attitude our generation loves won't fly when it's all said and done.

Common sense has my back, too. Let's think about it:

spray-can cheese and avocado-free "guacamole dip" versus carrots and potatoes pulled out of the ground yesterday; do we need to ask WJWD? (Hey, Jesus! What about the mound of pork slime we developed called Spam? Who wouldn't want a mouthful of meat-flavored Jello?)

As for me and my house, we will try to stop buying Oreos.

Day 8

"Just because I can have it doesn't mean I should."

I heard this recently and it stuck. The counterattack to this perspective involves a list of objections easily accessible to the standard American consumer:

- It's no big deal.

- I can afford this.

- I've worked hard for my money, so I can spend it how I want.

- I want this, back off.

- I deserve this.

- Other people spend way more.*

- I still have money in the bank.

- What's the big deal?

- (* Jen's excuse of choice.)

So we spend, spend; amass, amass; indulge, indulge item by item, growing increasingly deaf to Jesus who described a simple life marked by generosity and underconsumption. Over time a new compartment develops for our spending habits, safely distanced from the other drawers like "discipleship" and "stewardship" (which has been helpfully reduced to *tithing*).

And listen, I am first in line. Don't imagine my life has been characterized by financial simplicity. I wish I had back so many indulgent purchases; specific ones grieve me endlessly. The irresponsible and selfish and vain spending I've endorsed is so staggering, I hope never to know the actual number lest I sink under it. I am in this right now, neck deep. This isn't a sage's manifesto but a sinner's repentance.

I used to say, "But we tithe, and that money goes to stuff Jesus was all into." Except many churches use it for marble floors and shiny buildings and cool videos and expensive mailers and pretty landscaping and fancy sound equipment and, in one recent case, an awesome multimillion- dollar jet.

Journey with me on a quick sidebar for a moment: How have we let the church deteriorate like this? How is this okay? How can we endorse these expenditures? When did this become standard protocol for the Bride of Christ? We've engineered an elaborate two-step to justify this egregious spending *on ourselves*. We are far from Jesus' original vision; the whole enterprise would be unrecognizable to our early church fathers. The earth is groaning, and we're putting coffee bars in our thirty-five-million-dollar sanctuaries. Just because we can have it doesn't mean we should. I marvel at how out of place simple, humble Jesus would be in today's American churches.

But for now, let's discuss our share in this, since you don't control your church's checkbook (although you *do* get to choose a church stewarding tithe money for the greatest good, but there I go again). Let's address that original objection: "But I tithe." This basic obedience exempts the rest of our spending, assuaging our consciences and checking the stewardship box. With that drawer comfortably shut, the others can be opened at our leisure.

But you know Jesus, with the quick retort:

When he finished that talk, a Pharisee asked him to dinner. He entered his house and sat right down at the table. The Pharisee was shocked and somewhat offended when he saw that Jesus didn't wash up before the meal. But the Master said to him, "I know you Pharisees burnish the surface of your cups and plates so they sparkle in the sun, but I also know your insides are maggoty with greed and secret evil. Stupid Pharisees! Didn't the One who made the outside also make the inside? Turn both your pockets and your hearts inside out and give generously to the poor; then your lives will be clean, not just your dishes and your hands. I've had it with you! You're hopeless, you Pharisees! Frauds! You keep meticulous account books, tithing on every nickel and dime you get, but manage to find loopholes for getting around basic matters of justice and God's love. Careful bookkeeping is commendable, but the basics are required." (Luke 11:37–42, The Message)

I like this *Message* version, with the kick-you-in-the-teeth quality Jesus always nailed. "I know your insides are maggoty with greed" is the very un-PC way Jesus basically put it. And He hammered that "but I tithe" excuse, too. As

He pointed out to the Pharisees, they never, ever missed a penny of tithing but shamelessly neglected justice and totally missed the point. The outside was shiny while their insides were a hot mess, but lucky for them, Jesus had the remedy: "Give what is inside the dish to the poor, and everything will be clean for you."

Crickets.

I'm starting to wonder if Jesus actually meant that. Was He serious about sanctification through extreme generosity? Is He really advocating redistribution? I don't know if He knows this, but this would mean completely retooling the way we live and spend.

News flash, Jesus: Almost zero people I know live like this. I feel safer with the prosperity groupthink than with Jesus' ridiculous plan. The justification of the Christian community is happy to oblige me. (A recent statement following an expose of a massive luxury purchase with church funds: "We operate in a manner that is worthy of the calling of Christ and have no apologies." Oh, Jesus endorses this? Carry on then.)

What if we're buying a bag of tricks? What if wealth and indulgence are creating a polished people rotting from the inside out, without even knowing it? Is there a reason Jesus called the rich blind, deaf, unseeing, unhearing, and foolish? Jesus never utters a positive word about the wealthy, only tons of parables with us as the punch line and this observation: It is terribly hard for us to receive His kingdom, harder than shoving a camel through the eye of a needle. *That's really hard.* If this is true, then more than fearing poverty or simplicity, we should fear prosperity.

Shall we stop imagining these sad, sorry rich people belong to a different demographic? A brave believer admits, "He's talking about me." Look at our houses, cars, closets, our luxuries; if we are not rich, then no one is. If we aren't swept up in entitlement, indulgence, and extravagance, then Jesus is a fool, and let's get back to living. If tithing the minimum and consuming the rest is okay, then we can dismiss Jesus' ideas and act obsessed about other stuff He said.

But what if?

What if we are actually called to a radical life? What if Jesus knew our Christian culture would design a lovely life template complete with all the privileges and exemptions we want, but even with that widespread approval, He still expected radical simplicity, radical generosity, radical obedience from those with ears to hear, eyes to see?

What if we are camels, on this side of the needle, dangerously content with our fake gospel and avoiding the actual Christian life described in Scripture? What if the number of Christ followers is a fraction of those who claim to be? What if only some have ears to hear and eyes to see, and Jesus was not exaggerating when He predicted few would choose this narrow path and folks will be shocked on judgment day?

I'm exhausted thinking about this. Jesus' brother James had some similar ideas, but I'm too freaked out to unpack them. Literal obedience would require such a radical overhaul, my head is pounding. The ramifications are overwhelming. Today is a good day to steer clear from David Platt or Mother Teresa or Francis Chan or Martin Luther King Jr. And anything Jesus ever said. And the prophets. And the disciples. Or God.

Day 10

Austin New Church is less encapsulated on Sundays and mostly represented through tribes we call Restore Groups. Ninety-five percent of attenders are in Restore Groups, because otherwise, they'd be like, "What does this church even do?" since we are super-light on programs (pretty much none) or Sunday pizzazz (pretty much none). We have some churchwide stuff like Serve Austin Sunday and, um, Sunday church, but nearly all projects and Bible studies happen through Restore Groups.

Our own group morphed from one troop into four, thanks to a solid neighborhood domination strategy, executed through the novel concept of "being a good neighbor" (Thanks for the idea, Jesus!). So three groups band together once a month, take our grills downtown, and feed the homeless under the bridge at I-35 and Seventh Street.

There are hilarious nuggets to share about these evenings, including the absolute normalcy this is to all our kids. Like today, Molly's four- and six-year-old skipped around, jumping over a sleeping man on a cardboard box over and over, oblivious to social boundaries or fear. They are surrounded by dirty men who swear and sing, under a bridge ripe with urine, and you'd think they were frolicking at Sea World. The kids are so eager to help (handing out napkins, granola bars, bananas, water), we have to physically hold them back so they don't gang rush our homeless friends. We broke up three fights because the kids were elbowing for position.

This is precious, of course. Proximity to the marginalized is transforming our children. Unaffected by social conventions, they neatly sidestep the thousand reasons we adults bypass this involvement. They pass out full hugs, conversations, and endless handshakes with such un-self-consciousness, they'll lick their hands the next second and wonder why the moms are batting their fingers out of their mouths.

A homeless man clarified this once: "You know? We've lost so many things: dignity, security, our marriages, our jobs. But one thing we all miss is kids." A tighter safety net exists around homeless children; society won't stand for their vagrancy so they are whisked into foster care leaving parents on the streets. "But you guys always bring your kids down here, and it makes us happy. It's a bright spot in our dark lives."

Children bring joy to the homeless for the same reasons they bring joy to us. There is something so dear about a little voice singing or the cutest little bow in the cutest little ponytail or watching kids play football in utter innocence, breaking into dances and making everyone laugh. Plus, our kids aren't repelled by their poverty, which is a welcome change from the disgust and apathy the homeless endure daily.

I told my kids, "You being here is a wonderful gift. The greatest offering is your presence—your sweet, funny, adorable presence." Yes, we've had to explain why that man is talking to himself or why that woman is crying out or why that guy is dressed like a girl. Our kids are getting a street education, but they are also developing a heart for the outcast and even getting bossy about it. For instance, here's a recent comment from Sydney: "Mom? These hot dogs are cheap calories! We say we care, but we are serving unhealthy food! We need to bring homemade food next time." *Someone* has been brainwashed.

So after our time together, when the men headed to Salvation Army to get in line for a bed, our band of families planned dinner together, like we always do. As everyone piled into cars and hollered out directions, I pulled the kids aside and reminded them we weren't spending money on restaurants. My girlfriends—conditioned as I am *never* to allow our kids to miss out—all offered to pay, but this was a teaching moment, important to 7.

If a fast doesn't include any sacrifices, then it's not a fast. The discomfort is where the magic happens. Life zips along, unchecked and automatic. We default to our lifestyle, enjoying our privileges, but a fast interrupts that rote trajectory. Jesus gets a fresh platform in the empty space where indulgence resided. It's like jeans you wear every day without thinking, but take them off and walk outside, and you'll become terribly aware of their absence. I bet you won't be able to forget you are pantsless, so conspicuous will this omission feel. While that metaphor is in shaky theological territory, that is basically the result of a fast. It makes us hyper-aware, super-sensitive to the Spirit.

So while our friends went to dinner, the kids and I drove home, talking about 7 and struggling through the concept of self-denial. My kids' generation has never been told "no." This is a hard sell. Not quite old enough to grasp obedience to Jesus in a self-serving culture, we listed the tangible results of 7 so far, including:

• We are eating 100 percent healthier.

- We gave a ton of stuff to people who had nothing.

- We maintained several reforms from media month.

- Our carbon footprint is cut in half.

- We learned to garden, and we love it.

- We've pared down our rooms, our drawers, our closets, our stuff.

- We're thinking about, praying for, sharing with, and spending time with marginalized people.

- We sponsored a new child through Help End Local Poverty with money we reallocated.

- Lots of our friends have joined us.

- Our prayers are changing.

We came up with this list and then some, culling lessons out of 7 thus far. We talked about how fasting helps us think differently. We remembered the lifestyle of our Ethiopian kids, which centers us immediately. I validated their sadness at missing dinner, telling them my hardest 7 moments, too.

As usual, Sydney was most engaged, my spiritually sensitive bleeding- heart child. She will live in Haiti or adopt ten children or translate the Bible into an obscure language one day. She carries her emotions close, and they leak out at the slightest provocation. She thinks deeply. She cares sincerely. She worries about homeless people on cold nights. She cries over dead squirrels (well, he should have looked both ways).

Then there are my boys. I desperately worry they'll have to provide for a family someday. Where thoughts on Scripture and life aspirations reside in Sydney's brain, there is a black hole for the boys, crowded out by football and Nintendo and whatever is shiny in front of their faces. I can hold them in deep territory for about forty-three seconds.

After a twenty-minute discussion on fasting, I noticed all three kids staring pensively out the window, thinking their thoughts. I decided to mine their conclusions to show my readers how well I parented through this experiment. "Hey guys? Whatcha thinking?"

Sydney: You know? We only missed one dinner out with friends. Big deal. Think how many meals the homeless people miss, Mom. Instead of feeling sorry for myself, I'm going to think about them tonight. At least we have a home to go to and food in our kitchen to eat.

Caleb: Mom? If I had to pick a superpower, I would teleport. Awesome.

Day 13

Phone call from my girlfriend Stephanie:

Steph: You want to meet for lunch at Torchy's Tacos?

Jen: I can't this month. 7.

Steph: Oh yeah. I'm paying.

Jen: See you at noon.

Day 17

The Karpophoreo Project, our gardening partners through Community First, launched the concept of "Family Dinner," a gathering of residents (formerly homeless) and KP volunteers once a month for dinner. Ideally using fresh produce from our gardens, backyard garden hosts cook a meal in the RV park community trailer to share with the residents.

For the first Family Dinner, I volunteered to sous chef alongside my girlfriends Amy and Lynde. We assembled a menu of minestrone (thank you, Pioneer Woman!), crusty French bread, green salad chock-full of goodies, and homemade raspberry cobbler. We gathered our produce bounty and drove to the RV community, approximately four inches from the airport where planes just *insist* on taking off and landing constantly.

The community center is a jazzed-up FEMA trailer with a beautiful three-hundred-square-foot deck built by my adorable, tall, supercute brother Drew. As we chopped and cooked and baked and roasted, the residents chatted us up with glasses of sweet tea because that is what we drink in Texas, amen.

Most of the residents have worked in our backyard gardens so we've been in each other's lives for a year. This was a gathering of friends: Gordy, Brooke and Robin, Ms. Rosa, Jimmy, Kenneth and James, Gary, Avon.

And then there was Ben.

Ben has what we call "a little alcohol problem." On this evening Ben had indeed consumed a little alcohol, enough to tranquilize an elephant. After showing my kids the broken-finger-magic-trick twelve times, I noticed their strained laughter and rescued them. Which is to say I became Ben's new target. The bone of contention he picked was my ridiculous plan to adopt.

Jen: We're adopting two children from Ethiopia.

Ben: Excuse me, ma'am. Excuse me, with all due respect, did you say you're adopting? ADOPTING??

Jen: Yes, Ben.

Ben: Excuse me, ma'am, ma'am, with all due respect, are you *#@!-ing crazy?? You're going to adopt kids who are not like you and bring them into your home? Now I'm about to be the dumbest guy in the world [Ben's other favorite drunky phrase], but this is the worst idea I've ever heard. Do you know what you're doing?? DO YOU?? I'm Puerto Rican! [I don't know how this is relevant, but he included it often.]

Jen: They're in an orphanage, Ben. We're going to be their family.

Ben: Excuse me, ma'am, with all due respect, but you are an IDIOT! That's like adopting ME. Do you understand that? Like bringing ME into your home and expecting that to work!

Jen: It would be exactly like that, Ben, if we were adopting a middle-aged Puerto Rican alcoholic, but these are kindergartners.

Ben: Ma'am, with all due respect, and I'm about to be the dumbest guy in the world, but you're about to *#@! up your life.

After a half hour of this dialogue, Ben was escorted (read: strong-armed) to his trailer to sleep it off. Upon a stern scolding the next morning, Ben couldn't remember a thing, but he was extremely embarrassed and remorseful, which is something I want you to know. Ben is human, capable of regular emotions and reform, just like the rest of us. I, too, have woken up the next day and thought, *My gosh, did I really say that?* His social misstep was no different from any regrets I've suffered from poor choices or flawed discernment. Ben sent his deepest apologies, the most noble response to failure. He messed up, then he asked forgiveness—it's the oldest song of humanity, one we've all sung.

Jen and Steven, the KP directors, declared Family Dinner a colossal failure. (Jen's e-mail to me: "*I was mortified. I felt like my children were misbehaving. I have no idea how to play the role of mother at the ripe young age of twenty-six to the residents.*")

Failure? I totally disagree.

First of all, "Family Dinner" implies some dysfunction. I call as my witness thousands of American Thanksgivings, full of drama and infighting, barely held together by a roasted turkey. Families fly their freak flags with one another; it's what families do. We *expect* Uncle Albert to drink too many rum and Cokes and start telling whacked-out stories. Families circle the wagons around this behavior, balancing concession and reprimand. Oh, Uncle Albert! You did NOT invent Facebook, you crazy old loon! Stop telling that to people! Gah, I love Uncle Albert.

Community First teaches chronically homeless people damaged by the streets how to live respectfully and responsibly together. Pragmatically, they are being parented again through manners, fiscal stability, home ownership, and healthy habits. This is a long, messy process that requires grace and patience. If parents gave up on their kids after the first failure, no child would make it past fifteen months old.

Because the community wouldn't tolerate this behavior, Ben learned a lesson; he lost out on Family Dinner. By next year, who knows how consistent modeling and boundaries will affect Ben's addiction? He is a member of a healthy community for the first time in his adult life; we'll be patient while God works on his transformation.

The other residents were absolutely lovely. Dinner discussion was perfectly sane on the other end of the table. They were thankful and gracious, complimenting the chefs and protecting the spirit of community. My kids sat outside with the smokers, entertaining the men and cautioning them against the dangers of nicotine. (They are a true credit to their public school Red Ribbon campaign.) Gordy, who has the mental capacity of a nine-year-old, enjoyed a long lament with Caleb, discussing their moms' *annoying rules*; just two brothers under maternal oppression, trying to get by. Ms. Rosa marveled at Sydney's Bible knowledge, holding an impromptu Sunday School class. Gimme that old time religion; it's good enough for me.

The kids ran around the street climbing trees, their laughter drifting in the window, the men patted their full bellies and retired to the deck with cobbler, while the women packed up leftovers and cleaned the kitchen, and I thought, *Family dinner indeed.*

Day 18

7 caused the worst trauma in memory today. It started with a problem called: My oldest son needs a haircut because he looks like a stoner. His blond, shaggy hair had taken over his head. Brandon, as if scales fell from his eyes like Saul, stared at Gavin, tossed his book down and said, "That's it. Get in the car.

You're getting a haircut."

Wait a minute.

Supercuts isn't an approved line item. As Keeper of the Tenets of 7, I put the brakes on this excursion, but Brandon was on a mission. He came downstairs with clippers, positive he could knock this out himself. According to Brandon, this need not be left to the professionals. No money? No problem. Gavin resisted, of course, but with pressure from Brandon, they headed to the driveway for a shaving.

Ten minutes later all good feelings were gone.

Forty times shorter than he wanted and fairly wonkety, Gavin went from shaggy soccer cool to boot camp special. I can't possibly overstate how upset he was. He ran outside screaming, assuring us that not with every ounce of our power, nor threat of dismemberment, nor brute force would we get him to school the next day. He didn't speak to us for three hours. The look on his face was as brutal as a sack of dead kittens.

While he hunkered in the backyard, we threatened our other children's very lives if they said one word about his hair; nay, if they made the slightest face, we would drive them to the local jail. I texted my friend taking him to football practice later to feign blindness, as if she couldn't see his haircut but could miraculously only see to drive.

This was an epic fail; a bad haircut to a seventh grader feels like the end of the world. He is certain everyone is thinking about him 72 percent of the day anyway. I explained this to Brandon, who has no patience for drama, especially since Gavin's hair looked fine; it was just too short for his liking. There is no reasoning with a preadolescent in a tailspin. Just let him pull out on his own.

And he did. Unprompted, Gavin apologized to Brandon for acting like a psychopath (paraphrased). I laid out hair products, cool hats, pictures of short-haired studs like David Beckham and Ashton Kutcher and George Clooney. ("Mom! He's like a grandpa!" You shut your mouth, kid.) We cooed and cajoled and tested to see if we could joke about it yet (no). He forgave, but trust me, he won't forget. He plays for keeps.

So Gavin will probably reduce 7 to one sound-bite: "My parents wouldn't pay for a haircut, and Dad sheared me like a sheep."

Day 20

Wow. We spend a lot of money. Combing through a year of bank statements, we are not big-ticket item buyers; we nickel and dime ourselves to death. We spend almost everything we make, and honestly, I can barely account for half of it.

This is why spending has flown under my radar; it is subtle, incremental, seemingly inconsequential. Just this little thing here, and that small thing there. I don't feel like cooking; let's just get this. Individually, nothing too egregious, but together our spending amounts to a startling number.

Big deal, right? Do I really need to care about this high-end lipstick? Does it actually hurt someone if I buy these jeans or help someone if I don't? Let's say I cut spending down and work toward less consumption. So what? Is there even a chance my choices would matter?

I think they might.

Let's imagine a whole group of us, maybe thousands or even millions decided to challenge an unjust economic system with these sorts of discrepancies:

Annual U.S. spending on cosmetics:	$8 billion
Basic education for all global children:	$6 billion
Annual U.S. and European spending on perfume:	$12 billion
Clean water for all global citizens	$9 billion
Annual U.S. and European spending on pet food:	$17 billion
Reproductive health for all women:	$12 billion[3]

Consider this report from The United Nations:

Today's consumption is undermining the environmental
resource base. It is exacerbating inequalities. And the
dynamics of the consumption-poverty-inequality-
environment nexus are accelerating. If the trends continue
without change—not redistributing from high-income
to low-income consumers, not shifting from polluting to
cleaner goods and production technologies, not promoting
goods that empower poor producers, not shifting priority
from consumption for conspicuous display to meeting
basic needs—today's problems of consumption and human
development will worsen.

The real issue is not consumption itself but its patterns
and effects. Inequalities in consumption are stark.
Globally, the 20 percent of the world's people in the
highest-income countries account for 86 percent of total
private consumption expenditures—the poorest 20 percent
a minuscule 1.3 percent.[4]

That's us: That 20 percent at the top-buying 86 percent of
the stuff. So no, maybe one person pulling out wouldn't
matter. But if hundreds and thousands then millions of
us challenged the paradigm, let's say we said "no" for
every two times we said "yes," if we acknowledged the
power of our consumer dollar—to either battle inequality
or reinforce it—then our generation could turn the ship
around.

I see three easy shifts we could make, starting today:

One, nonconsumption.

This is the simplest and hardest. It takes true courage to

rage against this machine. Could we be countercultural enough to say, "We're not buying that. We don't need that. We'll make do with what we have. We'll use the stuff we already own." If this causes anxiety, I'm with you, trust me. Because who else does that? Who curbs their appetites anymore? Who uses old stuff when they could buy new stuff? Who sews patches on jeans or uses last year's backpacks? Who says 'no' when they can afford to say "yes"?

We could. We could wisely discern needs from wants, and frankly, at least half of those line items are misfiled. Let's take advice from Matthew Sleeth in *Serve God, Save the Planet*: "My grandmother has hundreds of axioms. One of them was 'If you think you want something, wait a month.' One of three things will happen if you follow this sage advice. One: You will forget. Two: You will no longer need it. Or three: You will need it more. Most often, numbers one and two will happen."[5]

We can simply stop spending so much, use what we have, borrow what we need, repurpose possessions instead of replacing them, and—the kicker—live with less. Like Barber noted, "The challenge is to demonstrate that as consumers we can know what we want and want only what we need; and that, with the rest of our lives we intend to live as lovers or artists or learners or citizens in a plethora of life worlds in which consumption need play no role."[6]

Two, redirect all that money saved.

Humor me: What if we lived on 75 percent of our income and gave the rest away strategically? Or what if we downsized to 50 percent, bringing fresh meaning to Jesus' command to "love our neighbor as ourselves." Pulling out of a lopsided market is one thing; redistributing wealth to the world's vulnerable is a whole 'nother level. Global microlending, anyone? Go to www.kiva.org to learn about microfinancing for small businesses, for as little as $25. There is a 98 percent repayment rate. Astonishing. Empowering indigenous people to transform their own communities is the most effective weapon against global poverty.

Your giving can effect extraordinary change. Pick a need, country, people group, an organization focused on empowerment and sustainable independence. You could be an answer to countless prayers. The poor don't lack ambition, imagination, or intelligence; most simply lack resources. We have what they require and more than we need. We could share.

Three, become wiser consumers.

We get to choose our vendors. It's simple to find out if products are made with integrity or on the backs of slaves and children. With watchdog groups like Not For Sale, free2work.org, change.org, and others now that consumers are denouncing human trafficking and slave labor, there is no excuse for ignorantly supporting a corrupt supply chain. The reason a shirt is $4 is because a worker was paid $.10 to make it; insistence on the cheapest prices is at the expense of freedom or living wages for workers.

Boycotting vendors who refuse public accountability and conceal their supply-chain records is a demand-side tool of responsible citizenship. This civic consumerism involves thoughtful shoppers who use consumer clout to shape what is sold and how it is sold. Joining watchdog groups, signing online petitions, making a twenty-second call to your senators, buying from responsible producers . . . these are simple steps with potential for massive reform. Exercised strategically, this demand-side power will eventually affect the supply-side manufacturers, insisting on "corporate responsibility in which the producers wear civic caps while captaining their corporate vessels, steering companies away from obvious abuses and profiteering selfishness of the Enron variety toward responsible decisions that benefit society as well as shareholders."[7]

On the positive side, there are marvelous companies who not only guarantee a slave-free product but economic leverage for some of the most vulnerable workers. Free-trade organizations, living-wage employers, Third World suppliers, companies with a conscience—your dollar can accomplish more than making the rich richer. (At the end of the book, I included a nice, long, delicious list of companies you'll be super thrilled to purchase from, so definitely check it out as a starting place.)

While it is easy to become paralyzed by the world's suffering and the inequalities created by corruption and greed, we actually hold immense power for change, simply by virtue of our wealth and economic independence. Because we decide where our dollars go. Never has so much wealth been so concentrated; our prosperity is unprecedented. If enough of us decided to share, we would unleash a torrent of justice to sweep away disparity, extreme poverty, and hopelessness.

The world is waiting. Our kids are watching. Time is wasting.

Are we willing?

Day 25

I am a word girl. I'm English/Language Arts/creative writing/history. I am fully right-brained; the left is a dormant holding cell for the Pythagorean theorem and something about isotopes I forgot twenty years ago, three seconds after I learned it. I correct misspelled words when I text. When the PowerPoint has a grammatical error during worship, I have to close my eyes to avoid this language failure. If I lost access to a thesaurus, I would undoubtedly quit writing.

Consequently, words move me. God and I do our best business in the Bible, and stories have changed my life. One well-crafted sentence can sustain me for weeks. Like this one we sang Sunday at ANC:"

God, may we be focused on the least, a people balancing the fasting and the feast."

I almost came undone.

That statement sums up all my tension and hopes for the American Christ follower, the American church, the American me. With good intentions but misguided theology, the church spends most of our time, energy, resources, prayer words, programs, sermons, conferences, Bible studies, and attention on the feast, our feast to be exact.

Now certainly, there is a feast, and thank you God for it. Where brokenness and starvation once consumed us, God sets us at a new table:"

Your love, O Lord, reaches to the heavens, your faithfulness to the skies. *Your righteousness is like the mighty mountains, your justice like the great deep. O Lord, you preserve both man and beast. How priceless is your unfailing love! Both high and low among men find refuge in the shadow of your wings. They feast on the abundance of your house; you give them drink from your river of delights. For with you is the fountain of life; in your light we see light."* (Ps. 36:5–9)

This is the feast of the redeemed; Jesus made it possible for the wretched to dine with the Most High, neither offending His holiness nor compromising His justice. For those adopted by grace and faith, He no longer sees our failures or omissions; He only sees the righteousness Jesus covered us with. We stand safely behind Christ, made white-as-snow perfect from His substitution on the cross.

The currency of salvation includes blessings, redemption, fulfillment, peace, healing, sustenance, forgiveness, and hope. It's a spiritual jackpot. For those salvaged from the gutter by Jesus, these are new mercies every morning. We are easily overwhelmed by the goodness of God, which knows no bounds. The gospel is so liberating; it is worthy of adoration every single second of every single hour of every single day forever. We will never be the same. This is indeed the feast, and to celebrate it is utterly Christian.

But the feast has a partner in the rhythm of the gospel: the fast.

Its practice is unmistakable in Scripture. Hundreds of times we see reduction, pouring out, abstinence, restraint. We find our Bible heroes fasting from food—David, Esther, Nehemiah, Jesus. We see the Philippian church fasting from self-preservation, sending Paul money in spite of their own poverty, a true sacrifice. John the Baptist says if we have two coats, one belongs to the poor. The early church sold their possessions and lived communally, caring for one another and the broken people in their cities. We see God explain his idea of a fast: justice, freedom, food for the hungry, clothes for the naked. This balance is a given in Scripture.

If we ignored the current framework of the church and instead opened the Bible for a definition, we find Christ followers adopting the fast simultaneously with feast. We don't see the New Testament church hoarding the feast for themselves, gorging, getting fatter and fatter and asking for more; more Bible studies, more sermons, more programs, classes, training, conferences, information, more feasting for us.

At some point, the church stopped living the Bible and decided just to study it, culling the feast parts and whitewashing the fast parts. We are addicted to the buffet, skillfully discarding the costly discipleship required after consuming. *The feast is supposed to sustain the fast*, but we go back for seconds and thirds and fourths, stuffed to the brim and fat with inactivity. All this is for me. My goodness, my blessings, my privileges, my happiness, my success. Just one more plate.

Not so with the early church who stunned their Roman neighbors and leaders with generosity, curbing their own appetites for the mission of Jesus. They constantly practiced self-denial to alleviate human misery. In the Shepard of Hermas, a well-respected Christian literary work in the early 100s, believers were instructed to fast one day a week:

Having fulfilled what is written, in the day on which

you fast you will taste nothing but bread and water; and having reckoned up the price of the dishes of that day which you intended to have eaten, you will give it to a widow, or an orphan, or to some person in want, and thus you will exhibit humility of mind, so that he who has received benefit from your humility may fill his own soul, and pray for you to the Lord.

In the early 200s, Tertullian reported that Christians had a voluntary common fund they contributed to monthly. That fund was used to support widows, the disabled, orphans, the sick, the elderly, shipwrecked sailors, prisoners, teachers, burials for the poor, and even the release of slaves.[8]

The difference between Romans and Christians on charity was widely recognized by unbelievers. The pagan satirist Lucian (130–200 c.e.) mocked Christian kindness: "The earnestness with which the people of this religion help one another in their needs is incredible. They spare themselves nothing for this end. Their first lawgiver put it into their heads that they were all brethren."

These Christians did not limit their assistance to members of their own subculture either. The Emperor Julian, who attempted to lead the Roman Empire back to paganism, was frustrated by the superior compassion shown by the Christians, especially when it came to intervention for the suffering. He famously declared: "The impious Galileans relieve both their own poor and ours. . . . It is shameful that ours should be so destitute of our assistance."[9]

What would the early church think if they walked into some of our buildings today, looked through our church Web sites, talked to an average attender? Would they be so confused? Would they wonder why we all had empty bedrooms and uneaten food in our trash cans? Would they regard our hoarded wealth with shock? Would they observe orphan statistics with disbelief since Christians outnumber orphans 7 to 1? Would they be stunned most of us don't feed the hungry, visit the prisoner, care for the sick, or protect the widow? Would they see the spending on church buildings and ourselves as extravagantly wasteful while twenty-five thousand people die every day from starvation?

I think they'd barely recognize us as brothers and sisters. If we told them church is on Sundays and we have an awesome band, this would be perplexing. I believe we'd receive dumbfounded stares if we discussed "church shopping" because enough people don't say hello when we walk in the lobby one hour a week. If they found out one-sixth of the earth's population claimed to be Christians, I'm not sure they could reconcile the suffering happening on our watch while we're living in excess. They'd wonder if we had read the Bible or worry it had been tampered with since their time.

But listen Early Church, we have a monthly event called Mocha Chicks. We have choir practice every Wednesday. We organize retreats with door prizes. We're raising three million dollars for an outdoor amphitheater. We have catchy T-shirts. We don't smoke or say the F word. We go to Bible study every semester. (*"And then what, American Church?"*) Well, we go to another one. We're learning so much.

I think the early church would cover their heads with ashes and grieve over the dilution of Jesus' beautiful church vision. We've taken His Plan A for mercy to an injured lost planet and neutered it to clever sermon series and Stitch-and-Chat in the Fellowship Hall, serving the saved. If the modern church held to its biblical definition, we would become the answer to all that ails society. We wouldn't have to baby-talk and cajole and coax people into our sanctuaries through witty mailers and strategic ads; they'd be running to us. The local church would be the heartbeat of the city, undeniable by our staunchest critics.

Instead, the American church is dying. We are losing ground in epic proportions. Our country is a graveyard of dead and vanishing churches. We made it acceptable for people to do nothing and still call themselves Christians, and that anemic vision isn't holding. Last year, 94 percent of evangelical churches reported loss or no growth in their communities. Almost four thousand churches are closing each year. We are losing three million people annually, flooding out the back door and never returning. The next generation downright refuses to come.

Ironically, this is the result of a church that primarily feasts.

When the fast, the death, the sacrifice of the gospel is omitted from the Christian life, then it isn't Christian at all. Not only that, it's boring. If I just want to feel good or get self-help, I'll buy a $12 book from Borders and join a gym. The church the Bible described is exciting and adventurous and wrought with sacrifice. It cost believers everything, *and they still came.* It was good news to the poor and stumped its enemies. The church was patterned after a Savior who had no place to lay his head and voluntarily died a brutal death, even knowing we would reduce the gospel to a self-serving personal improvement program where people were encouraged to make a truce with their Maker and stop sinning and join the church, when in fact the gospel does not call for a truce but a complete surrender.

Jesus said the kingdom was like a treasure hidden in a field, and once someone truly finds it, he will happily sell everything he owns to possess that field, a perfect description of the fasting and the feast. It will cost everything, but it is a treasure and an unfathomable joy. This is the balance of the kingdom; to live we must die, to be lifted we bow, to gain we must lose. There is no alternative definition, no path of least resistance, no treasure in the field without the sacrifice of everything else.

Oh Lord, may we be focused on the least; a people balancing the fasting and the feast.

Day 30

This. Month. Was. *Hard*. But good. It's one of those. A good hard.

Vast consumption is so ordinary that its absence was shocking. I didn't realize how casually I "grab lunch," or "run through the bookstore," or "pick up that little scarf." I admit: I have a compulsion to buy something somewhere. My craving is nonspecific; it just involves being in a store or restaurant and handing my debit card over and getting something back.

Specifically, I have never cooked so much. With zero restaurants on the list, I've spent forty thousand hours in my kitchen this month, and I'm a little sick of it. That's right, the girl who loves fresh ingredients and cookbooks and sauté pans wants Chick-fil-A sauce on a fried sandwich. I want to *not* figure out what to do with collard greens. I want to call Pizza Hut. I want to sit on the deck at Serrano's with my girlfriends and soak up this delicious weather over a massive intake of chips and salsa.

I'm missing the convenience of consumption, but I missed the camaraderie more. I've created conjoined twins out of *buying* and *connecting*. Time with another human meant eating at a restaurant or buying a four-dollar latte. My friends and I habitually bond over meals at our favorite haunts. Food brings us together with ease.

For the first week I holed up in my house, turning down invitations like a neurotic recluse. It didn't dawn on me to suggest an alternative connecting point. (I am slow.) Finally, I recognized *time together* was the real prize, not the $5.99 lunch special. Enter the rest of the month:

- Breakfast at Jenny's with four of my girlfriends.

- Lunch with my friend Stevie Jo. I pulled a sandwich right out of my purse.

- Amy, Lynde, and Alissa over for brunch.

- Long walks after hours with Jenny and Shonna. (We are "training" for a half marathon. It's next weekend. I don't want to talk about it.)

- Tuesday Night *Glee* Fest at Molly's. You know she has it recorded.

- Reciprocal brunch at Amy's with Lynde and Alissa. I invited us over.

- National Night Out with my neighbors.

- Potluck dinner with my oh-so-beloved Restore Group.

- Family four square tournaments. ("Someone" is a cheater, and his name rhymes with *Paleb*.)

- Longhorn football party on our deck. We're polishing up the phrase "rebuilding year."

So yes, eating is still a starting player, but being in each other's homes, cooking and sharing food together is delightful. Eating a meal in a restaurant is one thing, but friends padding around barefoot in your kitchen and chopping carrots for your soup and sipping their coffee on your deck is another creature altogether. This exits the expediency of consumerism and enters the realm of hospitality.

There is something so nourishing about sharing your living space with people where they see your junk mail pile and pee wee football schedule on the fridge and pile of shoes by the front door. Opening your home says, "You are welcome into my real life." This square footage is where we laugh and hold family meetings and make homemade corn dogs and work through meltdowns. Here is the railing our kids pulled out of the wall. This is the toilet paper we prefer. These are the pictures we frame, the books we're reading, the projects we're undertaking—the raw material of our family. It's unsanitized and truthful. We invite you into this intimate place, saturated with our family character.

Maybe this is why hospitality was big to the early church. Living life together in the sacred spaces of our homes is so unifying. When our Christian forerunners were persecuted and misunderstood, when belief in Jesus was dangerous and isolating, they had one another. They had dinner around the table. They had Sabbath together. They had soft places to fall when they traveled. Safe in the home of a fellow Christ follower, they could breathe, pray, rest. What a gift.

So here at the end of the month, I have some sweet memories, mostly in my own and my friends' spaces. There were hilarious stories confessed around my table, which I shall go to the grave with under threat of beheading. I let my girlfriends inspect all my closets one morning, which is like going to work naked. People rummaged in my pantry and used my chopping board. I examined Amy's garden and lounged on her couch over five cups of coffee, enjoying our XM Radio Coffeehouse Channel obsession. I've dropped seven pounds, thanks to the absence of restaurant food and walks with my girlfriends. My little tribe enjoyed double the evenings around the dinner table, laughing through *High/Low.* (Caleb: My low is that my feet really stink right now.) We put a chunk of money into adoption savings and gave a few hundred away, because guess what? When you don't spend money, you have more at the end of the month. This financial wizardry is brought to you free of charge.

I've discovered reduced consumption doesn't equal reduced community or reduced contentment. There is something liberating about unplugging the machine to discover the heartbeat of life still thumping. Maybe we don't need all those wires after all. Maybe we're healthier unhooked from the life-support of consumerism than we imagined. Is there a less-traveled path through our me-first culture that is more adventurous and fulfilling than the one so heavily trod? One that sacrifices none of the good parts of the story but inspires us to reimagine the sections that are bleeding us all dry?

I think maybe there is.

It is no accident that despite the fact that bazillions of dollars are spent telling us we are just consumers, and that's all the story we could ever need, people by the thousands and sometimes even millions are frustrated and looking for a better story. And it is here. Is it any wonder, if you live your life like a baby bird with your mouth open that what gets dropped into it every time is a worm? People will attempt to reshape your worm and convince you that it is extra yummy this time, but it is still a worm. And the story of consumers is still boring.

If you are going to get better than that, we're going to have to participate, and go out and seek new sources and resources and options, we're going to have to replace much of our consumption with rituals of non-consumption. We're going to have to write a good and compelling story with our lives. The good news is that it is a lot more fun to be a citizen than a consumer, and rituals of non-consumption are just as satisfying as retail therapy. The good news is that there are better stories out there for the claiming and the living, and events are conspiring to keep our times interesting. The good news is that we can do better than worms.[10]

Month 7

STRESS

- Conferences and retreats
- Airports
- Conference calls
- Radio interviews
- Meet the teacher
- Jersey Boys
- Coffees (tons)
- Lunch dates (gobs)
- Brunches (lots)
- 5th-grade parent meeting
- KP Garden maintenance schedule
- Restore Group Tuesday
- Meals delivered to sick/new baby/grieving friends
- Paint the hays county food bank
- Garlic greek game night
- Middle school
- Wyldlife meetings
- Pee wee football practice/pictures/games
- 7th-grade flag football league
- Elm grove open house
- Adoption dinner party
- Grill-outs for the homeless
- Marathon "training"
- CSA pick up on fridays
- Birthday parties
- Neighborhood national night out
- ANC girls' noght in
- Dinner parties
- Carb-load spaghetti supper for the marathon team
- Shabbot with friends
- HALF MARATHON
- College friends in for the weekend
- Orthodontist appointments
- Ninja club(don't ask)
- Youth group
- Pumpkin patch visitation
- Ten thousand hours of correspondence

I inspected my calendar for the last two months and compiled this list. I counted five blank squares in eight weeks. This doesn't include the daily labor that keeps our children from flunking out, like Sydney's character sketch of Mother Teresa with handmade costume and biography bag or Gavin's report on the history of American coins (yawn). Also not listed is marriage maintenance to keep the hubs from turning into a roommate, because honestly? A little heat is mandatory so he is okay with making concessions for my impulsive, *oops-I-forgot* approach to life, and in exchange I'll act graciously when our DVR is filled with seventy episodes of *The Unit* and *River Monsters*.

Add leading a church.

Add 7.

Add Brandon's first book due next Monday.

Add this manuscript due in five weeks.

Add a daughter whose love language is quality time.

Add sons who need supervision so they don't die.

Add midnight bedtimes and 6:00 a.m. wake-up calls.

We are the center attraction at the Freak Show Circus. Ladies and gentlemen, boys and girls, step right up! Be amazed by the family juggling flaming batons while riding a unicycle on a tightrope with their heads stuck in a lion's mouth! No net! Duh, duh, da-da-da-da, duh duh da-duh!

For the love of Barnum and Bailey, we have too much going on.

We are short fused, stressed out, overextended, and unrested. This pace is not sustainable. I don't want it to be. This season of life is passing me by, accelerated by a lack of boundaries. Most days I just try to keep the wheels on, not living in the moment at all; I'm just getting it done while thinking about what's left. My kids and husband get half answers, and eye contact is a crapshoot. Every day I could take a two-hour nap, so exhausted do I feel at 1:00 p.m. I have considered abandoning my career over the volume of e-mails.

Such is the ridiculous American life. Every one of my friends has a similar story. None of us are happy about it, yet we keep filling the calendars. Yes, I'm in; we'll sign up; I'll do it. We race from one activity to another, teaching our children to max out and stress out. Nice legacy.

This biblical concept of rest is whispering to me, "You're ignoring me." And I am. Not only do I *not* take God's command for rest seriously, but I act like its not in the Bible. Ah, Sabbath. How cute and archaic. It's adorable how the Hebrews obeyed that. Good for them.

Clearly I believe my labor is more encompassing than the ancients, what with their little cultivating the land and harvesting their own food and making their supplies and raising gobs of children and traveling to festivals and worshipping at the temple and dodging enemies and getting captured and released and whatnot. Oh, you Israelites don't even know busy! I have thirty-one unanswered e-mails from yesterday! Perhaps you managed *rest* between the spring harvest and impending war, but I have to write three thousand words today *and* meet someone for lunch. I don't mean to be condescending, but God expected more from you because of your lack of discipline and little idolatry problem.

Ahem.

There are six days when you may work, but the seventh day is a Sabbath of rest, a day of sacred assembly. You are not to do any work; wherever you live it is a Sabbath to the Lord. (Lev. 23:3)

Well, that's Old Testament. That law doesn't apply to us. Or something.

There remains, then, a Sabbath-rest for the people of God; for anyone who enters God's rest also rests from his own work, just as God did from his. Let us, therefore, make every effort to enter that rest, so that no one will fall by following their example of disobedience. (Heb. 4:9–11)

Oh. But hey! Jesus was always breaking the Sabbath with healings and such!

Jesus: The Son of Man is Lord of the Sabbath. (Matt. 12:8)

Jen: Um, so?

Jesus: Are you Lord of the Sabbath, Jen?

Jen: I'm not sure.

Jesus: You're not.

Jen: Okay, then.

Evidently, this thing still stands. And maybe for good reason. Maybe this isn't just another spiritual task to wear us out. Perhaps God designed this as a gift, not an obligation. What if God understood our tendency to overwork and underrest, so He made it mandatory for believers to *breathe . . . pause . . . pray . . . relax* every week? Maybe Jesus meant it when He said, *"The Sabbath was made for man, not man for the Sabbath"* (Mark 2:27).

God ordained the Sabbath *for* us, not as just another requirement *from* us.

After six months of 7, I am ready to tackle resting and prayer. On the seventh day God rested, and in the seventh month we will too. The kids are thrilled, instinctively understanding that fasting from a fast life has "marvelous" written all over it. Plus, it won't mess with their Gameboys or access to Double Dave's Pizzaworks for the Wednesday buffet.

We will follow the ancients, the monastics, the Benedictines, and the contemplatives into the practice of honoring the hours through seven prayer pauses every day: midnight, dawn, midmorning, noon, midafternoon, twilight, and night. Those humble enough to pause and touch the grace of the hour have hallowed these rhythms for centuries. Some of these come from traditions and even language outside the typical evangelical experience, but they are most definitely characterized by the practice of resting before God, which is rarely cultivated by the evangelical writers and speakers of our day. These hours, echoed in Scripture, have been revised and expanded in many ways, known by several names: the canonical hours, the Divine Office, the Prayer of the Hours, the Divine Hours, the Liturgy of the Hours.

For Month Seven, our guide will be *Seven Sacred Pauses*, written by Macrina Wiederkehr, member of monastic community St. Scholastica, whose wisdom is so profound, I underlined nearly every sentence in the book. She describes the pauses as "breathing spells for the soul," an oasis to remember the sacredness of life, who we are, how to offer God the incredible gift of our lives, and learning to *be* in the midst of so much *doing*.[1] We will pause and pray seven times a day:

The Night Watch (midnight)

The Awakening Hour (dawn)

The Blessing Hour (midmorning)

The Hour of Illumination (noon)

The Wisdom Hour (midafternoon)

The Twilight Hour (early evening)

The Great Silence (bedtime)

Each pause has a focus, and like Wiederkehr explains, "Each day we are summoned to be creators of the present moment. Artists know the value of white space. Sometimes what isn't there enables us to see what is. Perhaps you are being called to the spiritual practice of bringing a little of the white space—of *nada*—into your workday. There in that white space you will find your soul waiting for you. Allow the anointing rhythm of the hours to touch and teach you each day."[2]

In addition to these daily pauses, the Hatmakers will observe the Sabbath from sundown on Saturday to sundown on Sunday. Traditionally, Sabbath begins on Friday evening, but we are adhering to the spirit of the day, which calls for corporate worship and family rest, and for us that is Sunday (unless the country would like to move church services to Saturday and push all games, tournaments, birthday parties, and community events to Sunday). Additionally, Saturday is sometimes a work day in our family, as ministry requires. We have a weird life. For us the day of rest is Sunday when we gather with the saints, pack up the week's work, and claim the treasure of the Sabbath.

We're shutting down the circus, people. For this month, rather than Barnum and Bailey, we'll be the low-budget sideshow carnies without a big production and a fraction of the star power. We've been a sorry bunch of clowns, running around like idiots, cramming into cars, driving in circles and getting nowhere. We're exhausted (and we suspect the elephants are plotting a coup). It's time to breathe and pray and learn to be still and rest. Now *that* sounds like The Greatest Show on Earth.

Day 1

O Pilgrim of the Hours

Each morning
Night's curtain
Opens on a new day.
You are invited
To join the great opening.
Open your ears.
Open your heart.
Open your eyes
To the sacred path
You travel every day,
The path of the hours.

Greet the hours
With joyful awareness.
Greet the hours
With faithful presence.
Greet the hours
With a reverential bow.
Greet the hours
With a sacred pause.

Reverence each hour
As a small stepping stone
On your pilgrimage
Through the day.
Receive the gift
Of seven sacred pauses.
Practice waking up
Seven times a day.

—Macrina Wiederkehr[3]

I'm going to admit something to you: I'm not a good
pray-er, okay? I never have been. I love the Word; I connect
naturally to that medium. I like words on paper. I like
a tangible passage. I like actual language to focus on. I
process through writing. Scripture is how I know God and
feel known by Him.

Prayer is harder for me. Whether it's a communication
weakness or an undisciplined mind, I don't know; but
I have to work hard at consistent, focused prayer. My

prayers include rogue parenthetical thoughts: (I'm so hungry.) (I forgot to order books for my event.) (Why do these pants feel so tight?) (When did I go to the dentist last?) I'm a concrete thinker, so ordering my thoughts without an anchor is a struggle. This final month of 7 is necessary for me.

The structure of the *Seven Sacred Pauses* is perfect for a wandering mind like mine. Every prayer has a rhythm, a focus, and—three cheers!—written prayers and psalms and readings. The language will tutor me. Here are the basics of each prayer pause:

The Night Watch

My eyes are awake before each watch of the night, that I may meditate on your promise. (Ps. 119:148)

Also called vigils, *which I love*, this pause is around midnight. "Like Jesus, keeping watch the night before he died, I keep vigil with those who wait alone."[4] This is a deep, even dark prayer of waiting and interceding, keeping vigil with Christ who never sleeps and guards us in our darkest hours (Isa. 40:28). The Night Watch advocates for others in a dark night of the soul: the suffering, abandoned, oppressed, lonely. "Perhaps some night when you get up to pray, something will turn over in someone's heart and find its voice all because of your small prayer. Perhaps our very waiting in the darkness gives some struggling unknown pilgrim the hour's hope."[5] Sometimes vigils are for waiting, when your struggle has been voiced and God's hand hasn't moved. The Night Watch is a time to say, "I will wait for you, Jesus."

Although there are beautiful prayers and psalms to use, this pause is also powerful silent—a simple, quiet connection with Jesus, staying awake together to shoulder the suffering that plagues this planet and our hearts. "For God alone my soul waits in silence" (Ps. 62:1 nrsv). It's like sitting silently together in the waiting room while a loved one is hanging on by a thread in the ER—words aren't necessary, but there is something powerful about your presence, your attention, the vigil you and Jesus are keeping.

Readings

Psalm 42

Psalm 63

Psalm 119:145–152

The Awakening Hour

"Satisfy us in the morning with your steadfast love; so that we may rejoice and be glad all our days." (Ps. 90:14)

At dawn it's time to begin our day in glory, remembering God's goodness. Even after the darkest night, the sun will rise. The Awakening Hour includes thankfulness for a new day, a fresh slate. It's the moment to pray for resurrection: What needs to rise in us today? Do we need to awaken to joy? Forgiveness? Should we pray for the resurrection of love in our hearts for our spouse or children? Ask for a dawning in our own soul: "Even in darkness light dawns for the upright, for those who are gracious and compassionate and righteous" (Ps. 112:4).

We enter a new day where our lives can become a living praise. Our desire to live this day well, for Jesus' glory, is an offering. After the Night Watch this moment celebrates God's intervention, His redemption. We never have to look far to see what He has repaired and whom He has transformed. Night vigils are for waiting and interceding; the Awakening Hour is for praising and celebrating. "This day is Yours, Jesus. Awaken Hour love in my heart so that I am a vessel of light today."

Readings

Psalm 19

Psalm 95

Psalm 147

The Blessing Hour

Let your loveliness shine on us, and bless the work we do, bless the work of our hands. (Ps. 90:17)

This mid-morning pause has two emphases: The first is mindfulness of the Spirit's abiding presence. It was the middle of the morning when the Holy Spirit came upon the waiting disciples with gifts of courage for birthing a church (Acts 2:15). For this reason the early church commemorated the coming of the Spirit during the midmorning hour of terce, or "third hour," a fixed time of prayer in almost all Christian liturgies.

At this hour the opportunities are still endless, making it the perfect time to invite the Spirit to stir our souls. This pause can redirect our morning trajectory from "efficient" to "inspired." We invite the Holy Spirit deeply in before the day gets away from us.

Second, the Blessing Hour is about the sacredness of our hands and work. Whatever our work looks like—an office, raising children, working from home, a classroom, ministry—we ask the Spirit to bless us with creativity, composure, inspiration, love. Kahlil Gibran said, "Work is love made visible"; what if we approached our work as an opportunity to show love? To our coworkers, those we serve, our children, to our students . . . visible love is possible if we work mindfully, as carriers of the sweet Spirit of Christ.

What a lovely moment to share over a fresh cup of coffee with a Christian coworker or a midmorning snack with our kids. Together, we ask Jesus to bless our hands and reveal the sacredness of our work, inviting the Spirit to breathe fresh wind into our tasks. We turn our affections to the Spirit, receiving the affection He feels for us.

Readings

Psalm 67

Psalm 84

Psalm 121

The Hour of Illumination

You are the salt of the earth . . . you are the light of the world.
(Matt. 5:13–14)

At midday, the brightest moment of the day, we honor the hour when Jesus embraced the cross (Matt. 27:45). Like Him we recommit to giving our lives away. We follow His leadership in servanthood, practicing peace in a world of violence and vowing to love this world like Jesus did. In the spirit of the hour, we pledge to shine brightly, becoming hope to the hopeless and light in the darkness.

During the Hour of Illumination, we ask Jesus to send light into our hearts so intensely that they break wide open, so we can make the decisions that lead to peace—from death to life, deception to truth, despair to hope, hate to love. We self-inspect our hearts for violence we are choosing to harbor—toward ourselves, spouses or family members, coworkers, community, those who are different, toward any part of creation. We ask God's love to illuminate the parts of our souls darkened with bitterness or anger or unforgiveness or apathy.

By all means enjoy this pause outside with your face turned toward the sun. We pray to be sons and daughters of the light, bringing joy to a dark world. We pray against the darkness that consumes and steals and ruins. We offer our hands and words as agents of change and justice. Like Gandhi said, "Be the change you hope to see in the world." This midday prayer is our pledge to pour out our lives, just like Jesus did at great cost.

Readings

Psalm 24

Psalm 33

Psalm 34

The Wisdom Hour

For to me, to live is Christ and to die is gain. (Phil. 1:21)

At midafternoon the Wisdom Hour embraces the themes of surrender, forgiveness and wisdom, and the impermanence of this life—including aging, maturing, and death. It is the hour Jesus died and gave up His spirit (Mark 15:34). This prayer acknowledges all things are passing, not in a macabre way but in the spirit of wisdom which knows this life is temporary, and we should live like we believed that. Frankly, who would like this day to never end? This season to never pass? For greater things to never be realized?

This hour is the prayer for wisdom to help us live like we were dying, which we are. Imagine the fearlessness we'd embrace with this understanding! Imagine the risks we would take, the love we would share, the forgiveness we would not withhold, the dreams we would chase. Envision the bitterness we would release, the hang-ups we would let go of, the beauty we would create.

With evening approaching, we pray for *perspective* on this short, fleeting day, this short, fleeting life and accordingly, we hold out forgiveness, release our grudges, and offer our gifts to the world, understanding we have only a few years to share them or they will be wasted.

Readings

Psalm 71

Psalm 90

Psalm 138

The Twilight Hour

Also called vespers, this is the much loved evening prayer, prayed for centuries at the end of the workday as dusk approaches. The main themes are gratitude and serenity as the evening lamps are lit. We invite God's peace as we leave work and transition into dinner, family, home, rest. Training our minds toward tranquility, we ask: What is the greatest blessing of this day? What one accomplishment can I smile over? What is undone I can gently lay down until tomorrow? Is there anyone I need to make peace with? The Twilight Hour is for exhaling, calming our minds, and transitioning into the evening.

A major theme of vespers is gratitude. No matter the chaos of the day, Wiederkehr reminds us, "If you search out reasons to be grateful, you may be amazed to discover that your gratitude room is overflowing."[6] We practice being thankful for the gifts of the day, the loveliness of the season we are in. Even with disorder at this hour, we say "thank you" for employment, for children and home, for our gifts. We say "thank you" for tomorrow, a perfect landing spot for unfinished tasks. We say "thank you" for hands to labor and love with and ask for grace for the work of the approaching evening.

Readings

Psalm 34

Psalm 139

Psalm 145

The Great Silence

By day the Lord directs his love, at night his song is with me—a prayer to the God of my life. (Ps. 42:8)

This prayer concludes the day; a beautiful time to pray with children as we tuck them in or with a spouse or friend before we sleep. Also called compline, from the Latin word for *completion*, it begins with a gentle evaluation of the day. The focus is on awareness, and we include not just weaknesses but the strengths and accomplishments of the day. The Great Silence teaches us to be healthy sinners, living in neither denial of our sin or despair because of it. God reminds us we are loved sinners. We learn to live with more integrity and obedience than the day before, as together in prayer we examine the day.

The second theme is darkness—protection from some forms and acceptance of other forms. We ask the Spirit to guard against our enemy, protecting our zeal and innocence in Christ. We pray our children are sheltered under God's wings. As sin is a darkness that envelops from within, we confess and repent from the tentacles that bind us. We intervene for those seized by darkness: suffering, sickness, death, disease. We pray for our brothers and sisters who need our intervention desperately.

On the other hand, we welcome the soft darkness that is exquisitely beautiful and healing. God dims the lights on our weary bodies, making the way for sleep, allowing us to see the stars. There is a beauty to the darkness, the natural rhythm of the earth that invites us to be still and rest. It is time to let go of the day and enter the Great Silence. ReadingsPsalm 23Psalm 91Psalm 134Here we go.

Day 2

I met Jenny and Christi for lunch at Fire Bowl Café. After yammering about whatever we yammer about, I slipped my Bible out of my purse. The table went silent.

Jenny: Are we about to get rebuked?

Christi: Are we having devotions?

Jenny: Is this an intervention??

Christi: Am I in trouble?

Jenny: Are you about to admit something bad?

Christi: Is this a Bible drill?

I reminded them about the Hour of Illumination (Christi: Geez o' pete, 7 is still going on??), and I read excerpts from *Seven Sacred Pauses* and opened Psalm 24. We let those beautiful words energize our midday while we passed Christi's teeny baby around, and the girls were thrilled we were just praying together, not holding an intervention.

Yay, me! I have friends I can do this with. I've prayed and studied so many times with these two. I know everything about their spiritual lives, and they know all the gory details of mine. We've wrestled through every issue imaginable and prayed through our best and worst times.

Christi was so smitten that my phone rang two hours later from our friend Laura:

"Christi told me all about the pauses. Tell me everything. I have a baby, a toddler, and a preschooler. My sharp mind has turned to cornmeal and I think I've developed an anxiety disorder. My hair is dirty. I've forgotten how to spell. I haven't gone to the bathroom alone in four years. I need God forty-nine times a day, but I'll settle for seven. Spill it.

"Thus continues the cannibalization of my friends by 7.

Day 6

I sent an SOS e-mail to the Council, admitting I'm having trouble observing all seven pauses each day, particularly the Night Watch, which is spectacularly meaningful but, um, at midnight.

Jenny to the rescue: "I am doing the Night Watch for you tonight. Just go to sleep and I'll take it." She sent me this the next day:

I read all the psalms for today: 42, 65, and 119. They were all awesome. I felt so excited about this after reading them! This time is not about me, but interceding for the forgotten:

Psalm 42:9–10, The Message

Sometimes I ask God, my rock-solid God, (Hear their cry, sweet Jesus) "Why did you let me down? (Why are you letting the orphan, oppressed, poor, and lonely down?) Why am I walking around in tears (Why are they all in tears?) harassed by enemies?" They're out for the kill, these tormentors with their obscenities, taunting day after day, (Lord, protect them from being tormented by the enemy) "Where is this God of yours?" (God, this question makes me feel so desperate for these people. And so sad that they probably ask this.)

Psalm 42:11

Put your hope in God, for I will yet praise him, my Savior and my God. (Thanks for being hope! God, I want to be hope too. And I pray these forgotten, lonely, and abandoned people will not give up hope.)

Tonight I'm praying for:

The women and children beaten by their husband/boyfriend or parent

The women and children being raped

The people thinking about ending their life b/c of hopelessness

The children that just lost their only living parent

The children dying from lack of food and water and lack of medicine and those still alive with aching bellies b/c we don't care enough

The twenty-seven million slaves and those driving the demand for them

The teenagers and adults addicted to drugs and alcohol

The lonely parents who have lost a child, and those sitting next to a child, knowing they are about to die

The abandoned children who are scared and alone

The widow or widower that just lost their best friend

The homeless who feel unloved and forgotten

The 147 million orphans Those that are feeling so dark and desperate

The children being held captive/kidnapped

The prisoners

The sick

This is NOT my writing for your book, stupid! But I loved these verses and wanted to share. Plus, I wanted you to know I was serious about taking your Night Watch!

How precious. Jenny kept vigil for millions suffering a dark night of the soul. She sat with Jesus, remembering them, interceding, naming their abuses and begging for justice. Her intervention has integrity because she is learning to shop "slave-free," is active in the foster system, sponsors orphans and supports widows, and loves wayward teenagers her kids befriend.

You participate sincerely in the Night Watch when your daytime hours maintain the same intervention. Like James said, "Suppose a brother or sister is without clothes and daily food. If one of you says to him, 'Go, I wish you well; keep warm and well fed,' but does nothing about his physical needs, what good is it? In the same way, faith by itself, if it is not accompanied by action, is dead. But someone will say, 'You have faith; I have deeds.' Show me your faith without deeds, and I will show you my faith by what I do" (James 2:15–18).

Note to future friends: If I ask you to participate in a social experiment, and you send me material and say it is "not writing for the book," I will ignore this and copy and paste it exactly as is, with complete disregard for your feelings.

Day 7

I haven't observed all seven pauses in a day yet. For crying out loud! Stopping in midstream is way harder than it sounds. It's not that I don't want to; I can't remember to. You would think since this concept is not only a spiritual exercise but book fodder, I would stay on it, but you would be wrong. I blink, and it's lunch. I blink again, and I'm cleaning dinner dishes. Seven pauses is kicking my butt and taking names.

Plus—BLEH—it is making me feel super guilty. At the end of every day, I count how many I missed and scold myself for prayer failure. I'm not the highest heel in the closet, but I think I'm missing the point. If prayer and rest equal guilt and frustration, then I'm doing something wrong. I can practically see God rubbing his temples.

Today I remembered something from *Seven Sacred Pauses*: "One of the things I have learned is the importance of the bell. The bell calls us to the Prayer of the Hours. The bell is annoying. The bell is good . . . When I hear the bell, I pray for the grace to put aside the work I am doing. In listening to the bell I am actually listening to an invitation for union with the Beloved. In answering the bell I am proclaiming by my actions that there is an even greater Love than the loving service I am performing."[7]

I need the bell! (Read: iPhone alarm.) Done. Alarms set.

While we're discussing failures, our first Sabbath was a hot mess. It started with me flying home at 8:30 p.m. on Saturday night. Kids were heading to bed. Dinner was over, meaning the chips my children ate while Brandon was sequestered upstairs to finish his book due Monday. Even if we tried to observe Shabbot around the dinner table, we couldn't have, since we sold it in the ABBA Fund Garage Sale. It only seated five and we're about to ratchet that up by two, so we have a rug with a light fixture over it.

Sunday morning Brandon dashed out earlier and zanier than usual, as the heater broke at church and the thermostat read 57 degrees. The kids and I came four hours later for the second service. Then we zipped to my mom's for lunch, finished our last bite, and raced Gavin to his flag football double header, which I bailed on for training at church where I'm leading a new initiative in which I have no idea what I'm doing. I got home at 7:30, and the kids asked, "What's for dinner? We're starving. No one fed us." (Brandon = book = deadline = anarchy.) So I dumped frozen soup in a pot, served it to everyone on the rug, and sent the kids to bed.

Sabbath fail.

Between the travel, football, Brandon's book deadline, and the training, this day was unsalvageable. Our redemption: That was my last event of the year, Gavin's final game, and the Internets will mercifully whisk the book away from our home tomorrow; thus Sabbath potential increased 100 percent for the rest of this month.

Gentle reader, I shall shake the dust off my feet from this first week of malfunctions and try again, starting fresh tomorrow.

I have seven daily alarms set.

I have a clear weekend calendar.

Brandon will return to life in twenty-four hours.

However, three to five pauses a day was better than none, and some were very, very sweet. (Jettison the guilt, Jen. You abandoned that response with its partners in crime: traveling revival evangelists and awkward attempts to clap in church.) These are not a yoke of bondage, but breathing spells for the soul. Remember the point. Don't miss the forest for the trees, even if the trees come in rapid succession all day, making them impossible to keep up with; then they conspire against you on the Sabbath like a haunted forest.

Day 8

Like Zach and Kelly and Screech and Slater, I'm saved by the bell! I set seven repeating alarms on my phone with text reminders on the themes, and we hit six out of seven (sorry, Night Watch, but you're so late). The monks have that bell thingy down; I should've listened.

Four of the seven prayers happen while the kids are home. Yesterday during the Wisdom Hour (right after school), Sydney prayed about forgiving a classmate, who has been *mean as the devil* to her. I don't know why I didn't pray first, what with my gift of discernment. I previously considered:

1. whispering to this kid that I'm sending psychotic fairies into her room at night to eat her legs off, or

2. just barely nicking her with my car, not enough to sustain a serious injury but enough to send a message (minor injury? gray area).

Evidently prayer was a better option.

Sydney came home today and said, "Mom! You won't believe this! Out of nowhere, Jill said, 'I'm really sorry I've been so mean to you. I don't even know why I acted that way. I really want to be your friend if you'll forgive me.'" The day after Sydney released her from this debt in prayer, she repented on her own.

What happens in the spiritual realm when we pray? It's such a mystery. What words prompt the Spirit to move? What goodness do we join Him on when we pray for peace? How powerful are our prayer words? They are a catalyst for miracles, the impetus for healing. Does God wait for us to pray in His will, primed to move for righteousness? How many relationships is He waiting to mend? How much turmoil is He poised to soothe? How much peace is He ready to administer? Are we withholding the necessary words to trigger God's intervention?

Perhaps this is why He urges us to forgive, release, lay down, let go, trust, offer, submit, and obey; these are the keys that turn the locks that bind. Like Jesus promised:

I will give you the keys of the kingdom of heaven; whatever you bind on earth will be bound in heaven, and whatever you loose on earth will be loosed in heaven. (Matt. 16:19)

Maybe after we say, "I'll forgive," He inspires repentance in the offender. Perhaps when we say, "I'll finally trust you," He delivers. Is He waiting to hear "I'll do it" before clearing the path? If we can bind and loose things in the spiritual realm, why are we squandering prayer words on football victories and temporary luxuries? What a waste! We could be binding evil, injustice, and hatred while releasing freedom, recovery, and healing—partners in mercy, not just consumers of it.

God is inviting me into this spiritual clout seven times a day—seven times the power, seven times the influence, seven times the effect. I'm frustrated I ruined the first week with legalism, missing the exquisite opportunity to join God in the work of redemption. I *knew* Jesus was offering something wonderful, but my drift into legalistic entropy is strong, people.

And good news! Now I won't be named in a personal injury suit against a minor.

Day 13

Sweet, sweet Sabbath. People, please enjoy this sacred practice with your little families. There is such beauty to it, a spiritual rhythm. It is different from just another dinner at home. There is something supernatural in this form of worship.

Beginning around 5:00 Saturday evening, Brandon and I joined forces in the kitchen, preparing dough and toppings for pizza plus a fig and goat cheese salad with toasted almonds and fig vinaigrette tossed with butter lettuce *from our own garden*. I would be remiss to mention this is the

best lettuce we've ever tasted. Ever. More delicious lettuce
has never been grown. May I also brag on our carrots, snow
peas, spinach, and potatoes? Please act impressed over
our first winter garden, because we are morons and still
managed to grow a bunch of our own food.

Everyone gathered to top their pizzas, layering goodies over
a brilliant homemade sauce, which I've included for your
eating pleasure:

> Sauté three garlic cloves and 1 tsp of red pepper flakes
> in 1/4 cup of good olive oil for 3 to 4 minutes. Add 1 28
> oz. can of Muir Glen organic crushed tomatoes—please
> trust me, this brand matters and it MUST be "crushed
> tomatoes" or you will regret it the rest of your life.
> Stir then simmer for as long as you want, add salt
> and pepper and a bunch of chopped fresh basil, put
> on your pizza and die of happiness. Set leftover sauce
> out for everyone to dunk their crusts or bread in. Now
> you're a hero. Everyone loves you.

The pizzas smelled up the house like heaven. We set out
the "nice" dishes, poured wine and grape juice, positioned
the candles, laid Shabbot readings on each place setting,
situated challah bread in the middle, and the family
assembled around our new lovely table, which now seats
eight. Oh yes, we will soon have two little new faces at this
gathering.

A mood accompanies the Sabbath dinner. It is festive and
affectionate, expectant and joyful. My littles had happy
faces; Sydney asked to do this every week forever. Relief
surrounds the evening; the meal is special, the mood is
light, and the next twenty-four hours are wrestled from
the grip of stress and frenzy.

Brandon led us through the readings, as I lit two candles representing *remembrance* (of creation and deliverance) and *observation (of rest and Sabbath)*. We drank our wine and juice; we ate the bread. Communion belongs in the home as certainly as it belongs in the church. We prayed. We closed with "Shabbot shalom! Shabbot shalom!" Peace on the Sabbath.

Then commenced movie night with popcorn and hot chocolate. The rest of Sabbath involved our beloved church, lunch with friends, then home for naps. Brilliant. We wrapped up Sabbath at my parents' house for dinner Sunday, feasting on homemade fried chicken and mashed potatoes for my brother-in-law's birthday.

Delicious food, family, church, friends, rest, worship . . . thank you, God. You're smart.

Day 14

During the first week of October, I suffered inexplicable sadness for our Ethiopian kids, yet unknown to us. I couldn't quit crying. I couldn't stop worrying. I felt heavy and dark without knowing why. With tears burning at the slightest provocation, I threw my emotions into the Facebook ring for some backup. From adopting friends a common thread rose up:

"God is prompting you to pray for your children for some reason. You don't know them yet, but he knows they are yours. Intercede for them this week; then write these dates down. Once you receive your referral, check their paperwork, and you might discover divine timing." A slew of similar stories were posted.

So Brandon and I prayed desperately for our kids. Were they losing a parent? Were they suffering? Were they tender and lonely? Were they especially hopeless? Their need was unknown, but the ache was acute. So I cried the tears I just knew they were crying, and I begged Jesus to be so near, so gentle in their younglives while they waited for us, wishing a family wanted them but too afraid to hope.

Sensitive to their fragility, I spent that week checking (obsessing over) the Waiting Children's List on our adoption agency's Web site. I've been drawn to these kids since the beginning of our adoption journey. These children have not been requested or matched, unwanted even within the adoption community. Their crimes: (1) too old—meaning over five; (2) too sick—HIV, TB, birth defects; or (3) too many—siblings.

This very week a new little face hit the WCL: a darling, bright and shiny seven-year-old boy. I instantly loved his personality. He looked like Gavin in an African way. He seemed ornery, which I adore. So I pulled him up every day. Every day. Every day. I sent the link to Brandon. I sent the link to friends. I checked back in. I watched other WCL kids move from "available" to "file under review" while his smiling face remained "available." On a Wednesday I sent this to our family coordinator:

Hi Caitlin!

Sweet adorable Beniam is a healthy seven-year-old on the WCL. He totally falls within our request range; and since he's on there, I'm assuming there are no other requests for a seven-year-old boy. Would AWAA consider placing him with an unrelated younger girl and allowing us to consider them together?

We were exactly hoping for a seven-year-old boy and a younger girl. We would be so happy to apply for unrelated kiddos if this is a possibility.

Thoughts?

Jen Hatmaker

For a week we e-mailed back and forth about unrelated kids (sweet, precious Caitlin—extra jewels in her crown for fielding my relentless e-mails). I cannot explain how drawn to Ben we were. Every time we looked at him, he became more beautiful, more precious, more Hatmaker-ish. Our social worker needed to approve us for an unrelated placement, as we were approved for siblings. That, friends, *sounded* like a formality, so we got our ducks in a row to speed that process up.

Exactly one week after that e-mail, my phone rang the following Wednesday with that heart-attack-inducing-breath-stealing caller ID: "AWAA—Caitlin" (**A**merica **W**orld **A**doption **A**gency). Adopting parents with submitted dossiers wait for that with such anxiety and anticipation, that should we be on a conference call with the president of the United States, we would scream in his ear, "I GOTTA GO!!!!!" and click over. Parents call their agencies ten billion times; they call us never, but when they do, this is what they say:

"Jen? It's Caitlin. Sit down . . . this is your referral call."

The world stopped spinning.

Time froze.

Nothing else existed.

"SHUT UP!!!" is how I responded as a mature, emotionally controlled girl. Our dossier was submitted forty-eight days ago; this referral was fast. I couldn't think straight. The referral call includes sitting at your computer while your family coordinator introduces your child with the highly anticipated e-mail file, including pictures.

I told Caitlin I'd call her back in ten minutes because I needed to get Brandon home. Ring-ring:

"Are you stalking me? I just left! You know you can't live without me."

"Brandon, zip it! *We. Just. Got. Our. Referral. Call.*"

(Insert screeching brakes.)

We called Caitlin back and discovered our referral was one gorgeous, unbelievably perfect five-year-old girl. She was beautiful in every way. Brandon fell especially hard. With her little chicklet teeth and her shy smile, it seemed we might finally get a "gentle child," which required adoption since our gene pool squashed that characteristic.

But besides "adopting" and "Ethiopia," the other crystal-clear detail was "two children." Back in December when adopting from Ethiopia was imminent, Brandon kept bringing up *two kids*. Normally the bleeding heart, I was reluctant (could also be defiant, obstinate, terrified) to consider two, knowing we are already a circus and doubting my ability to parent five kids. But Brandon couldn't shake it; so we spent a week praying and fasting about one versus two.

On the final day of our fast, unknown to anyone but us, one of my dearest friends called: "Jen? I've been praying about your adoption. If this is irrelevant, just forget it; but every time I pray, I get the feeling you and Brandon are considering siblings . . ."

Jen stops breathing.

". . . I don't know why I keep getting this message. But if you are, we've prayed about it, and we want to pay for the second child. Whatever the cost increase is for adopting two instead of one, we'll cover the entire amount."

Jen bawls eyes out.

God? We're fasting to hear from you: one or two kids?

Insert: The Most Obvious Answer Ever Received In Our Lives.

Without question we knew God had two kids for us, so this referral for just one was terribly confusing. We were starved for clarity, staring at each other like one of us had an explanation, the key to unlocking this baffling development. Our strategy has been, "Go back to what you know for sure. What was the last thing you heard?" The marching orders for two children was iron-clad, so I went three weeks back to those dark days full of prayer and sorrow. I confirmed the dates then searched this beautiful girl's file:

It was the week she was brought to the orphanage.

Shipped twelve hours north of her village, her people, everything she knew to a crowded orphanage with children and workers who spoke a different language, it must've been devastating. She must've felt so alone. At age five. Except Jesus never leaves His little ones, His most vulnerable. He was there in the scary van ride north. He was there in her confusion and fear. He was there as she was assigned a bed and communal clothes and had her beautiful head shaved. He was there that first heartbreaking night. And He made sure we were there in spirit, too.

I am telling you, we felt her grief. We carried her turmoil. We cried her tears. Jesus made sure we sat watch with Him over her. He invited us into the vigil He was keeping on her behalf. Exactly three weeks after her first lonely night in the orphanage, we got her referral.

She was ours. We knew it.

She was the "younger unrelated girl" we asked for when pursuing Ben. It all locked into place. Within hours of the call, we asked for him too. For four agonizing days, we fought for his referral, this bright, shiny boy who'd seen hundreds of babies and toddlers come and go while he waited for someone to want him. For four days we pleaded our case against staunch resistance. For four days prayers and e-mails and calls flooded in as our Christian community rallied for this boy.

Enter The Great Silence, compline, the prayer of completion. Every Sunday night at 9:00 p.m., the parents adopting through our agency join in prayer all over the world. We pray for our children, the nannies, our paperwork, referrals, court dates, traveling mercies, approvals, and grace. I told my adoption community: "Please pray for our expanded referral. We want this boy so desperately, but the resistance against his placement seems insurmountable."

We were hanging on by a thread. We knew God said adopt two children from Ethiopia. We knew He connected us in prayer to our daughter's traumatic abandonment. We knew He imprinted Ben on our hearts already, before we even had a referral. We knew these two children were the ones, but the approval looked hopeless.

From nearly every state and several other countries, we prayed at 9:00 p.m., the hour of The Great Silence. We interceded for one another and begged God to move for the orphan. We voiced our impossible circumstances and trusted Him to work the common, everyday miracles that surround adoption. We acknowledged His sovereignty over bureaucracy, embassies, social workers, and poverty. We prayed for completion: Our children home. Hesitantly, timidly, I said, "I trust you, God." At 9:27 p.m., our social worker sent this:

"I am going to approve this referral."

No words can describe the rejoicing in our house and certainly in the heavens. Another orphan found his home, despite the odds, regardless of "the rules." Yet again, God moved mountains for the very least. The day our Ethiopian children were born, the angels celebrated their immense value, the image of God they each bear. Their tragic circumstances didn't lessen their worth but raised them to the highest level of divine attention:

- The Lord is close to the brokenhearted and saves those who are crushed in spirit.

- I love the Lord, for He heard my voice; He heard my cry for mercy.

- I will not leave you as orphans; I will come to you.

- God sets the lonely in families.

- Blessed are you who are poor, for yours is the kingdom of God.

- Our God is a God who saves; from the Sovereign Lord comes escape from death.

We've been invited into a beautiful story involving hundreds of saints in prayer for the redemption of two treasures. God captured an entire community with love for two children whose names were headed into the oblivion of poverty and despair. As selfish plans fail daily, and greedy dreams burn out as God removes His hand from endeavors we are using His name to endorse, Jesus gently placed two African orphans in the center of a faith community, restoring their names from a statistic back to the loved, precious, essential children they are.

I want you to know their names.

Our Beniam is seven, and we'll call him Ben, the son we fought for. Our daughter's name is Matawi, which means "Remembrance." We will call her Remy because she was never forgotten—not by her Creator, not by her Savior, and not by us. God walked with our children through every sorrow; their plight was ever before Him. God never forgot, never slept, never stopped working until His children were restored.

He remembered them.

For the Lord comforts his people and will have compassion on his afflicted ones. But Zion said, "The Lord has forsaken me, the Lord has forgotten me." Can a mother forget the baby at her breast and have no compassion on the child she has borne? Though she may forget, I will not forget you! See, I have engraved you on the palms of my hands; your walls are ever before me. . . .

See, I will beckon to the nations, I will lift up my banner to the peoples; they will bring your sons in their arms and carry your daughters on their hips. Kings will be your foster fathers, and their queens your nursing mothers. They will bow down before you with their faces to the ground; they will lick the dust at your feet. Then you will know that I am the Lord; those who hope in me will not be disappointed.

Can plunder be taken from warriors, or captives be rescued from the fierce? But this is what the Lord says: "Yes, captives will be taken from warriors, and plunder retrieved from the fierce; I will contend with those who contend with you, and your children I will save." (Isa. 49:13–16, 22–25)

Day 16

Yucky post ahead

You've been warned.

You know what's lame? Jealousy in a grown woman. I work in a weird industry/ministry hybrid. The subject is God, but it involves contracts, marketing budgets, cover designers, PR directors, publishers, and some hype. It takes fussing to get a book into your hands. Like me, most writers are neurotic and paranoid about this, certain everyone else is getting a better contract, better everything. They are probably all having secret dinners without me. I'm already self-conscious about my work, so add the success of other writers and perceived slights, and I'm like a melodramatic character on the CW. (I'm grossed out by myself, too. It's not just you.)

Around 11:00 a.m., I heard about a friend's massively wonderful book deal. It involves a team of committed experts and a lot of zeros. The word *synergy* was used and I threw up in my mouth. I became instantly furious with everyone who ever collaborated on my contracts. Publishers, editors, PR directors, my agent . . . they are all in on it. With complete certainty I knew they'd been at the secret dinners conspiring against me. Not only do they not believe in me, but now I know they despise me. They actually wish harm to me since none of my contracts ever matched this synergetic one.

I may have pulled up my Amazon reviews, which confirmed the freefall.

Icky ick ick. Oh ego, you ridiculously fragile ballast! I thought I'd banished you by now. I hate when you show up all insecure, trying to garnish credit and edge into the limelight. You ruin things. You steal honor and joy that rightfully belong to others. You turn beautiful tasks into garbage, and you wrestle glory from Jesus' hands. I hate you. I mean, I really hate you. I wish you were dead. But you're so hard to kill.

And the bell tolled at noon—The Hour of Illumination. Uh-oh. Written by Jen Hatmaker twenty-two days ago:

During the Hour of Illumination, we ask Jesus to send light into our hearts so intensely that they break wide open, so we can make the decisions that lead to peace—from death to life, deception to truth, despair to hope, hate to love. We self-inspect our hearts for violence we are choosing to harbor—toward ourselves, spouses or family members, coworkers, community, those who are different, toward any part of creation. We ask God's love to illuminate the parts of our souls darkened with bitterness or anger or unforgiveness or apathy.

I walked outside with Lady Bird and turned my face to the sun, marveling at the ugly war that rages in me and God's unfathomable patience with it all. I thought about Jesus, who never angled for credit, ever. In fact, He had the most perplexing habit of telling people *not* to talk about His awesomeness, how He healed and saved. Jesus always deferred glory, redirecting people to one another and toward His Father and Spirit, who was to come. What Jesus didn't do was complain the other rabbis got more temple time or had better synergy.

I am commissioned to be a light, but I can't illuminate this world while competing with the lights of others. I mean, really? It isn't possible to miss the point any worse. Together we are a city on a hill. When one of us shines, it is a community victory. If we all lived radiantly, we simply couldn't be hidden any longer. This is not about individual wattage; our power is communal, or it is meaningless. "How good and pleasant it is when God's people live together in unity!" (Ps. 133:1).

God, this is the story you've given me to live. Write it with beauty and light. Banish the dark pockets of selfishness and jealousy with truth. Forgive me for choosing envy when I should have been thrilled your name will become even more famous. My gosh, I am a mess. Teach me peace in a violent world, already riddled with competition and greed. Give me a heart of flesh that contends for your glory through anyone, everyone, anywhere, everywhere. Reign over me until there is only you.

I am so grateful for this pause today because without it I would've continued the downward spiral, uninterrupted. I'm sure of it. I was four seconds away from Googling myself. This simple prayer stopped the hemorrhaging before I lost a whole day (week/weeks) nurturing my jealousy like a little pet. Maybe that's one reason Paul told us to "pray continually" (1 Thess. 5:17). Constant prayer interrupts our ego trips and disrupts our toxic trajectories. It says, "Whoa, missy, stop right there. Really? You're going to keep feeding this beast? Let's count to ten and rethink this. You know, Jesus always said . . ."

Who can argue with that? It's like seventh grade when mom let my sister get her ears pieced two years earlier than I did and extended her bedtime *that same week*, and when I was simply showing her the error of her parenting by yelling in her face about the injustice I lived with and the favoritism she was clearly showing Lindsay because obviously I was the most unloved yet high-achieving daughter in the house and maybe I should just go live with Gran . . . SLAP! Right across the face. Stunned us into silence until we both burst out crying.

That's how The Hour of Illumination was today. A nice slap in the face to shock me out of an old-fashioned hissy fit. Good medicine. Think of all the damage I wouldn't inflict if I prayed in the middle of all my episodes! Perhaps I'll keep these alarms set past next week. And maybe I'll delete this confrontational e-mail I drafted to my agent about a pending contract. Sorry. The devil made me do it.

Day 18

I marvel at the company I keep. My friends would be intimidating if they weren't so fun and occasionally naughty. My comrades are adopting, serving, raising money, raising awareness, sacrificing, advocating, giving away, sharing, fostering, sponsoring, fighting, dreaming. This planet is brighter for their presence. They are good people. (Do not believe what you have heard about them. Unless you've seen pictorial evidence, which may or may not exist.)

I have friends, including Council Member Trina, seized for the plight of refugees in Austin. Refugees were forced from their homelands by war, civil conflict, political strife, and/or gross human rights abuses. These survivors were persecuted—often tortured and brutalized, their families murdered—and ultimately displaced because of their race, religion, nationality, tribe, or social group and are unable to return home. Approximately fourteen million refugees have sought sanctuary in other countries, and roughly three thousand settle in Austin each year.

While they've escaped violence and instability of their homelands, they face daunting obstacles in America. Refugees receive a small stipend for four months, less than unemployment. In this amount of time, on an income below poverty level, they are expected to become self-sustaining. It is clearly impossible, and the odds are stacked against them heavily. With fragmented English and no context for American culture (computer skills, banking, enrolling kids in school, employment, junk mail vs. real mail, shopping, bus routes, homework, this list goes on forever), refugees get stuck in minimum-wage jobs with no tools to escape, and the cycle of poverty continues.

Keep in mind these are incredibly smart and resourceful people who've overcome unfathomable evils and lived to tell. Their station has nothing to do with work ethic or capabilities and everything to do with language barriers and cultural displacement. They simply need advocates to mentor them toward a stable place in the American economy.

Which brings me back to my friends who dreamed up a social enterprise called Open Arms, a for-profit business employing refugee women in Austin at a living wage, a company with a conscience. Using donated T-shirts, Open Arms repurposes discarded items and turns them into beautiful scarves, pillows, purses, bags, rugs, and more—a metaphor for the women who craft them. Additionally, Open Arms provides on-site seminars (computer skills, language, banking, budgeting), plus child care and early intervention for their young kids, breaking another link in the poverty chain.

Their debut is this weekend at the illustrious Christmas Affair, a ginormous four-day market organized by the Junior League with more than two hundred merchants and attendance north of thirty thousand people. Granted a coveted booth, Open Arms needs five hundred pieces to sell, and everyone is working their little fingers to the bone to make it. My friend Leslie, the engine behind Open Arms, wouldn't even let *the team* take a scarf in advance to start wearing, *not even if they paid for it*. She counted every day.

That girl runs a tight ship.

Jenny, Shonna, our friend Larkin, and I volunteered all morning, three days before the Christmas Affair. We received our task: take T-shirt scraps of scraps (*nothing wasted!*), cut them into 11 x ¼ strips, tie them through each Open Arms tag, and pin tags on every item ready for sale. While the international women hummed at their sewing machines doing the skilled work, we chattered and giggled and pinned the ever-lovin' business out of those tags.

At 10:00 a.m. sharp, my trusty bell rang, reminding me to pause for the Blessing Hour, including wonderful themes for our morning at Open Arms: an invitation to the Spirit, acknowledging his presence and recommitting the day to his glory, and a simple prayer to bless the work of our hands, all of our hands.

With my heart in my throat, we all paused together and prayed God's Spirit displayed in every scarf, each bag, that He become famous for His redemptive work in the lives of the most vulnerable. I asked God to bless the work of the hands in the room: Sudanese hands, Burmese hands, Congolese hands, Ugandan hands, American hands. I asked God to remember these women who have seen so much violence yet still work cheerfully, humbly. I petitioned the future work of their hands: raising children, creating beauty, embracing healing. I prayed blessings over this beautiful business of reclaiming, reimagining, repurposing shirts and lives. I thanked the Spirit for planting this dream in Leslie's heart then fanning to flames to others committed to living out his mission. (Tears? Maybe a few.)

Then back to work as our friend Lacey threw down the gauntlet earlier in her sweet, sweet voice: "We were hoping maybe everything could be tagged and boxed by 11:30 . . ." That sounded like a challenge packaged in sugar, and we took the bait. 11:30? Oh, we'll see your 11:30 and raise you "boxes loaded in cars."

Now reader, go to www.theopenarmsshop.com and buy something, or I will never speak to you again for the rest of my life.

Day 20

Leave it to the Hatmakers to dumb down something as sacred as Sabbath dinner. People, I just play the hand that is dealt me, okay? Brandon was out of town until midnight, so it was just the four of us, and we were leaving Sunday morning for eight glorious days off.

Gentle reader, if you are not a mother, here is the translation:

When transporting your family away from your quarters for longer than one solar period, you engage a marathon of preparations that make you question the decision to go anywhere the rest of your life. The list is exhaustive, and you will discover not one human on the planet who feels like being helpful. This is on you, Mom. You'll answer for every omission while getting zero credit for performing the duties of a packing mule for your tribe. It goes something like this:

"Get down your suitcase. We're packing for eight days, everyone. Remember, it's cold in the mornings and warm

in the afternoons. Did you get your suitcases down?
Everyone come get their clean clothes and put them away!
We are coming home to a clean house, do you hear me?
Where are your boots? Where is your toothbrush? What
do you mean, it's been missing "for awhile"? What have
you been brushing your teeth with?? Don't answer that.
Why are you playing Xbox right now? Pack socks! Pack
underwear! Why is your suitcase not down? Bring books to
read. Yes you will. Because I'll make you. Where is Lady's
leash? Why is it connecting your bikes? What is "slingshot
riding"? Pick out movies to bring! No, we are not bringing
Cats and Dogs: The Revenge of Kitty Galore. Because it makes
my brain shrink. So help me, are you still on the Xbox???
What do you mean you're done packing? I see one pair
of jeans and an air-soft gun in here. I'm coming up in five
minutes, and I'm giving away everything that is still on
your bedroom floor. Oh my stars, is your suitcase still not
down??"

This tirade continues until the second you pull out of your
driveway. It will take your husband ten miles before he is
speaking to anyone again, and you declare a moratorium
on all talking and sound until lifted by you, the keeper of
the details and the packer of the things. Approximately
one hour later, your teeth unclench. On the third day of
your vacation, you decide that you might possibly, maybe,
travel again with your family, but you're not sure yet. It's
too soon to tell.

So packing cut into my meal preparations for Sabbath.
However, we still wanted to inaugurate our day (week) of
rest, the launch of our little sabbatical.

We still had candles.

We still had the readings; Gavin read the "man" parts in lieu of Brandon.

We still used the nice dishes.

We had, um, chicken strips and macaroni and cheese.

We shared Communion with the last heel of sliced cinnamon bread.

And water, since we drank all our juice before leaving town.

But we put the water in fancy cups.

We got super tickled about all this, and I snapped a picture to commemorate what the kids dubbed "the Mom Sabbath." Amazingly, this jolted me out of drill sergeant mode and restored laughter to the house. We thanked God for the gift of time off, for the family ranch, for thousands of good days behind us and even better days ahead.

Shabbat shalom!

Day 23

On the last day of school in seventh grade, fifteen of my friends met at Shoney's for breakfast, dominating the restaurant while our moms pretended not to know us. Please try to remember seventh grade, especially if you are a girl. Recall the cruel awkwardness, the certainty you were tipping the scales at 102 pounds, the fear no boy would ever get past your home perm and lack of booby buds, and the feeling you were destined for Dorkville.

Population: only you. Remember how all your friends wore Esprit and Guess jeans, and your mom said she'd rather book a one-way ticket to commie Russia before shelling out $50 for jeans? (I was a tragic twelve-year-old stuck in lower middle class during the Cold War.)

That fine morning at Shoney's, my friends and I were showing off and making enormous nuisances of ourselves, when *a miracle happened*. Ron Coyle, the finest junior in the history of the world, oldest son of my parents' best friends, came behind me, wrapped his arms around me, and kissed me in front of everyone. My memory swears he got a centimeter of lip. Then he set me back down and walked away.

You could've heard a pin drop. Forks stopped in midair. Girls froze in mid-bite. A gorgeous high school boy just kissed a member of their prepubescent tribe in front of their faces. I tried to play it cool, but I didn't really have that skill set. Everyone gaped at me, not believing my good fortune while simultaneously wishing I were dead.

It was pretty much the greatest day of my life.

Sometimes the stars align to wrap up a season perfectly; you didn't plan it, but the universe throws you a bone, and everything congeals in perfect harmony. The bow is lovingly tied on top, and the circle of life is completed. You'd like to imagine you are responsible for this, but the truth is, it's dumb luck and coincidence, and you just get to stand in the winner's circle.

Similarly, thus begins the final week of 7.

At my parents' ranch.

For eight days.

During Thanksgiving.

A *literal sabbatical*, including the first two Sundays off since we started ANC in 2008.

A planner would've engineered this finale on purpose, finishing a month of rest and prayer with family, sequestered on 350 beautiful acres, happily meal-planning for Thursday when we'll break bread in total thankfulness for this month, this year, this blessed life. But this all just sort of happened to me.

Regardless, I'm happily typing on the porch of the barn as the breeze blows, watching Sydney and Lady leap across hay bales and listening to my boys gun the four-wheeler in the front pasture. My mom and dad are reading books in the afternoon sun, and Brandon is setting up mid- and long-range targets for a Hatmaker Shoot Off. We have no cell service. We have no Internet. There is no cable either, but we do have one spotty TV with a VHS player where we watch old movies every night, piled on the couches like puppies. We'll feed cows this week and move hay bales. The guys will hit the deer blinds and attempt to fill our freezers for the winter. (An armadillo already lost its life last night, thanks to Caleb's sharp shooting. It's Texas, people.)

We'll wear the same clothes over and over, and four days from now I'll ask if anyone has taken a shower. The answer will be no. I didn't even bring makeup. At least once we'll head "into town" to eat at the Rockin' J's in Comanche, a converted gas station where 95 percent of the patrons will have on camouflage. We'll order biscuits and gravy because we aren't imbeciles. We've been here less than twenty-four hours, and I've already read a book and a half. The kids brought bones and other treasures from their explorations. By 8:30 a.m., I'd already washed a load of filthy clothes after Caleb and Lady decided to "walk through the creek instead of go aaaaaaaaallll the way around it" (fifty additional yards). We'll enjoy coffee in the morning, sweet tea in the afternoon, and a glass of Cabernet Sauvignon on the porch at night, while the sun sets over the coastal fields.

This week will lovingly bookend 7, offering the best space to reflect, gear down, and express gratitude. I'm surrounded by my favorite people at my favorite place during my favorite week on earth. It's the proverbial public kiss, the finest possible ending to this incredible experimental year. I'll gratefully pray through the hours in the pasture, on the four-wheeler, and in the barn; while cooking breakfast for the hunters and dinner for the explorers; with my kids, my husband, and my parents; in the early morning on the porch and as we turn off the lights after movie night.

"Dear Artist of the Universe, Beloved Sculptor, Singer, and Author of my life, born of your image I have made a home in the open fields of your heart. The magnetic tug of your invitation to grow is slowly transforming me into a gift for the world. Mentor me into healthy ways of living. Help me remember to pause."[8]

Day 26

The rhythm of the ranch is healing to the frantic pace of normal life. It's also a tutor, teaching me the superior tempo of living well. At the ranch there is no hurry. There is no racing from one thing to the next unless you count trying to outpace Lady Bird on the four-wheeler. Thanks to its strategic geography, we aren't distracted by the Internet, TV, or phones (if you stand on a chair in the southwest corner of the barn while holding your phone to the heavens, you get one bar).

Friend, you might be imagining a luxurious, sheek, rustic ranch with overstuffed leather furniture and antler chandeliers. Please let me set the record straight. This is a working cattle ranch, no house, just a barn that houses a four-hundred-square foot office/living room/kitchenette/ bathroom. The utility sink, refrigerator, and washer and dryer are out in the barn, so during the winter we fight over who has to brave the frigid barn to fetch jelly from the fridge or—horror—hand wash the dishes while bundled like an Eskimo.

At night the two couches fold out into beds: voila, a bedroom. These beds are slightly less comfortable than sleeping on an inverted mat of ball bearings. Add a kid draped all over you, and we basically pray for each night to end. The TV only plays VHS tapes. "Why are the lines squiggly at the top of the screen?" the spoiled modernchildren ask. They don't know about tracking, a cross we children of the '80s had to bear. The pipes freeze at the first sign of a cool breeze, so we keep milk jugs of water in the bathroom so we can fill the tank up and flush. It's all very glamorous.

So believe me, the ranch life is a simple one, depleted of all the extravagances we're addicted to.

And yet.

None of us could wait to get out here. We've been talking about this week for two months. We love, love, love the ranch and every rustic detail. We crave the outdoor air and dirty farm boots. The boys were on the four-wheeler before we put the car in park. The kids explore for hours. We would have no clue where they were if not for the hilarious walkie-talkie communiqué we eavesdrop on.

Brandon and the boys experience pure bliss from their hunting endeavors, and why not? We have twelve deer blinds on the ranch, all ironically named: the Spongebob, the Bishop, Crow's Nest, Alaska Stand, North Creek, Penthouse, the Grove, and of course, the Bellagio, named for its opulence with its retractable windows, carpeted floor, and heater. (Caleb falls asleep in this deer blind every time.)

As the sun set and the hunters were returning, I started dinner and entered the Twilight Hour, that grateful transition from the activity of the day to the relaxation of the evening. I love gathering my chicks after days like today, when muscles and imaginations were stretched to their limits and flushed cheeks walk in the door competing for space to tell their tales. Hats pulled off and ponytails released, a mountain of ranch boots left by the door. The family assembled with fresh, new memories and an eager anticipation of the next day.

I read Psalm 145 and repeated a beautiful prayer from *Seven Sacred Pauses*:

> O You whose face is a thousand colors . . . look upon us in this twilight hour, and color our faces with the radiance of your love. As the light of the sun fades away, light the lamps of our hearts that we may see

one another more clearly. Let the incense of our gratitude rise as our hearts become full of music and song. May the work that we bring with us into this hour fall away from our minds as we enter into the mystical grace of the evening hour. Amen.[9]

Day 30

What a finale to Month Seven! Thanksgiving was epic: we ate our weight in honey ham and fried turkey, jalapeno cranberry relish and my Grandma's carrots, which are legendary and will go down in King family history. We cooked and laughed and napped and ate again. My mom made pumpkin cheesecake and homemade whipped cream. Clearly nothing can top that, so I'll end this food paragraph on that high note.

I'm thankful for the contemplatives who've stirred me: Henri Nouwen, Brother Lawrence, Macrina Wiederkehr, Mother Teresa, Richard Rohr; David, Isaiah, Jesus. Their noble embrace of prayer and stillness has inspired me into deeper communion with God. This mindfulness has been terribly stretching.

I've discovered I can fast from clothes and waste and spending easier than I can fast from busyness. Wear the same outfit six days straight? Sure. Garden and recycle? No problem. Pause seven times a day in the middle of my life? Now that's asking a lot. I found this month very challenging and equally beautiful. Evidently, I don't respond well to interruptions, Spirit-led or otherwise.

But these pauses, plus the Sabbath, plus the sabbatical taught me something: My heart craves a slower life. I want people to stop prefacing their phone calls with this: "I know you're so busy, but if I could just have a second . . ." I want to figure out what this means for our family. We can't live in the barn forever, nor we can pull out of work, ministry, school, community, mission, family, and all the activities that accompany them. But what can we do to cultivate a quiet ranch heart in a noisy urban world?

I know we'll be keeping the Sabbath. Um, hold your applause since we've been instructed to do this from Exodus to Hebrews. As God explained at the inauguration of the Sabbath:

Remember the Sabbath day by keeping it holy. Six days you shall labor and do all your work, but the seventh day is a sabbath to the Lord your God. On it you shall not do any work, neither you, nor your son or daughter, nor your male or female servant, nor your animals, nor any foreigner residing in your towns. For in six days the Lord made the heavens and the earth, the sea, and all that is in them, but he rested on the seventh day. Therefore the Lord blessed the Sabbath day and made it holy. (Exod. 20:8–11)

Is it coincidental that God named every person included in the rest? Sons and daughters, servers and animals, guests and visitors; we all need this. My neglect of the Sabbath doesn't just affect me but my entire household, my extended community. The pace we keep has jeopardized our health and happiness, our worship and rhythms. We belong to a culture that can't catch its breath; rather, we refuse to catch our breath.

God doesn't pull any punches here: The Sabbath is holy. Not lazy, not selfish, not unproductive; not helpful, not optional, not just a good idea. *Holy.* Like God demonstrated in Exodus 16, He'll provide for daily needs, but on the sixth day He'll rain down a double portion to store up for the Sabbath, covering our needs while we rest. The only day a double collection wouldn't spoil by dawn's light was the Sabbath; God made a way.

He still does. Originally, the Sabbath had to be planned for, food gathered a day in advance. It wasn't handed to the Hebrews on a silver platter. This principle remains. I still have to plan for the Sabbath, tying up loose ends and gathering what we'll need. I still have to prepare the family for rest, enforcing healthy boundaries and protecting our calendar. I still have to set work aside and trust in the wisdom of God's design. "Bear in mind that the Lord has given you the Sabbath" (Exod. 16:29).

My heart feels renewed at the completion of the month. Perhaps the greatest gift is clarity. My mission is concentrated: this matters, this doesn't, this counts, this doesn't. It's actually not that complicated. The Bible is true; no matter how contrary to reality it appears. I've discovered you can press extremely hard on the Word, and it will hold.

It is healing to forgive.

You *do* gain your life by losing it.

Love *does* truly conquer evil.

A simple life really *is* liberating.

As I wrap up Month Seven, I'll quote a prayer written by Henri Nouwen, which resonates so deeply, it's as if he stole my thoughts:

Dear Lord, you have sent me in to this world to preach
your word. So often the problems of the world seem
so complex and intricate that your word strikes me as
embarrassingly simple. Many times I fell tongue-tied
in the company of people who are dealing with the
world's social and economic problems.

But you, O Lord, said, "Be clever as serpents and
innocent as doves." Let me retain innocence and
simplicity in the midst of this complex world. I realize
that I have to be informed, that I have to study the
many aspects of the problems facing the world, and
that I have to try to understand as well as possible
the dynamics of our contemporary society. But what
really counts is that all this information, knowledge,
and insight allow me to speak more clearly and
unambiguously your truthful word. Do not allow evil
powers to seduce me with the complexities of the
world's problems, but give me the strength to think
clearly, speak freely, and act boldly in your service. Give
me the courage to show the dove in a world so full of
serpents."[10]

Conclusion

How do I summarize 7, an experiment that has forever altered our lives? My takeaways are so vast, I can't keep an idea still long enough to write about it. New thoughts have so usurped old thoughts, I can't remember what I used to think about. Then there are these ideas Brandon and I are dreaming about: community development, mixed-income housing, the three Rs (relocation, reconciliation, redistribution), downsizing. Of course, there is the poetic irony of our impending adoption, rounding out our family to *seven*. I'm regretting manuscript omissions already: my book collection eradication, the half-marathon I ran for adoption, James 5, the Global Voices Summit. There was just too much to tell.

Also swimming in my brain is the huge list of reforms with new habits and practices. Not to mention the crash course I've received on the economy and capitalism and alternative fuels and sustainable farming and neurological processes and industrialized food and local economics and consumer trends and ancient liturgy. I've read precision analogy by global economists and rhythmic prayer poetry by a monastic nun. I've digested articles by farmers, food lobbyists, social activists, missionaries, financial advisors, marketing analysts, pastors, insurgents, doctors, ecologists, waste managers, priests, advocates, nonprofit leaders, documentary makers, politicians, revolutionaries, troublemakers, and dreamers. I've ingested information through a fire hose and find myself sputtering and gasping. However, after curbing my appetites for so long, I've discovered my appetites have changed.

I realize some of you are hoping for a romantic ending here, something with aplomb, a juicy Twitter sound the bite (@jenhatmaker moved from the suburbs to a van down by the river with her five kids. Astonishing. #7 #readit). You're waiting for some surprise radical ending I've been saving to drop on my readers, like becoming missionaries or farmers or the quirky stars of a new "Simple Life" segment on *The Today Show* ("Welcome back, Hatmakers!" "Thanks, Matt! Good to be here again!" "Wow! Great dress, Jen!" "Thank you. I sewed it out of discarded plastic bags dredged up from the bottom of polluted lakes." "You are truly amazing." "It's all for Jesus, Matt.")

But that's not where we are. Honestly, we're not sure what's next for the Hatmakers. We know something new is coming; we recognize the winds of change that seem to blow on our little life with regularity. Brandon has that wild, itchy look in his eyes. 7 allowed us to slowly break up with some of our ideas, our luxuries. It was something of a long good-bye. It's not you, it's us. Well, it is you.

This was the beginning of a process, not a complete story by itself. We didn't live out 7 and cross the finish line. This adventure was something like being morbidly obese and unable to schedule a life saving surgery until losing weight first. We had to shed and cull and purge before God can even remotely begin to deal with the serious issues. This was presurgery business, the required fast before the real procedure.

However, even if I had a clear directive, I'm not sure I'd share it here. Whatever God has done or is doing in our family is certainly not a template, and I don't want it to be. We live in a certain city with a certain task, we have specific gifts, and we're horribly deficient in others. Our life looks like it does because we are the Hatmakers, and God is dealing with us the way He's dealing with us. We have history and sin issues and circumstances and geography that God takes into account as He stakes our place in His kingdom.

You have an entirely different set of factors. I have no idea what this might look like in your life, nor do I want that job. Your story is God's to write, not mine. Some of us are going to live in the suburbs, others downtown. I'm going to garden; you're going to take the subway. We're adopting, you're redistributing, they're downsizing. I use words, you use a hammer. There isn't a list here. There is no stencil we can all trace into our lives in perfect unison. Here is our baseline as a faith community:

Love God most. Love your neighbor as yourself. This is everything.

If we say we love God, then we will care about the poor.

This earth is God's and everything in it. We should live like we believe this.

What we treasure reveals what we love.

Money and stuff have the power to ruin us.

Act justly, love mercy, walk humbly with God. This is what is required.

Interestingly, as I write this a few weeks after the completion of 7, I've discovered something surprising.

I engaged a fast with my adoption community last week,

and *it wasn't even hard*. I couldn't believe it. I kept waiting
to feel desperate, but instead the fast was simple
and beautiful and focused on prayer rather than the
mechanics. Gone were the screaming voices in my head;
gone was the simmering anxiety. It was like putting on a
familiar sweatshirt. After saying "no" to things I wanted
for nearly a year, I guess I gained some control over my
emotions and impulses. God used fasting as a tool to curb
my appetites and regulate my reactions. It was a concise
realization: "Something in me has deeply changed."

Perhaps this is why Scripture calls us to the practice of
fasting—from food, from greed, from selfishness, from
luxuries. It isn't just the experience; it's the discipline. It
changes us. Fasting helps us develop mastery over the
competing voices in our heads that urge us toward more,
toward indulgence, toward emotional volatility. Like
consistent discipline eventually shapes our children's
behavior, so it is with us. Believe it or not, God can still
change us. Not just our habits but our hearts. Say "no" for
a year and see for yourself.

Steven, our KP partner, asked me this morning while
harvesting carrots and potatoes (!!) and lettuce: "Who is
your reader?" and that got me thinking about you. I'm
going to guess you are probably a middle- to upper-middle
class parent (but love to my nonbreeders!), and mostly
your life is terribly blessed. Your world is pretty controlled:
kids are in good schools, neighborhood is safe, jobs are
fairly secure, wardrobe is impressive enough. These
advantages cause you some tension, but you're not sure
why or what to do with it.

You're likely a believer, but whether you're a lifer or a
recent devotee, I'm not sure. A few of you are teetering

on the edge of faith, drawn in by Jesus but repelled by his followers. As for church, you probably go to one, but a bunch of you don't; the elitism and waste and bureaucracy became too much and you left, or you want to leave. Some of you are solid attenders, but you feel like crawling out of your skin sometimes, valuing faith community but worried yours is missing the point. A few of you have found the church of your dreams. Half of you read *Radical*, or *Crazy Love*, or *The Irresistible Revolution*, and since you're reading this, you might've read *Interrupted*. You loved and hated it.

I'm guessing you've cried over orphans or refugees or starvation or child prostitutes, heartbroken by the depravity of this world. It's not okay that your kids get school and birthday parties while Third World children get abandoned and trafficked, but you don't know how to fix that. You're wondering if your lifestyle is connected to these discrepancies, and you have a nagging suspicion that less is more but it's a muddy concept. Everyone has ideas. It's confusing and overwhelming. This creates a sort of war within, and it leaves you raw. Sometimes you're a full-blown mess over it.

Hear this: I don't think God wants you at war with yourself.

He sent the Prince of peace to soothe those tumultuous waters already. Self-deprecation is a cruel response to Jesus, who died and made us righteous. Guilt is not Jesus' medium. He is battling for global redemption right now; His objective hardly includes huddling in the corner with us, rehashing our shame again. He finished that discussion on the cross. Plus, there's no time for that.

We're so conditioned to being a problem that we've forgotten we're actually the answer. God is not angry at you; how could He possibly be? You are His daughter, His son; you're on the team. Don't imagine He is sitting us all down for a lecture. Rather, He's staging a rally, gathering the troops. The church is rising like a phoenix right now, collecting speed and strength and power.

I saw heaven standing open and there before me was a white horse, whose rider is called Faithful and True. With justice he judges and wages war. His eyes are like blazing fire, and on his head are many crowns. He has a name written on him that no one knows but he himself. He is dressed in a robe dipped in blood, and his name is the Word of God. (Rev. 19:11–13)

Something marvelous and powerful is happening in the church. The Bride is awakening and the Spirit is rushing. It is everywhere. This movement is not contained within a denomination or demographic, not limited to a region or country. It's sweeping up mothers and pastors and teenagers and whole congregations. A stream became a current, and it is turning into a raging flood. It is daily gathering conspirators and defectors from the American Dream. It is cresting with the language of the gospel: the weak made strong, the poor made rich, the proud made humble.

The body of Christ is mobilizing in unprecedented numbers. Jesus is staging a massive movement to bind up the brokenhearted and proclaim freedom for captives. The trumpet is blowing. We are on the cusp, on the side of the Hero. So while we're mistakenly warring with ourselves, Jesus is waging war on injustice and calling us to join Him.

This is way more fun than self-condemnation, no?

So imagine me linking arms with you, giving you an

affectionate Texas squeeze. Guilt might be the first
chapter, but it makes for a terrible story. Jesus gave us
lots of superior material to work with. If your stuff and
spending and waste and stress are causing you tension
like mine is, just do the next right thing. Ask some new
questions; conversation partners are everywhere (their
name is Legion, for they are many). Take a little baby step.
Tomorrow, you can take another. Offer yourself the same
grace Jesus has given you. We're no good to Him stuck in
paralysis.

For most American Christians, this will begin with
deconstruction, but the real thrill is in the reconstruction.
I don't want to base my life on what I'm against. How
boring. That's not inspiring enough motivation. I imagine
the sooner we untether from the trap of "more," the
clearer this will all become. We're building the scaffolding;
the real construction comes next.

I value you desperately, my sisters and brothers in this
adventure. I marvel at your gifts; you're so essential to this
conversation. I am stunned by the collective goodness of
the Bride. As I hear stories of intervention and reduction
and courage, I applaud Jesus in selecting you for your
tasks. We serve an unruly Savior on a recklessly wild ride;
I'm glad you're on it with me. May we embrace unity over
infighting, bravery over comfort, us over me, people over
principles, and God's glory over our own. Together, let's
become repairers of broken walls and restorers of streets
with dwellings.

*The Lord bless you and keep you; the Lord make his face shine
on you and be gracious to you; the Lord turn his face toward you
and give you peace. (Num. 6: 24–26)*

A Few Companies with a Conscience

- http://livefashionable.com
- http://www.cometogethertrading.com
- http://www.redearthtradingco.com
- http://www.furnacehillscoffee.com/index
- http://preemptivelove.org
- www.noondaycollection.com
- www.bethejoy.com
- http://goodnewsgoods.com
- www.theopenarmshop.com
- www.meadscorner.com
- www.commonthreadz.org
- www.Groobs.com
- www.globalgirlfriend.com
- www.cometogethertrading.com
- www.3seams.com
- http://www.ravenandlily.com
- http://www.numanainc.com
- http://www.pyxispath.com
- www.tradeasone.com
- www.thehungersite.org
- www.funkyfishdesigns.com

Acknowledgments

No one lost their lunch on this joyride more than Brandon and my family, swept up in another one of "my little ideas," as the hubs says. God love them. There are not four people I'd rather eat eighty pounds of avocados and learn how to compost with more than the Hatmaker tribe. Hey? I know! Let's add two more kids and become a full-fledged circus. I love you, Brandon, Gavin, Sydney, Caleb . . . and our two Ethiopian darlings who have no idea what they are about to get into. You are the family I've always dreamed of.

The second gaggle of people who invested in 7 is The Council. For reasons yet unclear, you joined the fray and kept the wheels on. You ate seven foods and wore seven clothes and gave your stuff away and shut down Facebook . . . *and you weren't even getting paid.* Your wisdom and enthusiasm were my fuel. Becky, Molly, Jenny, Shonna, Susana, and Trina: I love you, you crazy, wild, hilarious, inappropriate, loyal girls. Be mine forever.

Our little Austin New Church family has changed my life in such acute ways I can no longer envision my life without you in it. You are adopting, sacrificing, fighting human trafficking, dreaming, fostering, feeding, building wells, building orphanages, building the kingdom. In the context of ANC, 7 fit right in. I'm not even a weird girl around you people, and that is really saying something. I love you profoundly.

I want to thank the advocates and visionaries and dreamers and thinkers who guided me through the mazes of 7. I didn't understand demand-side economics. Now I do. I didn't know how sugar snap peas grow. Now I do. I've had so many teachers. Thank you for your books, your articles, your divergent and courageous lives. Keep saying what you're saying. It matters.

Notes

Introduction

1. See http://www.billbright.com/howtofast.

Month One: Food

1. I went to www.nutritiondata.com, but given how the Internet changes, a different site might be preferred depending on when you're reading this.

2. See http://www.sciencedaily.com releases/2009/05/090501162805.htm.

3. See http://www.ngonewsafrica.org/2010/01/ethiopia-rejects- warning-of-hunger.html.

4. See http://www.wfp.org/countries/ethiopia.

5. See http://derevth.blogspot.com/2008/10/types-of-theology.html.

6. See http://news.nationalgeographic.com/news/2004/01/0111_ 040112_consumerism.html.

7. Michael Pollan, *In Defense of Food: An Eater's Manifesto* (New York: Penguin Books, 2008), 13–14.

8. Ibid., 6–7.

9. Ibid., 10.

10. See http://www.eurekalert.org/pub_releases/2005-03/ chb-eoc 031605.php.

11. Barbara Kingsolver, *Animal Vegetable Miracle: A Year of Food Life* (New York: Harper Perennial: 2007), 126–27.

12. See www.sweetsurprise.com.

13. See http://www.sweetsurprise.com.

14. Pollan, *In Defense of Food: An Eater's Manifesto,* 150–52.

15. Richard Rohr, *Simplicity* (New York: Crossroad Publishing Company, 2003), 99–100.

Month Two: Clothes

1. Benjamin R. Barber, *Consumed: How Markets Corrupt Children, Infantilize Adults, and Swallow Citizens Whole* (New York: WW Norton, 2007), 9.
2. Ibid., 9–11.

Month Three: Possessions

1. Shane Claiborne, *The Irresistible Revolution* (Grand Rapids: Zondervan, 2006), 113–14.
2. See http://www.safeplace.org/page.aspx?pid=341.
3. Benjamin R. Barber, *Consumed: How Markets Corrupt Children, Infantilize Adults, and Swallow Citizens Whole* (New York: WW Norton, 2007), 11, 281.
4. Richard Rohr, *Simplicity* (New York: Crossroad Publishing Company, 2003), 59–60.

Month Four: Media

1. See http://www.nytimes.com/2010/06/07/technology/07brain.html?_r=1&pagewanted=all. 2. Ibid.

Month Five: Waste

1. Wendell Berry, *What Are People For?* (New York: North Point, 1990), 98.
2. See http://kprojectmlf.wordpress.com.
3. See http://www.sustainabletable.org/issues/eatlocal.
4. See http://www.localharvest.org/buylocal.jsp.
5. See http://www.time.com/time/business/article/0,8599,1903632,00.html.
6. See http://sustainableconnections.org/thinklocal/why.
7. See http://www.epa.gov/epawaste/nonhaz/municipal/index.htm.
8. See http://www.ehow.com/about_5125376_bottled-water-statistics.html.
9. See http://www.epa.gov/epawaste/conserve/rrr/reduce.htm.
10. Tracey Bianchi, *Green Mama* (Grand Rapids: Zondervan, 2010), 18–19.
11. See http://www.fueleconomy.gov/feg/current.shtml.

12. See http://www.fueleconomy.gov/feg/byfueltype.htm.

13. See http://e85vehicles.com/e85/index.php?topic=467.0.

14. Steven Bouma-Prediger, *For the Beauty for the Earth: A Christian Vision for Creation Care* (Grand Rapids: Baker Academic, 2010), 20.

15. Ibid., 182.

Month Six: Spending

1. See http://dictionary.reference.com/browse/consumerism.

2. See http://www.ota.com/organic/mt/business.html.

3. "The State of Human Development," United Nations Human Development Report 1998, chapter 1, 37.

4. Human Development Report 1998 Overview, United Nations Development Programme (UNDP).

5. J. Matthew Sleeth, *Serve God Save the Planet: A Christian Call to Action* (Grand Rapids: Zondervan, 2007), 83.

6. Benjamin R. Barber, *Consumed: How Markets Corrupt Children, Infantilize Adults, and Swallow Citizens Whole* (New York: WW Norton, 2007), 292.

7. Ibid., 293–94.

8. See http://www.christiancadre.org/member_contrib/cp_charity.html.

9. *Epistles of Julian*, 49.

10. See http://scienceblogs.com/casaubonsbook/2010/04/why_im_not_an_organic_purist.php.

Month Seven: Stress

1. Macrina Wiederkehr, *Seven Sacred Pauses* (Notre Dame, IN: Sorin Books, 2008), 13.

2. Ibid., 14.

3. Ibid., 17.

4. Ibid., 29.

5. Ibid., 32.

6. Ibid., 138.

7. Ibid., 8, 26.

8. Ibid., 177.

9. Ibid., 147.

10. Henri Nouwen, *Seeds of Hope* (New York: Doubleday, 1997), 112.

Take the
7 WEEK
CHALLENGE
AGAINST EXCESS

clothes spending waste
stress media possessions food

WORKBOOK

The 7 Experiment

Jen Hatmaker

PRIVATE FACEBOOK GROUP

the7experiment.com